Robin Boyd grew up in Northern Ireland, served on the staff of the Student Christian Movement in London, and taught – and learned – Christian theology in India (Gujarat State). A minister in newly united churches in both India (Church of North India, 1970) and Australia (Uniting Church in Australia, 1977), he was also Director of the Irish School of Ecumenics (1980–87). His previous books include *India and the Latin Captivity of the Church* and *Ireland: Christianity Discredited or Pilgrim's Progress?*

THE WITNESS OF THE STUDENT CHRISTIAN MOVEMENT

'Church ahead of the Church'

ROBIN BOYD

First published in Great Britain in 2007

Society for Promoting Christian Knowledge
36 Causton Street
London SW1P 4ST

British Library Cataloguing-in-Publication Data
A catalogue record for this book is available from the British Library

ISBN-13: 978–0–281–05877–8

1 3 5 7 9 10 8 6 4 2

Typeset by Graphicraft Ltd, Hong Kong
Printed in Great Britain by Ashford Colour Press

Contents

For Anne

Abbreviations

AACC	All Africa Conference of Churches
ACC	Australian Council of Churches
ASCM	Australian SCM
Aux	Auxiliary Movement
AV	Authorized Version
AVA	Australian Volunteers Abroad
BB	Boys' Brigade
BBC	British Broadcasting Corporation
BCC	British Council of Churches
BCCU	British College Christian Union
BEM	*Baptism, Eucharist and Ministry*
BMS	Baptist Missionary Society
CCA	Christian Conference of Asia
CEC	Conference of European Churches
CICCU	Cambridge Intercollegiate Christian Union
CIE	Confédération Internationale des Étudiants
CISRS	Christian Institute for the Study of Religion and Society
CMS	Church Missionary Society/Church Mission Society
CNI	Church of North India
CN-L	*The Christian News-Letter*
Copec	Conference on Christian Politics, Economics and Citizenship
CSI	Church of South India
CTBI	Churches Together in Britain and Ireland
CU	Christian Union
CWME	Commission on World Mission and Evangelism
DCSV	*Deutsche Christliche Studenten-Vereinigung*
DICARWS	Division of Inter-Church Aid, Refugee and World Service
EASY Net	Ecumenical Asia–Pacific Students and Youth Network
EGGYS	Ecumenical Global Gathering of Youth and Students
ERCDOM	Evangelical Roman Catholic Dialogue on Mission
ESR	European Student Relief
EU	Evangelical Union
EUCU	Edinburgh University Christian Union
GB&I	Great Britain and Ireland
ICC	Irish Council of Churches
ICE	Institute of Christian Education
ICF	Irish Christian Fellowship
IFES	International Fellowship of Evangelical Students
IMC	International Missionary Council

IRO	Inter-Regional Office
ISS	International Student Service
ITCU	Irish Theological Colleges' Union
IUCU	Inter-University Christian Union
IUS	International Union of Students
IVF	Inter-Varsity Fellowship
IVP	Inter-Varsity Press
JPIC	Justice, Peace and the Integrity of Creation
LMC	Life and Mission of the Church
LMG	London Medical Group
LMS	London Missionary Society
MEUT	*Mission and Evangelism in Unity Today*
MOW	Movement for the Ordination of Women
NCC	National Christian Council/National Council of Churches
NCYC	National Christian Youth Convention
NSCC	National Student Christian Congress
NUS	National Union of Students of England and Wales
PACE	Protestant and Catholic Encounter
PCR	Programme to Combat Racism
QUB	Queen's University Belfast
RBC	Religious Book Club
RSC	Rapid Social Change
SCM	Student Christian Movement
SMH	Student Movement House
SODEPAX	Joint Committee on Society, Development and Peace
SPCK	Society for Promoting Christian Knowledge
SVM	Student Volunteer Movement for Foreign Mission (USA)
SVMU	Student Volunteer Missionary Union GB&I
TCD	Theological Colleges Department
Tearfund	The Evangelical Alliance Relief Fund
UCA	Uniting Church in Australia
UCCF	Universities and Colleges Christian Fellowship
UCD	University College Dublin
UCM	University Christian Movement
UFT	United Faculty of Theology
Unesco	United Nations Educational, Scientific and Cultural Organization
WCC	World Council of Churches
WEA	Workers' Educational Association
WFDY	World Federation of Democratic Youth
WSCF	World's Student Christian Federation/World Student Christian Federation
WSR	World Student Relief
YMCA	Young Men's Christian Association
YWCA	Young Women's Christian Association

ERRATA

(1) *Acknowledgements*, p ix: A line of type is missing from the final sentence, which should read: "Above all I am indebted to my late wife Frances (Paton), to all my SCM colleagues and friends down the years, including current members and staff, to my wife Anne Booth-Clibborn (Forrester), and to our two families – Irish-Australian-Indian and Scottish-English-African."

(2) p 122, 10 lines up, should read "Hawke and Keating Labor Governments".

(2) Students and leaders at the Ecumenical Institute, *c*. 1949: Suzanne de Diétrich, Hendrik Kraemer and seated centre; James Blackie, second right, front row. (*Phot Blackie*)

(3) Crossing the Atlantic on the way to WSCF General Co Whitby, Ontario, Canada, 1949. Group includes Margaret F Nansie Anderson (Blackie), Davis McCaughey and Philip Potter. (*courtesy Nansie Blackie*)

(4) Lesslie Newbigin and Anne Forrester (Booth-Clibborn) at a Scottish SCM conference *c*. 1950. (*Photo courtesy Anne Booth-Clibborn*)

Acknowledgements

I should like to acknowledge the help I have received in writing
book – through conversations by phone or in person, and through le
and emails – from the following friends and colleagues:

Margaret Acton, Bobby Anderson, Bruce Barber, Robin and Marg
Barbour, Richard and Ray Baxter, David Beswick, Nansie Blac
John Bowden, Kenneth and Pat Boyd, Lawrence (Nana) Brew, Ma
Conway, David Edwards, William Emilsen, Alan Falconer, Duncan
Margaret Forrester, Ian Fraser, Kathy Galloway, Brian and Renate Ho
Alistair Hulbert, Michael Hurley, Alistair Kee, Christine Ledger, M
Levison, Owen and Jenefer Lidwell, Steven and Annebeth Mackie, A
Martin, John Martin, Jacques Matthey, Jean McCaughey, Tim McClu
John Morrow, Andrew Morton, Mary Niven, Slaine O Hogain, I
Parsons, David Philpot, Betty Preston, Liam Purcell, Kenneth Ro
Martin Rowan, Ulrich Seidel, Edward Shotter, Martha Smalley, Geraldin
Smyth, Salters Sterling, Mary Tanner, Michael Taylor, Ian Telfer, Dougl
and Elizabeth Templeton, Michael Wallace, Kevin Ward, Harry Wardla
Alan and Margaret Webster, Charles West, Jane Yule, Jean Yule, Sandy Yu

In addition I should like to thank the Faculty of Divinity (as it th
was) of the University of Edinburgh for the award of an Honor
Fellowship (2001), which opened many doors of study and conversati
my colleagues at the Centre for the Study of Christianity in the N
Western World, New College, Edinburgh; and my former colleague
the Irish School of Ecumenics, Dublin. I am most grateful to my p
lishers, SPCK, and particularly to Ruth McCurry, Louise Clairmonte
Yolande Clarke; and – for assistance in publication and distribution
Yannick Provost of the World Council of Churches and Hilary Re
and Hugh McGinlay of the Australian Theological Forum. Above
am indebted to my late wife Frances (Paton), to all my SCM collea
and friends down the years, including current members and famili
Irish–Australian–Indian and Scottish–English–African.

Robin
staff; to my wife Anne Booth-Clibbom (Forrester) an
our t

Cover credits (from top downwards):

(1) World Student Christian Federation Asia-Pacific Region memb
Hong Kong join a demonstration against the World Trade Organiza
education policy, 2005. (*Photo courtesy WSCF Inter-Regional Office, G*

Introduction

This is not a history of the Student Christian Movement; if it were, it would need to be a multi-volume work like Kenneth Scott Latourette's magisterial *A History of the Expansion of Christianity*. The history of the Movement's international manifestation as the World Student Christian Federation has been well covered by John R. Mott, Ruth Rouse, Suzanne de Diétrich and the joint work of Philip Potter and Thomas Wieser. Some national movements have histories which cover at least part of their existence, like Tissington Tatlow's massive yet eminently readable story of the British Movement up to 1929. Other histories, like that of the Australian SCM, are being prepared.

The present book is different, and I am not a professional historian. Yet for some years, and especially since my participation in the centenary celebrations of the Australian SCM in 1996, I have been uncomfortably aware of a kind of conspiracy of silence about what happened to the SCM in the late 1960s and early 1970s, as a result of which it dwindled in membership and support in many countries, and ceased to be the force in the life of the churches which it had hitherto been. Risto Lehtonen's book *Story of a Storm* (1998) broke that silence, but left many questions unanswered. In this book I have attempted to convey something of the joy and exhilaration experienced by many thousands of students over many years through their membership in the SCM; through their finding in it a community and a movement where they could be themselves, could ask any questions, could be pointed towards the best sources of biblical, theological, political and social scholarship, could find their way into – or more deeply into – the life of the Church (while not ceasing to be its loving critics), and could offer themselves to God to endeavour to carry out God's mission to the world in Christ's way. I have also tried to give brief portraits of some of the leaders of the Movement (far fewer than I could have wished), and of the contribution they made both to the Movement, and later – all over the world – to church, university and society.

The book is necessarily very 'bitty', and the bits selected are largely ones of which I have had personal experience, while the huge gaps, like Africa, China, Japan, Latin America, the United States – and Wales! – are the areas with which I have had least contact. My own experience of the Movement has been mainly in Britain, Ireland, India, Australia and 'the Federation', as well as – to a limited extent, and largely through conferences – France, Germany, Holland and Switzerland. And while my student and staff experience belongs to what I have called 'the golden age', I have endeavoured over the years to keep in touch with what is happening in the Movement as it continues to maintain, question and forge anew 'the SCM tradition'. For the book is really the story of that tradition, as it began and developed; as it wrestled with the challenge of being Christian in the world of the university, its own special mission field; as it suffered division, flourished, struggled and perhaps went astray; as its vision of mission and unity, of justice and peace spread to many successor organizations; as it has sought to rediscover its roots; and as it now – one tradition with many manifestations – faces the future in hope.

1

Students evangelizing the world
(c. 1890–1920)

Young people have been at the heart of most of the great movements in the life of the Christian Church. Jesus, we are told, was about 30 years old when he began his ministry. Mary was considerably younger when she said 'Yes' to the promise that she would be his mother. The twelve apostles were young men when Jesus chose them; so was St Paul when the murderers of Stephen – another young man – piled their clothes at his feet. And so it has been with the Christian movement among students.

The Student Christian Movement (SCM)[1] – with its varying names in many countries – and the World[2] Student Christian Federation (WSCF) of which it is a part, can claim to be one of the major movements which have changed the course of the Church, and enriched its life, in the past three centuries.[3] The mention of *three* centuries implies that the SCM's claim can stand in such august company as the Methodist movement of the eighteenth century and the Tractarian movement of the nineteenth; and it forms a highly significant part of both the modern missionary movement and the ecumenical movement. Its claim to uniqueness lies in the fact that it was the first truly ecumenical Christian community of modern times – a community committed to mission in Christ's way, committed to the unity of Christians, yet honouring the many different Christian traditions included in its membership. Not only did it become the model for the World Council of Churches (WCC): it also provided the major impetus – in personnel and in theology – for the unity of such churches as the Church of South India, the Church of North India and the Uniting Church in Australia. Few movements in the history of the Church have contributed so effectively to the unity of Christians. Its contribution to the mission of the Church – cross-cultural, socio-political, and more especially in the context of the university – has few if any parallels.

Beginnings

The last quarter of the nineteenth century witnessed a dynamic combination of three elements – university students, personal Christian awakening, and the call to missionary service overseas – which led to

1

an explosion of missionary enterprise greater than anything in earlier times. That combination had already been at work here and there in eighteenth-century Europe, for example in the 1706 Danish Lutheran mission to Tranquebar in India, led by Ziegenbalg and Plutschau of the German University of Halle, and with the significant co-operation of the Society for Promoting Christian Knowledge (SPCK), founded in England in 1698. A generation later came the 'Holy Club' of Charles and John Wesley at Lincoln College, Oxford, followed by their mission to Savannah, Georgia, in 1735. William Carey (1761–1834), the Baptist pioneer of English-speaking Protestant missions, was never a university student, though he later became a renowned scholar, and founder in 1818 of the well-known Serampore College near Calcutta. The work he started in India in 1792 marked the beginning of a whole series of mainly denominational missionary societies, including the Baptist Missionary Society (BMS, 1792), London Missionary Society (LMS, 1795), Netherlands Missionary Society (1797), Church Missionary Society (CMS, 1799), and the Basel Mission (1815). Several interdenominational societies, whose object was to help the work of all the missionaries, were quick to join in, like the Religious Tract Society (1799) and the British and Foreign Bible Society (1804). But not all Christians were keen to support overseas missions, and the missionary societies were not overwhelmed by recruits. In 1796, for example, the Church of Scotland Assembly rejected a proposal that the church take steps for 'the diffusion of the Gospel over the world'.[4] How was the missionary enthusiasm of a few to be changed into a movement which would challenge and engage the young people who would eventually become the leaders of the churches?

As early as 1706, on the other side of the Atlantic, a group of students at Harvard College led by a young man called Recompense Wadsworth had founded a Christian society, and 10 years later this had grown and developed under the strong and attractive personality of Cotton Mather. Similar groups, largely devoted to prayer and personal spiritual growth, can be traced right through the eighteenth century.[5] But the beginning of a definite, if for some decades sporadic, Christian 'student movement' is probably best traced to 1808, and a group of five students of Williams College, Massachusetts, led by Samuel J. Mills, who sheltered from a storm under a haystack, and there and then decided to dedicate their lives to missionary service overseas.[6] They were part of a wave of religious revivals which swept through America in the last decade of the eighteenth and the first of the nineteenth centuries.[7] Mills and his friends formed themselves into a group called 'the Brethren', whose purpose was 'to effect in the persons of its members a mission or missions to the heathen'. Out of this group – especially through the efforts of Mills, joined by Adoniram Judson (later to become famous as the Baptist pioneer missionary in Burma) – there eventually arose the American Board of Commissioners for Foreign Missions (1810).

There was still, however, no major student-led group at work in the universities of the world. In 1844 George Williams (a young man in his twenties) founded the Young Men's Christian Association (YMCA) in London, but it was directed towards white-collar workers rather than university students. The YMCA soon spread to the United States and Canada, and in 1855 the World Alliance of YMCAs was constituted in Paris. It was in America that the YMCA began to branch out on a large scale into the world of universities and colleges, and it was an association organized by the students of the University of Virginia in 1858 which can lay claim to being the first Student YMCA in the world.[8] In that same year, in England, the Cambridge University Medical Students' Association was founded, while in Scotland the Edinburgh University Medical Students' Christian Association began in 1865, paralleled, 40 miles further west, by the Glasgow University Students' Christian Association.[9]

There was a remarkable reciprocity between events in the United States and in Britain. The great American evangelist Dwight L. Moody visited Britain in 1873 and again in 1882, and as a result of the second visit the famous 'Cambridge Seven' volunteered for mission service with the China Inland Mission (founded in 1865 through the work of J. Hudson Taylor). The Cambridge Seven were a group of popular if somewhat elitist young graduate sportsmen – cricketers and oarsmen – whose example encouraged many others to answer the call to missionary service overseas. One of their number, J. K. Studd, visited the United States in 1885, and it was through him that the young John R. Mott, then a student at Cornell University, was won to Christ. The Student Volunteer Movement quickly spread to Britain, where it was greatly strengthened by the work of Prof. Henry Drummond of Glasgow,[10] 'the most powerful student evangelist Britain has ever seen'.[11]

Henry Drummond, who died at the age of 45 in 1897, just as the movement was beginning to become organized on an international scale, was probably the most important figure, in Britain at least, in pioneering its outstanding features. Although he became professor of natural science in the then Free Church's theological college in Glasgow, and although his books, especially *Natural Law in the Spiritual World*, *The Ascent of Man* and *The Greatest Thing in the World*, became bestsellers, he was not primarily an academic theologian. Rather he was a man of deep personal holiness, steeped in the Bible and wholly committed to Christ and his Kingdom, with a rare gift for personal evangelism which was equally effective with individuals and with large crowds of students. Recruited at the age of 22 by Moody to help him in his evangelistic mission of

1873–75 in Britain, he later finished his theological studies in Edinburgh, and in 1884 began what was to become a ten-year evangelistic movement among university students in Edinburgh, throughout the British Isles and in America and Australia. Working with C. T. Studd (brother to J. K.) and Stanley Smith, the cricketing and rowing leaders of the 'Cambridge Seven',[12] he urged students to answer the call to overseas missionary service, and they responded in their hundreds.

In his earlier evangelistic work with Moody, Drummond had not yet wrestled with the great theological issues of the time, especially the questions raised by critical biblical scholarship and by the relation of science (especially evolutionary science) to the Christian faith. By 1884, however, when he began his work among students in Edinburgh, he had come to accept – and to advocate strongly – an attitude of openness to science and to critical textual scholarship. He firmly believed that it was essential for the Church to accept a positive attitude to science; and it was largely because of this perceived honesty that university students all over the world flocked to hear him, and many who had given up their faith as discredited found it restored.[13]

Drummond's advocacy of the Christian faith started a major and unprecedented movement among university students. It differed from the older orthodoxy, and so became an object of controversy. But it brought a great renewal of life to the churches and to the missionary cause: it was a true 'movement', though that word – frequently used by Drummond – had not yet acquired its specific reference to the SCM. Yet already it included many features which were to be characteristic of the SCM. It was firmly based on Scripture, interpreted according to the most scholarly and up-to-date methods. It was also firmly based on personal commitment to Christ; and indeed Drummond – when challenged, as he often was – was always prepared to affirm a simple statement of the atonement, though without specifying a particular theory of it.[14] It affirmed the need for Christian living. Drummond held that 'the evidence for Christianity is not "the Evidences"' (the traditional proofs of the existence of God from the orderliness of creation and the inner presence of the moral law). 'The evidence for Christianity', he said, 'is *a Christian*'.[15] Drummond saw no contradiction between true science and true Christianity. He saw science rather as an instrument for deepening our understanding of God's creation, which can lead us to modify Christian teaching, by penetrating more deeply into the workings of God's creation. And he stressed the importance of prayer; though for Drummond this was perhaps more the earnest prayer of one or two people, or of a group, rather than the regular and formal liturgical prayer of the Church. He was committed to the mission of the Church, especially overseas but also among the poor, underprivileged and oppressed.[16] And he was committed to Christian unity, though here Drummond thought rather in terms of non-denominational co-operation or 'spiritual unity' than of commitment to organic church unity.

It is little wonder that, in the years when the headquarters of the British SCM were at Annandale in Golders Green, north London – the house bought for the Movement by its first general secretary Tissington Tatlow, and rebuilt into a large and attractive brown-brick neo-Georgian mansion – the first sight to meet a visitor's eyes in the entrance hall was a large bronze medallion of Henry Drummond.[17] Though his memory was soon eclipsed by the large personality of John R. Mott, it is fair to say that no one left a stronger imprint on the *thought* of the Movement than he did. And his effectiveness was helped by his early alliance with Moody: both were able to stir up the latent faith of childhood in their hearers, while Drummond was able to convince sceptical students that they could maintain that faith and deepen it while taking on board the findings of modern science and biblical scholarship.

It was in America that the organized beginning of a specifically student Christian movement took place, largely through the pioneering work, from 1883, of Robert Wilder and his sister Grace, to whom, more than anyone else, Mott in later years attributed the origin of the student missionary movement.[18] 'To Wilder I trace the great interest in missions in the colleges more than to any other man', he wrote, and 'to his sister, more than to him, the spirituality and higher success of the Movement'.[19] In 1886 a student gathering, under the auspices of the YMCA, was held at Mount Hermon, Massachusetts, with D. L. Moody as the leading speaker, and before it ended 100 of the 250 students present (including Mott) decided to offer for foreign missionary service. Wilder was one of the student leaders, and he immediately began to tour the universities, colleges and theological seminaries of the US and Canada and enrolled more than 200 'volunteers'.

In 1888 the Student Volunteer Movement for Foreign Missions (SVM) was officially set up, with Mott as chairman.[20] In that same year a young Princeton student leader called Luther D. Wishard set off to visit universities and colleges all over the world on behalf of the intercollegiate YMCA, first visiting Britain and Germany, and then going on in 1889 to Japan, where he spoke at several missionary colleges. That summer a student conference was held in Kyoto on the theme 'Christian Students united for World Conquest', attended by 500 students, of whom 96 were women. Since the YMCA summer student conference was being held simultaneously at Northfield in America, the Japanese students sent their American counterparts a three-word telegram: 'Make Jesus King'. This telegram led to action which spread from Japan to America, and thence to Sweden, Norway and Denmark, where a series of student conferences ensued, culminating (as we shall see) in 1895 at Vadstena Castle in Sweden with the foundation of the World's Student Christian Federation.[21]

Meantime the Student Volunteer Movement grew rapidly, first in America, and soon afterwards – at first under American leadership – in the British Isles, where its first manifestation, as the Students' Foreign Missionary Union, was founded in 1889,[22] with its members signing the declaration, 'It is my earnest hope, if God permit, to engage in foreign missionary work'.[23] Sinclair Stevenson of Dublin and later of Gujarat in western India, who went up to Lincoln College, Oxford, in 1886, claimed that he was the first student in the United Kingdom to sign the declaration.[24] In 1892 'the Student Volunteer Missionary Union of Great Britain and Ireland' (SVMU) was founded, the earlier organization gladly giving way to the new one, and the declaration eventually taking the form, 'It is my purpose, if God permit, to become a foreign missionary'.[25] A travelling secretary (A. T. Polhill-Turner) was appointed, and in 1893 the quarterly *The Student Volunteer* appeared for the first time; by the end of that year the SVMU had 491 members in Britain, 25 of whom had already sailed for service overseas.

But the feeling was spreading that the focus of the movement was too narrow; a nationwide Christian student organization was needed, whose appeal would be wider than simply to a missionary vocation. And so, at the Keswick[26] summer conference in 1893, the Inter-University Christian Union (IUCU) was founded, sharing with the SVMU the services of Polhill-Turner as secretary. The following year the name of the new organization was changed to the British College Christian Union (BCCU). Donald Fraser of Glasgow University succeeded Polhill-Turner as secretary of the SVMU in 1893 and as BCCU secretary in 1894: the joint career of the SVMU and the BCCU (which in 1905 would become the SCM) had begun.

The American Methodist layman John R. Mott (1865–1955),[27] whom we have already met working for the American YMCA, was the leading figure in the founding of the international World's Student Christian Federation (WSCF), with its slogan (they called it 'the watchword') 'The Evangelization of the World in this Generation'. As Mott later explained, the watchword did not imply an expectation that the whole world would be converted to Christianity within 30 years or so. It meant rather that the Gospel must be communicated to all people everywhere – especially since new methods of communication, commerce and colonialism had made this a practical possibility – and that each generation of Christians must recognize this vocation as its own.[28] But there was an urgency about the call to evangelism, and the slogan-makers did not hesitate to use strongly military metaphors: 'Evangelize to a finish and bring the King back!' was one, and 'Students – strategic points in the world's conquest' another. The link between C. T. Studd and Mott is, like that between Moody and Drummond, a significant one. It is a case of the conversion of a young man with an open, inquiring, perhaps 'liberal' mind through the personal influence of another, slightly older young man with a more traditional faith, involving them both in a commitment to overseas service in mission. Mott in his own way became a missionary first and foremost, whose field was the world, beginning with the university, and the promotion there of 'the recognition of the supremacy of the Lord Jesus Christ and of his work as the only sufficient Saviour'.[29] Here, in the beginnings of the SCM, there was a conscious double relationship between the Movement and the Bible: first, obedience to the great commission of Matthew 28.19–20, 'Go ye therefore, and make disciples of all the nations' (RV); and second, the basing of the Movement's methodology on Bible study ('study circles' as they were called) and on prayer for grace and power to carry out the missionary obligation.

The United States will not figure largely in this book, as the author's experience of the Movement has mainly been in other countries. But the immense debt of the Movement to its American pioneers must be acknowledged, as must also be the vast numbers of missionaries, and leaders in the missionary and ecumenical movements, whom the American SCM (frequently and familiarly operating as the Student YMCA and YWCA)[30] has given to the world.[31]

A man whom a senior church leader described as 'the young man who deals in worlds and archbishops' joined the staff of the British Movement in 1896. His name was Douglas Thornton,[32] and he was an evangelical Anglican from Cambridge, fired with enthusiasm for mission overseas, and a highly effective advocate of the Movement. He not only became a friend of many Congregationalists, Methodists and Presbyterians, but was instrumental in persuading the Catholic wing of the Church of England to support the work of the SVMU. He was on the staff for just two years, and in that time became a doughty advocate of the 'watchword', especially through his promotion of a 'Memorial' to the churches, urging them to accept the watchword officially, and to give support to the SVMU which was finding more candidates for overseas work than the churches and missionary societies could afford to send. Although the churches and societies gave their support to the Memorial, and the Anglicans passed it on with a commendation to the Lambeth Conference, the Movement was disappointed by the response. The churches seemed to be saying, 'This has always been our aim, but what more can we do than we are already doing?' The Movement had wanted them to say, 'We accept the watchword: the world can and should be evangelized in this generation: this is not just our *aim*: it is our *duty*, and we shall see that it is done, and that the resources are provided.'[33] Yet the SCM was showing the way ahead, and in its energetic advocacy of mission was beginning to show its capacity to be what later came to be called the 'church ahead of the Church'.

Thornton's passion was for what is now called cross-cultural mission, especially in the Muslim world, and in his short time on the staff he became an effective producer of study material on other faiths and on the prospects for Christian mission in different cultures. His 1895 book *Africa Waiting* can claim to be the first book ever published by the British SCM, many years before the official birth of the SCM Press in 1929; a careful study of the African continent, it was crammed with facts – including what to wear and what not to eat – and was reprinted three times.[34] After influencing many students to dedicate their lives to mission overseas, Thornton himself went to Cairo, where he died in 1907 at the age of 34. His friend and colleague Tatlow said of him simply, 'He was the greatest prophet the Student Movement has ever had'.

In 1899 the British Movement published a paperback edition of Mott's book *The Evangelization of the World in This Generation*, which managed to reach railway station bookstalls, where it sold for sixpence.[35] It was in that year that my father Robert Boyd went as a student to Queen's College, Belfast (in the old Royal University of Ireland), and through joining the college Christian Union soon became a student volunteer, engaged to serve overseas. Here are some sentences from a memoir he wrote towards the end of his life:

> I remember well the occasion on which, with my Bible open before me at the 6th chapter of Isaiah, I knelt in prayer, and said as definitely as I was capable, 'Here I am, Lord, send me'. I left the room and went straight to the Christian Union meeting at Queen's College, and set down my name.[36]

He wondered about wasting time in academic study, when he could be useful in the mission field straight away, and continues:

> While I was debating the question, the Rev. Dr. John G. Paton, the veteran missionary of the New Hebrides Mission, visited Belfast . . . He advised us to get fully trained as ministers, doctors or teachers, and he urged us, if at all possible, to become missionaries of our own Church.[37]

My father took John G. Paton's advice. He completed his university degree, followed by theology at Princeton and Belfast. He then offered for missionary service, but had to wait for several years, as there were so many volunteers in the queue ahead of him, before he finally got to India in 1909, where he spent the next 13 years. For the rest of his active service he was the home convener of the Foreign Mission of the Presbyterian Church in Ireland. Already in that early twentieth-century vignette there are four strong SCM themes: the Bible; the missionary call; academic integrity; and commitment to the Church.

In 1908 the SCM held a national conference in Liverpool with no fewer than 1,640 delegates from the different university and college branches. The platform at this meeting still carried a banner with the original watchword; but another banner had now been added – significantly over the Exit! – with words which were to become the motto of the international Movement, *Ut omnes unum sint*, 'that they all may be one' (John 17.21, AV). *Unity* was already being added to mission.

It was not only in Britain and America that the Movement spread. Its Australian beginnings, for example, were in 1896, when Mott visited that continent and in Melbourne recruited a young German-speaking Presbyterian ordinand of Lutheran background, Johannes Heyer, to attend the forthcoming conference at Northfield (USA). Shortly after the conference Heyer was able to visit the Pietist leader of the German Movement, Count Pückler, and helped to overcome his deep suspicion of the Anglo-Saxon origins of the SCM.[38] It was an early example of the way in which a constant process of dialogue, sharing of ideas, and changing of attitudes went on between the different national Movements. Development of the SCM in Australia was rapid, and in the various university branches the emphasis was, as elsewhere, strongly on Bible study, prayer and volunteering for missionary service. Heyer's brother-in-law Frank Paton served for seven difficult years (1896–1902) on the island of Tanna, Vanuatu (then the New Hebrides); and in a book called *The Message of the Student Christian Movement*, published in Melbourne in 1910, he wrote:

> Bible study must be part of our daily life all through our student days . . .
> The Christian Union always rightly puts the supreme emphasis on Bible
> Study as the main factor in the formation of character.[39] The purpose of
> our Bible Study is that we may know the kind of Man Jesus was, and in
> order that we may become the kind of men He wants us to be.[40]

Eric Fenn, in his 1939 history *Learning Wisdom: Fifty Years of the SCM*, says that the Movement of those early days meant above all two things to its members: the Morning Watch, and Foreign Missions. 'They devoted a definite time each day (seldom less than an hour) to the deliberate renewal of their touch with Christ through prayer and Bible study; and they set out to give their lives in the cause of foreign missions.' Already by 1910 hundreds of former SCM members, men and women, from many national movements, were serving as missionaries all over the world.

The Basis

For the first two or three years of the British Movement's history there was no attempt to define a 'basis' for its work: there was too much to do in promoting the growth of Christian Unions in colleges and universities all over the country, and recruiting volunteers for work overseas. At the summer conference in 1895, however, a brief basis was adopted: 'A belief in Jesus Christ as God the Son and only Saviour of the world'.[41] The question then arose, 'Is this a *personal* basis, which every individual wishing to become a member of the Movement must affirm? Or is it rather a description of the belief of the Movement itself, indicating the kind of community a new recruit is joining?' Tatlow and Donald Fraser were strongly in favour of the latter view, and a committee meeting in 1898 resolved

> (1) That the act of joining a college Christian Union be taken as expressing assent to the basis of the BCCU.
> (2) That the interpretation of the basis be left to the judgement and conscience of the individual.

This expressed the position which the Movement would eventually adopt, though not until after World War 1. Meanwhile, however, Mott and other leaders favoured a 'personal basis', and at the Matlock conference of 1901 this was accepted, the new Basis of Membership reading:

> I desire in joining this Union to declare my faith in Jesus Christ as my Saviour, my Lord, and my God. Any student in becoming a voting member of an affiliated Union, or signing the declaration of the SVMU shall be understood thereby to express his acceptance of the above.

To this was added a paragraph on the object of the Movement:

> The object of the Union shall be to lead the students of British universities and colleges to become disciples of Jesus Christ; to unite them in seeking a fuller spiritual life; and to enlist them in the work of extending Christ's Kingdom throughout the whole world.

For some years the Movement went ahead happily with this Basis: in fact for most of the SCM's history it has gone ahead with little reference to its Basis, until some issue has arisen which sparks off a period of self-examination. In the first decade of the twentieth century an effort was made to describe in rather more detail what the Movement was about. It was a long process, involving not only students and staff members like Mott, Tatlow, and Wilder, followed by Ruth Rouse, Winifred Sedgwick, Bill Paton and Kenneth Kirk (later theologian Bishop of Oxford), but also leading theologians like E. S. Talbot (Bishop

of Winchester), the Methodist J. H. Moulton and, from Edinburgh,
H. R. Mackintosh. The process finally led, in 1913, to the adoption of a
new Aim and Basis:

> The Aim of this Movement is to lead students in British universities and
> colleges into full acceptance of the Christian Faith in God – Father, Son
> and Holy Spirit; to promote among them regular habits of prayer and Bible
> study; to keep before them the importance and urgency of the evangel-
> ization of the world, the Christian solution of social problems, and the
> permeation of public life with Christian ideals; and to lead them into the
> fellowship and service of the Christian Church. Any Christian Union becom-
> ing affiliated shall incorporate in its Constitution the following clause: 'The
> corporate activities of this Christian Union shall be in harmony with the
> Aim of the Student Christian Movement'.

To this was added a personal Declaration of Membership, which began
with the words, 'In joining this Union I declare my faith in God through
Jesus Christ, whom as Saviour and Lord I desire to serve'.

Lay leadership

Most of the leaders of the student missionary movement in its early years,
certainly in America and Britain, were lay people,[42] and many of them
continued to serve the churches and missions without ever being
ordained, like Robert E. Speer of the American Student Volunteer
Movement and later of Presbyterian missions, and John R. Mott himself.
The tradition of lay leadership would continue in Britain, notably with
J. H. Oldham[43] and a group of outstanding women like Zoë Fairfield, Ruth
Rouse, Kathleen Bliss and Marjorie Reeves, to whom the door of
ordination was not open.

By 1910 the Student Christian Movement (SCM) – which in Britain
had finally, in 1905, decided to use those three words as its official title,
instead of 'British College Christian Union' (BCCU) – was strongly
established in countries all over the world, in a series of national Movements linked together in the World's Student Christian Federation.
At first the Federation had offices in New York and London as well as
Geneva, and it was only much later that the headquarters staff was
concentrated in Geneva. In America, Britain, many European countries
including Russia, the Middle East, South Africa, India, China, Japan,
Australia and New Zealand the Movement was flourishing. The different national Movements were in constant contact with each other by
letter, telegram and the printed word, as well as through travelling secretaries. And a steady stream of academically and professionally qualified
young men and women was passing into the service of the Church and
its mission overseas and at home.

Edinburgh 1910: mission demands unity

The Edinburgh World Missionary Conference of 1910 is often hailed as the birthplace of the modern ecumenical movement.[44] But it was much more than that: it was the culmination of a century of cross-cultural missionary enterprise, which had already produced a remarkable degree of inter-church co-operation, symbolized for example in the decennial missionary conferences held regularly in India in the later decades of the nineteenth century. Yet the modern English-speaking missionary movement had very modest origins, represented by William Carey, the Nottingham cobbler who, through his sheer ability and devotion, was able to exercise a profound influence on the great East India Company itself. Being a missionary in the early and middle years of the nineteenth century was by no means a glamorous occupation: critics were many, and supporters in the sending countries were seldom numerous. It was the rise of the student movement in the last quarter of the nineteenth century which brought about a profound change, and gave the missionary calling a certain glamour and popularity which it had previously lacked – especially through figures like the Studd brothers with their public school and cricketing image, and their background of comfortable family stability. They were familiar with the world of colonial and commercial expansion and prosperity where the consolidation of political power, especially British power, seemed capable of proceeding hand in hand with evangelization. Edinburgh was building on a century of missionary pioneering and consolidation, and the way forward to a much better world seemed to be wide open.

Much of the initiative for Edinburgh came from John R. Mott, who, while continuing to work for the student Movement, had begun persuading the churches themselves to come together for co-operation in overseas mission, and – with the significant help, as organizing secretary, of the British SCM's educational secretary J. H. (Joe) Oldham (1874–1969) – set up the 1910 Missionary Conference, which he himself chaired. Edinburgh was an astonishingly sophisticated, high-powered and open-minded meeting, as anyone who has looked at the massive preparatory volumes and later reports will know; but the centrality of the Bible and the missionary calling was never in doubt. Edinburgh was first of all about *mission*, about Matthew 28.19 – 'Go and make disciples of all nations'. *Unity* – 'That they all may be one' (John 17.21, AV) – was a by-product; important certainly, but a means to an end – 'that the world may believe'.

Richey Hogg, historian of the International Missionary Council, noting the wide spectrum of churchmanship at Edinburgh (largely the result of the persuasive powers of Oldham and Tatlow) mentions how an Anglo-Catholic bishop there described himself as 'a lion in a veritable den of Daniels', and comments, 'The SCM made Edinburgh not simply a gathering of likeminded Christians, but a truly representative assembly'.[45] Tatlow, Mott and Oldham, all still young and two of them laymen, were in fact showing great courage, as well as critical judgement, in modelling the Movement as 'church ahead of the Church', seeking to bring reluctant bishops and other church leaders to the point of working together for the evangelization of the world.

Joe Oldham is a figure whose name will occur frequently in this story, for he was active in the SCM and in other movements and groups associated with it, many of them largely inspired by him, from the Movement's earliest days in the mid-1890s until his death in 1969. Mission, unity, higher education, personal relationships, social ethics, politics – on each of these areas of the Church's life and witness this strong, effective, yet unobtrusive Scottish layman left his mark. Edinburgh was very much a product of people whose lives had been influenced by the SCM, and who were still deeply involved in it. Indeed Charles McLaren, in the jubilee history of the Australian SCM, *Other Men Laboured*, says without qualification, 'The modern oecumenical movement is the outcome of the worldwide Student Christian Movement'.[46] At the time when McLaren's book was published, 1946, few would have questioned that statement. But the roots of both the SCM and the ecumenical movement went back to the great Protestant missionary movement, whose beginnings, as we have seen, were more than two centuries before Edinburgh 1910.

Yet already at Edinburgh there were signs of a division in the Movement, between those, like Henry Drummond, who believed that their commitment to academic integrity was driving them to take seriously the findings of critical biblical scholarship and of evolutionary biology, as well as the pursuit of social and political justice, and on the other side the more conservative wing of the Movement which gave centrality to a personal conversion experience, and to a particular understanding of salvation. Edinburgh, to them, seemed to represent a victory for the more 'liberal' view of mission and the more 'catholic' aspect of churchmanship, and so was suspect. It is significant that neither in Oliver Barclay and Robert Horn's recent account of the Cambridge Intercollegiate Christian Union (CICCU) *From Cambridge to the World: 125 Years of Student Witness* (2002), nor in Geraint Fielder's *Lord of the Years: 60 Years of Student Witness, 1928–88* (1988)[47] which tells the story of the IVF/UCCF), does Edinburgh 1910 rate so much as a mention. Already in that year the division between the seemingly more liberal leaders and members of the Movement and the more conservative CICCU had come to a head, and in March 1910 the CICCU disaffiliated from the SCM and WSCF.[48] The Movement's annual report for 1910, acknowledging the CICCU's 'great influence for good in the life of the University', comments how the Cambridge Union depended largely on

> the complete unanimity of its members in the details as well as the fundamentals of their religious positions, [and] had for some time been feeling the difficulty of combining the fuller interdenominationalism of the Student Movement with the traditions and ideal of which it was justly proud. As the result of a mutual agreement between the Student Christian Movement and the CICCU the latter withdrew from affiliation; and the Movement is now represented in Cambridge by a committee on which all types of Christian thought are represented.[49]

The CICCU, founded in 1878, had undoubtedly been a pioneer in the student movement; it had affiliated with the nascent SCM in 1893, and so with the WSCF in 1895. In 1910, however, it was simply one among many affiliated Christian Unions, and Barclay contrasts its 200 disaffiliating members with the 150,000 members of the worldwide WSCF.[50] Its disaffiliation was a sad event, and a foretaste of what would happen on a global scale in years to come.

Following shortly after Edinburgh, and stemming from the WSCF rather than from Edinburgh itself, though involving many of the same leaders (notably Mott himself) came the 1911 Federation Conference in Constantinople. This event was remarkable in that it included active participation by the Orthodox churches. The Ecumenical Patriarch gave it his blessing, with the words, 'I consider such a conference to draw Christians into fellowship and co-operation as one of the most sacred causes, and I will help it in any way in my power'. Already from about 1903 a Russian SCM, with both Orthodox and non-Orthodox members, had come into existence under the leadership of the Lutheran Baron Paul Nicolay;[51] and Mott reported that there were delegates from the Orthodox churches of Greece, Russia, Romania, Bulgaria and Serbia, as well as the Gregorian, Syrian, Maronite and Coptic churches.[52] The British SCM's annual report for 1910 noted that 'a wholly new factor has been introduced into the student life of South Eastern Europe and Asia Minor'.[53] The Movement was pioneering a new road of ecumenical friendship across the ancient division between the churches of the East and the West; it was a road which the churches themselves would eventually follow, with significant results. In Constantinople in 1911, as in Edinburgh in 1910, Mott's contribution was outstanding. He was, in Ruth Rouse's words, 'the man who, if any deserves the title, may be called the pioneer of the modern ecumenical movement'.[54]

Men and women: an equal partnership

From the beginning of the student Movement, women as well as men were involved in it, though at first the men heavily outnumbered the women, as they did in the universities. The usual pattern was to have separate men's and women's branches, and in their joint committee discussions it was often customary for the women to make their contribution through a spokesperson, giving them only one voice among many male ones. Things in the British scene began to change, however, with the appointment in 1909 of Zoë Fairfield as assistant to the general secretary Tissington Tatlow.

Zoë Fairfield had been a student at the Slade School of Art in 1898, had been secretary of the Art Students' Christian Union, and, as a strong advocate of women's rights, had taken a leading part in the London Women Students' Committee. After her appointment to the staff in 1909 she became a powerful force at the heart of the Movement's activities, where she remained for the next 20 years; and in the index to Tatlow's monumental history of the SCM she rates more mentions than William Temple or even John R. Mott. Tatlow tells how people who expected her simply to bear the burden of day to day business in the office 'soon realized that a first class mind was being brought to bear on the problems of the Movement'.[55] Quietly and firmly she achieved her aim of the equality of women and men in the SCM. With her coming, 'the emancipation of the women was complete . . . [She] fought no battle, but simply took her place in the councils of the Movement with complete ease, and the women followed her example'.[56] Already before World War 1 she had been a supporter of the suffragette movement, and early in the war she completed the editing and publication of a book entitled *Some Aspects of the Woman's Movement*, including two of her own contributions. The book was widely studied in the SCM.[57]

It was not only among women and fine-art students that her influence was felt. Over the years she became the chief maker of programmes for the great summer conferences, usually held at Swanwick in Derbyshire, and it was often she who suggested themes and speakers. She made sure that the range of speakers was not curtailed by the limitations of the students' experience, but was as wide and representative as possible. This marked the emergence of a strong 'SCM tradition' of close co-operation between students, SCM staff and leaders in church and university, characterized by an awareness of the contemporary issues – theological, missionary, social and political – which needed to be approached, a knowledge of who the best experts were in the different areas and a conviction that in every area the speakers should be people of the highest academic integrity.

'Swanwick' was to become a famous word in the history of the SCM, and as it will recur frequently in these pages, a brief description is essential. Among Tissington Tatlow's many contributions to the life of the Movement was his purchase of the large house known as The Hayes, near the Derbyshire coal-mining village of Swanwick, whose management, under the name of 'First Conference Estates', came under the aegis of the SCM. In early years much of the accommodation, and the major meeting-place, was under canvas, but later a large wooden chalet-type building was added, and a conference hall. Already by the late 1920s Swanwick had acquired the atmosphere and the reputation which were to continue to attract students for many years.

Beyond racism

In theory there was, from the first, no place for racial discrimination in the SCM. It was a missionary movement, seeking to bring people of every race and culture into the Christian family. From an early date it had adopted the motto *Ut omnes unum sint*, with its clear implication that in Christ there is neither Jew nor Greek, just as there is neither male nor female. Certainly colour was not a category that gave rise to discrimination for the SCM, any more than it did for Kipling when he spoke of 'lesser breeds without the law' to indicate his contempt for the methods of German imperialism. And it is significant that even between German and Allied members of the Movement there was a rapid and dramatic reconciliation after the end of the war in 1918, just as there was after World War 2.

Yet in practice there were difficulties regarding race, especially in the USA and South Africa. Christian Unions had been formed in both white and black American colleges, but in the earliest years the American movements had not been able to arrange for black students to be present at white conferences or vice versa. The fact that a WSCF conference at Williamstown in 1897 was an international event, with people from many races present, made it possible for an African–American student to attend; and another was present at the Tokyo conference in 1907. But the numbers remained minimal. In 1913 a conference was due to be held at Lake Mohonk. The Federation, encouraged by the leaders of the American movement, made it clear that the inter-racial principles of the Federation would not permit it to accept the American invitation to Lake Mohonk unless 'coloured' students were admitted to the conference on the same basis as whites.[58] And so in the event 13 African–American students were there. A principle had been established; and although racial issues would often be high on the agenda of the Federation thereafter, it would normally be because the whole Movement was fighting for the rights of people suffering from racial discrimination.

One of the leaders at the Tokyo WSCF conference in 1907 was a distinguished Indian woman, Lilavati Singh; and three years later S. K. Datta, also of India, was a major colleague of J. H. Oldham in organizing the Edinburgh missionary conference.[59] Oldham made his own special contribution to the struggle against racism, as to so much else, by his book *The Race Problem*, published by the SCM in 1924, and studied widely in the British Movement. Through his experience in India, and later in Africa, and through the wide SCM network of well-informed missionaries with whom he kept in touch – medical, educational and agricultural as well as evangelistic and pastoral – he was able to exercise influence on Indian and colonial policy, and at the same time developed his own creative concern and expertise for the social issues which he would later work on so effectively in the Life and Work movement.

In the following decades the participation of students and staff from across the whole spectrum of race and culture would be a common feature of the Movement's life; and in places as diverse as the USA, South Africa and Australia the SCM would take a leading role in the fight against racial discrimination.

The Great War and its aftermath

Four years after Edinburgh 1910 came the terrible carnage of World War 1. Thousands of students on both sides were in the trenches, whose horrors were shared by many military chaplains. Some of these, on their return home, became student and church leaders of their generation – men like Studdert Kennedy in Britain and Frank Rolland[60] and Frank Paton[61] in Australia. The life of the Federation in the war years is vividly described by Ruth Rouse, who was herself badly injured by a bomb at Étaples in May 1918.[62] Most of the young men in Britain, France, Germany and eventually the USA were in the forces; others, including SCM members, were put in prison as conscientious objectors. As a result, women began to take a leading part in the life of the Movement: Leo Viguier of the French SCM, for example, and Dora Irons, the first woman chairperson of the British SCM general committee.[63] The care of prisoners of war – both one's own and those of the enemy – became a vast field of work, largely carried out by YMCA secretaries whose roots were in the Movement.

Large numbers of refugees also had to be cared for, especially in Switzerland, as well as students cut off from their home countries. Despite wartime restrictions Mott, as an American, was able to continue his world travel until 1917, even visiting Germany late in 1914.[64] Students in the forces, on both the Allied and the German sides, tended to be uncritically supportive of their own national cause, though the ethics of making war at all were questioned by some, often at the personal cost of imprisonment. In 1916 Tatlow estimated that there were at least 10,000 past and present members of the SCM in the British forces;[65] yet the Movement was able to carry on with its normal programmes, and in fact about a quarter of the 24,000 students in the various colleges were SCM members.

One interesting new British enterprise in 1917 was the opening of Student Movement House (quickly to be known as SMH) in London's Russell Square (it later moved to Gower Street). It was Zoë Fairfield who, with the help of Henri-Louis Henriod (originally of the Swiss Movement, but then working in London) and F. A. (George) Cockin, persuaded Tatlow to set up SMH, on the model of the pre-war and war-time student *foyers* in France, Switzerland and London. There were a great many foreign students in Britain, especially from India, and this was a place where students of any race or faith could feel welcome. Donations for SMH flooded in, especially as it was planned as a memorial to students killed in the war. The casualties in all the warring countries were appallingly high. Among those lost – and it was a severe loss to the whole Federation – was Charles Grauss, general secretary of the French SCM, killed shortly before the end of the war.

Strangely, there is evidence that, at least in the English-speaking world, the unbelievably awful massacre of 'the Great War' had less effect on student thinking and theology than did the Vietnam war 50 years later. Yet there *were* changes, and they affected the theology of the coming decades. It was hard for soldiers to believe that their somewhat blasphemous yet brave and unselfish mates should, after suffering the fatal hell of the trenches, find themselves in an even worse and unending theological hell. More helpful was the conviction that God was a suffering God, sharing as the crucified Christ in the agony of the trenches, and in some strange way taking its burden upon himself. It was a view of the atonement that would later be developed and become well known through the writings of student leaders like C. S. Paul in India (whose book *The Suffering God* was published in 1932) and Dietrich Bonhoeffer in Germany.

The first post-war task to be tackled by the Federation was that of relief for the vast numbers of students who were ex-prisoners, or displaced persons, or simply people whose homes and livelihoods had been destroyed. The story of how this problem was tackled, which is also the story of the early development of international ecumenical relief agencies – in the first instance for the relief of students in Europe – is brilliantly told by Ruth Rouse in her 1925 book *Rebuilding Europe: The Student Chapter in Post-War Reconstruction*.[66] The book was published by the SCM for the Federation, which, right through the war, held in its fellowship such diverse countries – friend and foe – as France, Germany, Denmark, Finland, Hungary, Italy, the Netherlands, Norway, Russia, Sweden and Switzerland, as well as China, Japan, and India, to say nothing of Britain, the USA, Australia and New Zealand. The WSCF was in fact the only international student society to survive the war, and it did this even though many of its affiliated Movements were on different sides of the struggle.[67]

So it was a new and practical chapter in the Movement's hitherto somewhat academic and elitist life which began in February 1920 when Ruth Rouse, then on the Federation staff, and Eleonora Iredale of the British SCM visited Vienna and found 'despair, suicide, one meal a day or less, no underclothing, no overcoats, broken shoes in the winter slush, sleeping in restaurants or lavatories', among the 15,000 college students in Vienna, 1400 of whom were women.[68] In Ruth's chilly room, and at her invitation, five young women – who frankly owned that they hated to meet, since one represented the German National Student Society, two were from Jewish associations, one from the Socialist Union and one from the Catholic Student Society – met, became friends and decided to send out an appeal through the WSCF. The Federation responded, set up a committee called European Student Relief (ESR), and put Conrad Hoffmann in charge of it. An American who had worked for prisoners of war throughout the hostilities, he had amazingly been allowed to stay in Germany even after America entered the war in 1917. ESR worked across all barriers of religion as well as denomination, yet it did not hesitate to take as its own the motto of the Federation, Christ's prayer *Ut omnes unum sint.*

Ruth Rouse and Conrad Hoffmann made a remarkable team, and were successful in enlisting the good and great of church and state in many countries to help in raising the large sums of money needed to get the students – and the collapsed universities – of Europe into action once more. There was a small Geneva staff, with 'field representatives' scattered all over Europe, in Poland, Czechoslovakia and Bulgaria as well as Smyrna in Turkey. In 1921 they helped to transport 1500 Russian refugee students from Constantinople across Hungary to Prague. In many countries, like Poland, anti-Semitism was rife, and Jewish students needed special help. Hoffmann, with his experience of prisoner-of-war camps, had to admit that conditions in student hostels in Poland, Hungary and Czechoslovakia were often even worse.

For women, the sordid misery and danger of their homeless condition was appalling. Women students were sleeping in the railway waiting-rooms amongst rows of demobilised soldiers on the floor; if a friendly soul intervened to offer them a bed, it was often a prostitute. What wonder that some of these women committed suicide.[69]

In Germany the ESR promoted the development of *Wirtschaftshilfe*, a scheme for economic self-help which, with the hard-won support of the trade unions, made it possible for impoverished students to work in mines, factories and farms and so pay for their studies. In the process it broke down the social barriers which had previously separated students from the working classes. Similar schemes were developed in Latvia, Hungary and Poland. In other places, for example Hungary, ESR was able to break down long-standing differences between political, religious and racial groups. Other 'Christian' groups specifically excluded Jews, but ESR – following the policy of the Federation – was adamant that they must be included, and so was able to build up a truly cross-cultural student community.

ESR's work soon spread beyond Europe, especially into the Near East. In September 1922 came the catastrophic order to all Christians to quit Turkish soil. The ancient Christian communities of what was known as 'Asia Minor' were wiped out, and a million refugees made their way to Greece, including many students from Christian colleges in Turkey. 'Within a day or two of the burning of Smyrna, every Christian student and professor was either dead, or on his way to the interior, "deported" as of military age, or a refugee in Athens or the islands.'[70]

But the largest of all ESR's ventures, in these years just after the 1917 Russian Revolution, was in Russia itself where, with the failure of the 1921 harvest, famine struck. Dr Fridtjof Nansen, the Arctic explorer, appealed to ESR on behalf of the League of Nations for 'your help to rescue the Russian youth decimated by famine' and ESR responded, in 'the greatest investment made by the world student fellowship on behalf of any country'. It was a peculiarly difficult operation, as the ESR insisted on the principle of impartiality of distribution, while the Soviet government had already adopted a policy of what Ruth Rouse, in a sinister foreshadowing of later 'ethnic cleansing', described as 'so-called cleansings of the universities' by which students and professors with dissident religious or political views were excluded.[71] Nevertheless, a great deal of help was given, until in April 1925 ESR was informed by the government that its contribution was no longer acceptable, and the staff had to withdraw at once. Writing her account that same year, Ruth Rouse asks, 'How many of these capable and self-sacrificing students will be permitted to take part in the rebuilding of their country?'[72] It is a question that even today is not easy to answer, though any answer would certainly have to take account of the great contribution to Christian thought made by the Russian theologians of the émigré community in

Paris between the wars, like Berdyaev, Bulgakov, Solovyov, Zernov, Zander and others, most of them with strong SCM associations.[73]

There is no doubt that ESR's work in helping the shattered universities of Europe to recover their strength after the war did more than save lives and help thousands of students to equip themselves for their future professional lives: it helped to preserve and enhance the intellectual tradition of Europe; and even more, it helped to inaugurate a new era of intellectual co-operation between the scattered universities of Europe and America. In Ruth Rouse's perceptive words, the Federation Jack-of-all-trades at Geneva had relieved intellectual famine.

ESR had been organized with such astonishing imagination and efficiency that by 1924 its emergency work was virtually completed. Thereafter it was able to give more attention to organizing international conferences where students from different countries and religious and political traditions could meet each other, for the barriers between relief-providing and relief-receiving students had been broken down. In the 1920s the climate of active opposition to the Christian faith, from committed Marxists to equally committed 'freethinkers', was much more actively antagonistic than is the indifference of the early twenty-first century. It was important to create friendships between students of every point of view; and so these ESR conferences were not specifically 'Christian', like SCM or WSCF conferences, but were deliberately intended to promote international friendship across the barriers. And they were *student* conferences, with the entire programme left to the students themselves. In 1925 it was decided that the name European Student Relief should be changed to International Student Service (ISS). It remained in association with the WSCF until 1931, when it became a separate organization – one of the Movement's numerous offspring. Later, in order to help refugees from Nazi Germany after 1933, and from China after 1937, the Federation founded a new European Student Relief Fund in 1940, which became World Student Relief (WSR) in 1943, working in co-operation with ISS and with the Roman Catholic international student secretariat Pax Romana.

ESR/ISS was a highly successful and truly pioneering venture, and was indeed the world's first fully ecumenical relief programme. Christian Aid in Britain, and the relief arm of the WCC, which has operated under a succession of names through the Division of Inter-Church Aid, Refugee and World Service (DICARWS, 1960) to Unit IV: Sharing and Service (1992), and including the Programme to Combat Racism (PCR) are descended from it, as are similar organizations in many countries. And it all began with two SCM secretaries, Ruth Rouse and Eleonora Iredale, and the five young women from mutually antagonistic student organizations who met in a chilly room in Vienna in 1920.

Ruth Rouse, who as early as 1895 had been editor of *The Student Volunteer*, the magazine of the British SVMU, left the SCM staff in 1929 to work for the Auxiliary Movement ('the Aux'), the British SCM's senior friends' organization. In 1948 she put the Movement still further in her debt by publishing a history of the Federation's first 30 years (1895–1934).[74] And, having affirmed that the Federation was the 'experimental laboratory of ecumenism',[75] she went on six years later to publish the results of those experiments by editing, with Stephen Neill, the ground-breaking *A History of the Ecumenical Movement, 1517–1948*, which takes the story, in which she herself played such a significant part, from Luther at Wittenberg in 1517 to the WCC at Amsterdam in 1948.[76]

One more sequence of events in the immediate post-war period is worth recounting. The first meeting of the Federation's general committee after the war was held in July 1920 at Beatenberg in Switzerland. Twenty-four countries were represented, and they included Germany; we are told that 'there was the same atmosphere of goodwill, frankness and vital interest in spiritual issues to which we are accustomed in the Student Movement'.[77] At this meeting Mott expounded the principles of the WSCF, which at that time included, interestingly, 'the maintenance of the non-political character of the Federation'. It was not to be long before this principle would be considerably modified, for at the Beatenberg meeting financial provision was made for relief work (which was in fact already being carried out) provided that it was in harmony with the Christian purposes of the Movement; and it was at this meeting that European Student Relief (ESR) was officially founded by the Federation. Meantime in France a fully secular International Student Confederation (CIE) had been founded, and invitations to join were sent to other countries, including Britain and the United States. British university students, especially those at the newly founded universities, were anxious to be able to take part in the meetings of the CIE, and in order to make this possible the National Union of Students of England and Wales (NUS) came into being in 1922. The SCM gave its encouragement to this new venture, secular as it was, and for some years representatives of the NUS were invited to the Swanwick conferences to make its work known.[78] For the SCM was beginning to be involved in public issues. At the 1921 Glasgow Quadrennial (so called because it was one of a series of conferences held every four years, the name persisting even when the sequence was broken by events like wars!), with no fewer than 2448 delegates,[79] a motion was passed repudiating the 1919 massacre of unarmed Indian civilians at Jallianwallah Bagh in Amritsar, with the words, 'We sympathise with your aspirations for a self-governing India, and we earnestly hope that the reforms now initiated may lead surely and rapidly to the attainment of that goal'.[80] Tatlow comments:

I believe that this was the first message the Movement sent to another Movement which dealt primarily with public questions and the relation to such of the Student Movement. It was a further symptom of the newly awakened sense of responsibility in relation to international questions in the Movement.

The ending of the war in 1918 marked the emergence of a world which had changed for ever: but instead of the apocalyptic gloom one might have expected there was, at least in the universities of the English-speaking world, an air of hopefulness, as thousands of ex-servicemen (and not a few women) flooded the universities, including many with government grants, who before the war could not have afforded a university career. In the SCM there was an outlook of problem-solving liberal evangelicalism, reflected, for example, in the popularity of two books by Harry Emerson Fosdick, *The Manhood of the Master* and *The Meaning of Prayer*. Another popular book, for which Tatlow persuaded Randall Davidson, Archbishop of Canterbury, to write a foreword, was T. R. Glover's *The Jesus of History* (1916). These were all published by the Movement's publications department – forerunner of the SCM Press – which, under the leadership of Hugh Martin of the Baptist Church, was pioneering a new type of low-priced, accessible theological books. As Tatlow said, 'It has been our pride that we have never published a book, however brief and simple, behind which there was not sound scholarship'.[81]

The Basis again

In the closing stages of the war, and especially after thousands of returning servicemen and women began to flood the universities, there was a feeling that the Aim and Basis ought to be expressed in less technical terms, and with a stronger emphasis on the now wider scope of mission. There was also a conviction, contested by some, that the 'personal basis' restriction should be lifted: the Movement was not just for 'finders', but should also be open to 'seekers'. The debate resulted in the adoption, in 1919, of a new Aim and Basis:[82]

> The Student Christian Movement of Great Britain and Ireland is a fellowship of students who desire to understand the Christian faith and to live the Christian life.

> The Movement seeks to set forth Jesus Christ as the supreme revelation of God and of the true nature of man.

> It sees in Him the one sure guide for all mankind in every sphere of thought and conduct, in art and industry, in politics and the professions, in science

and education; the source of power for the overthrow of evil and the renewal of all human life.

The Movement challenges students to recognise the urgent need of the whole world for Christ, without limit of race or nation, and to respond by dedicating their lives to His service as He may guide them.

It calls them to explore his teaching, and to follow the guidance of His Spirit in the pursuit of truth, beauty and righteousness; to prepare them-selves by study, discipline and prayer for the tasks of the future; joyfully to accept God's gift of deliverance and life for themselves; and to enter the fellowship of worship, thought and service which is the heritage of the Christian Church.

Membership

The membership of affiliated Christian Unions and of the Student Volunteer Missionary Union shall be open to students who, having con-sidered the aim and basis, desire to enter the fellowship of the Student Christian Movement.

At the same time a change was made in the wording of the SVMU declaration, if anything making it even more demanding than before. It now read: 'It is my purpose, if God permit, to devote my life to mis-sionary service abroad.'

Reflecting on this period, Eric Fenn, writing in 1939, could say:

The temper of the immediately post-war generation of students was one of optimistic expectation of social change, coupled with a sense of human inadequacy. We thought in terms of the Kingdom of God, and understood by that a better ordering of society, which *we* could build – with God's help.[83]

Throughout the 1920s the Kingdom of God, and the human contribu-tion towards building it, would remain a dominant theme of the Move-ment's life.

24

2

'Poisoning the student mind'?
(c. 1920–35)

Many SCM graduates from American, British, European and Australasian universities had gone overseas on missionary service before World War 1, and many more followed in the immediate postwar period, some in the service of churches and missionary societies and others (without the 'missionary' label) under governments or business houses. Their achievements were remarkable. In Africa, India, China, Japan and the Pacific they planted and developed churches, set up medical and educational institutions great and small, and won notable victories for the social advancement of women, children and the disadvantaged. The world *was* evangelized in the sense that Christian churches were established in virtually every country, and the stage was set for the development of those churches in the following century to the point where Christianity's greatest strength would eventually be found in the 'global South'.

By 1928, when the second World Missionary Conference (successor to Edinburgh 1910) was held in Jerusalem, there was still a great deal of optimism about the world mission of the Church. The continental European representatives had grave doubts about this optimism, which they saw as being driven simply by the 'social gospel'. Yet a great deal that was good had been achieved: there was a far higher proportion of delegates from the 'younger churches' at Jerusalem than at Edinburgh; women played a larger part; there was serious discussion of the problem of racism; people of other faiths were regarded as potential or actual allies in the development of a better world and in the fight against secularism; and already the reunion of the churches was on the agenda, as the negotiations which would lead to the formation of the Church of South India had started in 1919, and those leading to the Church of North India were about to begin. 'The world Church' had arrived.

A parting of the ways: SCM and IVF

But there were problems. Right from the time of the founding of the YMCA in 1844 there had been among students an acute intellectual conflict between religious orthodoxy and a liberalism which sought accommodation with the claims of natural science.[1] 'Liberalism' in the

SCM did not imply a break from an earlier evangelicalism. The Movement's earlier days, strongly influenced by Henry Drummond, were certainly evangelical, but they were not conservative, in the sense of an unwillingness to face the implications of biblical criticism, or the insistence on a particular interpretation of Christian doctrine. The division between liberals and conservatives, anticipated by the disaffiliation of the CICCU in 1910, and which led to actual separation in the 1920s, did not come from any sudden radical forward move, but rather from a call to stand still by the more conservative members of the Movement, who 'trembled for the ark' and were afraid of where this type of open-minded biblical interpretation might take them. The very success of the SVMU and of Edinburgh 1910, with their effective interchurch co-operation for mission, was viewed by some with suspicion. The SCM leadership was thought to be naive in its belief that 'the missionary spirit would bring doctrinal agreement as it had, in measure, helped to bring new life'.[2] The counterpoint to the evangelical liberalism of the Movement in the 1920s is the development of a conservative evangelicalism which paralleled, though it by no means reproduced, the rise in America of biblical fundamentalism.

Davis McCaughey, in his 1959 book *Christian Obedience in the University*, points out how in the first 20 years of the British SCM these two groups of very different outlook, one more liberal and one more evangelical, were able to exist within it, side by side. After that, however, strains began to be felt, partly through increasing participation in the Movement by the Catholic wing of the Anglican Church, and partly because of a growing radicalism on the liberal side.[3] In Geraint Fielder's words, there was fear on the evangelical side of an ecumenism that would combine the Protestant liberal view of the Bible and the Roman view of the Church.[4] Gradually the split became formalized. It was a very sad division, characterized by David Edwards as being quite as grave as any within the churches.[5]

In an effort to overcome the division, talks were held in 1919; and indeed 17 years were to elapse between the 1910 disaffiliation of the CICCU and the foundation of the Inter-Varsity Fellowship (IVF) in 1927. Already it was clear that there was a difference in language, and in the methods of interpretation applied to biblical passages (the word hermeneutics had not yet come into vogue). The evangelical leader Norman Grubb wrote that the SCM refused to 'consider the atoning blood of Jesus Christ as the central point of their message', and therefore 'had not maintained its original witness to the truth of God's Word'; and so, 'as a movement it had apostasised from the truths on which it had been founded, and the CICCU must remain absolutely separate'.[6] David Edwards, writing in 1960, points out that ' "the atoning blood of Jesus Christ", understood as "the life of Jesus Christ summed up in his death, making-at-one God and Man", *is* central to the SCM – and to all Christianity'.[7] The question at issue here is not the authority of the Bible, but rather the question of whether the Bible is to be interpreted as the literal meaning of selected texts and even words and phrases, or by a hermeneutic which interprets scripture by scripture, searching for the meaning underlying the literal text. The SCM had not moved away from the Bible: it was seeking to apply the highest standards of academic integrity and scholarly rigour to its understanding of the Bible.

The IVF, however, insisted that all its committee members should subscribe to its Doctrinal Basis, which among its eight points included (a) the divine inspiration and infallibility of Holy Scripture as originally given; (c) the universal sinfulness and guilt of human nature since the Fall, rendering man subject to God's wrath and condemnation; (d) redemption from the guilt, penalty and power of sin only through the sacrificial death (as our Representative and Substitute) of Jesus Christ, the Incarnate Son of God; (h) the expectation of the personal return of the Lord Jesus Christ.[8] As Edwards says, 'Such beliefs would probably be accepted by a good many individuals in the SCM, but most SCM members would wish to put the truth in them differently'.[9] The current (2005) version of the Doctrinal Basis is expressed in 11 points, in a different order, and in somewhat different phraseology, but is substantially unchanged.

The division between the SCM and what in Britain was variously called the Christian Union (CU), the Evangelical Union (EU), the Inter-Varsity Fellowship (IVF) and eventually the Universities and Colleges Christian Fellowship (UCCF) (and world-wide, since 1947, the International Fellowship of Evangelical Students) has been a tragic one, which has never been healed, and from which both sides have suffered. Gradually the positions have hardened, as they have become globalized, to the point where, all over the world today, the relation between liberals or ecumenists (it is hard to find a satisfactory term) on the one hand and evangelicals on the other is one of the most difficult there is. The division is a sad and damaging one, and facing it in the Spirit of Christ is perhaps the most important of all dialogues between Christians. It is a division which the Protestant and Anglican churches have found very difficult to tackle, since each of them is deeply affected by it. The Roman Catholic Church made a good beginning in the *ERCDOM (Evangelical–Roman Catholic Dialogue on Mission)* Report of 1984,[10] and it is significant that that notable dialogue came about because of a common commitment to mission.

The 'liberalism' of the Movement in the 1920s did not lead to a departure from Bible study as a central activity of the branches and of conferences. But it did mean that the mission to which students felt called by God took a more comprehensive shape. In addition to the under-standing of evangelism in the traditional sense of the verbal proclamation of the gospel, students were attracted to missionary service in medicine and education (as indeed were members of the IVF), to development and social justice projects overseas, and to political and economic witness and service at home, especially concerning unemployment and pacifism. These became the great issues of the 1920s and 30s. And they secured an astonishingly wide arena of discussion in the university through the SCM, whose official British membership in 1935 stood at no less than 11,500 out of a total student population of 72,000. In Adrian Hastings' words, the SCM was at the time 'easily the principal organ of the ecumenical movement'.[11]

Lesslie Newbigin went up to Queens' College, Cambridge, in 1928, and gives an interesting account of his first experience of the Movement, and how, as a virtual unbeliever, he was drawn to it rather than to the Evangel-ical Union:

> There was a lively branch of the Student Christian Movement and several of its members became my friends. I found their company very attractive. They were committed to their faith and ready to talk about it, but also open to difficult questions and ready to take me as I was – interested but sceptical and basically unconvinced. I never felt that they were trying to 'get at' me, as I did about the 'evangelical' group . . . I was more and more drawn into the company of the SCM, and in that company I *did* want to believe . . . By the end of my first year I was committed to the SCM and had become one of the college representatives.[12]

Meanwhile he had discovered that the college chapel was 'the only place where the SCM and the CICCU could pray together, for the official evangelical view was that the SCM members were unbelievers'.[13] That was a charge often made against the SCM. Henry Drummond had suffered from such attacks even before the SCM as such came into being, though D. L. Moody always defended him because he knew the true quality of Drummond's faith, life and witness. During the 1920s and 30s the SCM was often attacked for being too liberal, and on one occasion, apparently in Saskatchewan, Canada, in the 1930s,[14] an article appeared in a local newspaper accusing it of 'poisoning the student mind'. The SCM response, at a subsequent conference, was typical: it put the whole episode into a comic song, beginning with the words

> The SCM has found its true vocation –
> It's poisoning the student mind.
> Its leaders, with astute manipulation
> Are poisoning the student mind.

And the verses – capable of magnificent variation every year – went on to detail the theological aberrations of all the main speakers, whether they were liberal or evangelical, missionary or political, Barthian or Niebuhrian. By the 1940s and 50s the song had become an annual feature of Swanwick and other conferences, and somehow symbolized the SCM's gift for pushing forward radical frontiers while at the same time ensuring that the communication lines with the centre of the Christian faith remained open and functioning. The Movement never took itself, or even its distinguished speakers, too seriously. The seriousness of its commitment to the faith, however, was not in question. In the later words of the British Movement's 1950 Aim, the SCM was a community which called students 'to bear witness as responsible members of a particular church, in personal commitment to Jesus Christ as their Saviour and Lord'.

Mission demands justice

From the beginning, the SCM had concentrated on recruiting students for missionary work overseas. But issues of social justice at home gradually became a concern. Even before the official beginning of the Movement, Drummond and others (following the social teaching of Charles Dickens, Charles Kingsley and F. D. Maurice) had been involved in the creation of 'university settlements' in the depressed slum areas of large cities, where students, while following their courses, could undertake social service activities.[15] At first the SCM took little notice, but two speakers at the Matlock conference of 1900, George Hare Leonard and Miss A. W. Richardson, made such an impression by their presentation of the claims of social work that the issue came on to the Movement's agenda, and in 1901 Tatlow produced the first SCM publication on the relation of Christianity to society, *Outline Studies in Social Problems*.[16] Most university students at this time came from well-to-do families, with little experience of how other people lived; but at a 1909 SCM conference at Matlock to discuss 'the social problem' (attended by William Temple who was then a young teacher in Oxford) the participants had the grace to record their conclusion that '*We* are the social problem'.[17] The next major development, however, did not come until after World War 1, when Eric Scarlett, who had himself studied at Manchester Technical College, was appointed in 1922 as special secretary for technical colleges. He did this work for two years, and by the time he had finished there were SCM branches in about half the technical colleges in Britain. In a report, he wrote – with a perception of 'normality' unusual for the time – that he believed that technical students would help the Movement 'achieve an increasingly vital contact with more normal categories of humanity and more commonplace strata of life than are to be found in the cloistral humidity of our more "rustic" universities'.[18] Yet Scarlett's own calling was to China, where he went as an LMS missionary in 1924, and was shot by bandits six years later.

The postwar situation of the 1920s saw widespread poverty and unemployment in most countries. Edinburgh 1910 had advanced the cause of overseas mission, and the dream of Christian unity of Bishop Charles Brent of the American Methodist Church had begun to be fulfilled when his church called for a world conference on Faith and Order, which was eventually held at Lausanne in 1927. But it was the Swedish Archbishop Nathan Söderblom who, shattered by the failure of the churches to do anything positive to secure peace and social justice after the war, arranged for a 'universal conference on the Life and Work of the Church', which was held in Stockholm in 1925.

The SCM's first response to the situation of unemployment and poverty was to organize summer work camps, where students could work alongside unemployed miners and others. It was an experiment which helped to increase students' understanding of the conditions under which so many people were living, and for many – including Lesslie Newbigin – it was a traumatic experience. But it did little to deal with the underlying problems of economic justice and social ethics. Neither the students who went to work camps in South Wales nor those who revelled in driving railway engines as strike-breakers in the General Strike of 1926 were really dealing with the problems of unemployment. We shall see later how the Movement began to make a more considered and effective approach.

The 1920s also saw (among students as among the more radical missionaries) an increasing interest in other religions for their own sake. Through the writing of Rudolf Otto, J. N. Farquhar[19] (a YMCA secretary in India) and others, this became the era of comparative religion, an emphasis evident in the popularity among students of C. F. Andrews, friend of Mahatma Gandhi (who held that the initials CFA stood for 'Christ's faithful apostle'), staunch supporter of Indian independence and of the rights of Indian indentured labourers in the sugar plantations of Fiji, and sympathetic interpreter of Hinduism. In addition to appearances at Swanwick, Andrews visited and influenced the 1918 Mittagong conference of the Australian SCM.[20] The 1928 Jerusalem conference of the International Missionary Council (IMC) marked the climax, for the moment, of this kind of thinking about interfaith relations. Many of the leaders and delegates at Jerusalem were SCM people, and their concern for understanding people of other faiths, for racial justice and for a fairer relationship between the 'older' and 'younger' churches was reflected in the SCM's own study and conference programmes. It was a phase of conscientious and well-informed study of other faiths, in which Christianity was seen, as in Farquhar's *The Crown of Hinduism* (1913), as the fulfilment of all that is best in other religions – an attitude later to be challenged by Hendrik Kraemer's *The Christian Message in a Non-Christian World* at the Tambaram Missionary Conference of 1938. It was a phase in which Bible study was still important.

Theological colleges

From very early days, theological students were involved in the life of the British Movement, and 1896 saw the appointment of the first theological colleges' travelling secretary, Fred O'Neill of the Irish Presbyterian Church, later a missionary in China. He was followed by a succession of theological college department ('TCD') secretaries, many of whom went on to become well known in the missionary and ecumenical life of the churches, such as Leslie Hunter, Ambrose Reeves, Nicholas Zernov, Oliver Tomkins and Anthony Hanson. In 1898 the first large conference of theological students was held in Birmingham. From the beginning it was realized that the SCM had a different function in theological colleges from that in the universities, and so instead of setting up 'branches' in theological colleges – where they might develop into exclusive cliques of like-minded people – the opportunity was given to colleges as a whole to 'associate' themselves with the work of the Movement. For association it was necessary to have the consent of both staff and students, and gradually, over a period of about 10 years, the majority of the theological colleges in the British Isles became so associated.[21] While many colleges were located close to universities, so that their students could take part in general SCM branch activities, others such as Kelham (Society of the Sacred Mission) and Mirfield (Community of the Resurrection) were physically isolated. Each college appointed an SCM representative, who kept in touch with the Movement through the TCD secretary at Annandale. The listed aims of the department, as they had developed by 1952, included the following:

- to deepen the understanding of the nature and implications of the Ministry by offering to students the opportunity of making contacts with members of other colleges both of their own and of other denominations.
- to assist in emphasizing the world-wide scope of the Church's activities through TCD's connection with the World's Student Christian Federation and the Missionary Societies, Councils and Committees of the Churches.

- to further the realization of the common doctrinal ground held by the various denominations, and in doing so to make clear the nature and importance of the differences between the denominations.
- to make known the current trends in ecumenical theology and practice through TCD's association with the World Council of Churches and the British Council of Churches.

The department promoted the formation of 'theological college unions' in centres where there were colleges of different churches; every second year, in midwinter, a large theological students' conference was held at Swanwick; theological students were encouraged to share in the summer Swanwick conferences; and opportunities were provided for international contacts through WSCF meetings, student work camps and, in later years, courses at the Bossey Ecumenical Institute. The department was able to present the missionary and ecumenical challenge to theological students who might otherwise have remained isolated from it; and many people who later became leaders in their churches were given a vision of the scope of the Christian mission which stood them in good stead in their subsequent service of the world Church. And always the SCM sought to be faithful: faithful both to the separated churches, and to the Church, whose unity it sought. It never tried to set itself up as an alternative church, but helped theological students to become good ministers of their own churches, while never losing the vision of Christian unity – unity-for-mission.

Conditions of membership: tighter or looser?

The tension between the SCM and what would eventually become the IVF was present all through the 1920s, and was focused on two areas: the doctrinal content of the SCM's Aim and Basis, and the conditions for membership. There were those who believed that the doctrines of the incarnation, Trinity and atonement should be spelt out in some detail – greater detail even than that demanded by the churches – and that students should be required to assent to these definitions before they could become members. And there were others who thought that their mission to students could be carried out more effectively if membership were open, and people were encouraged to join the community, and there learn to 'understand the Christian faith and live the Christian life'. In an effort to dispel the fears of the more conservative members the help of the Federation's doctrinal stance was sought, and the following wording was added to the Aim and Basis:

> This Aim and Basis must be interpreted in harmony with the object of the WSCF, of which the Movement is a part, namely: 'To lead students to

accept the Christian faith in God – Father, Son and Holy Spirit – according to the Scriptures, and to live as true disciples of Jesus Christ.'

One result of this long debate, however, was that the Aim and Basis fell into disuse and the branches, still called Christian Unions, tended not to keep membership rolls at all. And so, throughout the 1920s, the debate continued, this time with William Temple lending his considerable weight to the discussion. Finally in 1929 a new document was approved, reflecting the liberal 'Kingdom of God' theology of the time and perhaps, sadly, recognizing that the Inter-Varsity Fellowship had already, in 1927, separated from the Movement. The Aim and Basis is described as being 'an expression of the convictions which guide the thought and life of the SCM as a whole', and goes on:

> As a Christian Movement we affirm our faith in God, our Father, whose nature is creative love and power.
>
> God is made known to us in Jesus Christ, in whom we see the true expression of His being and the true nature of man.
>
> Through His life and triumphant death, and through the living energy of the Spirit, we share in the redeeming love which overcomes evil, and find forgiveness, freedom and eternal life.
>
> Faced with the need and perplexity of the world, we desire to give ourselves to Christ and to follow Him wherever He may call us.
>
> We seek the Kingdom of God, the recreation of all mankind into one family, without distinction of race or nation, class or capacity.
>
> We desire to enter into that fellowship of worship, thought and service which is the heritage of the Christian Church.

The affiliation with the WSCF was acknowledged, and its 'objects' stated, but without comment. And finally came the new Condition of Membership, expressed in words already familiar from the opening sentence of the 1919 Aim and Basis: 'The SCM is a fellowship of students who desire to understand the Christian faith and to live the Christian life.' To that were added the words, 'This desire is the only condition of membership'. They were words which in the years to follow enabled and encouraged countless students, including me, to join the SCM.

Nondenominational or interchurch?

In the late 1920s and early 30s a certain tension was obvious between the 'Catholic' and 'Protestant' traditions within the Movement. There was a gradual swing away from the 'nondenominational' position, which still characterizes the Universities and Colleges Christian Fellowship (UCCF), towards an 'interdenominational', 'interconfessional' or 'interchurch' one, to which the term 'oecumenical' would later be applied. As early as 1912 Archbishop Davidson of Canterbury, a great friend of the Movement, was able to say of the SCM:

> It is not undenominational but it is interdenominational. There is markedly and emphatically no sinking or ignoring of denominational differences, and . . . the care taken in this respect, and the thought devoted to the matter, have rendered possible . . . gatherings such as the Edinburgh Conference of 1910, in which different Christian leaders took part without the smallest loss of denominational distinctiveness, or even what is sometimes called 'the sinking of differences'.[22]

The SCM was taking the Church seriously, and one sign of the developing interest in ecclesiology was the holding at St Albans in 1927, with the prompting of Zoë Fairfield, of the first Anglican–Orthodox conference for theological students. Leaders included the Anglican Bishop Charles Gore and Fr Sergei Bulgakov of the Russian Orthodox Church, and on the organizing side was Ambrose Reeves, at that time theological colleges secretary of the SCM, and destined to return more than 30 years later as general secretary.[23] His contacts with the emigré Russian Orthodox community in Paris had provided this opening. Zoë Fairfield, together with Tatlow, Amy Buller and a young Orthodox staff member at Annandale, Zenia Braikevitch (later, with Ambrose Reeves, joint editor of the journal *Sobornost*) was instrumental in setting in train the events which resulted in the forming of the Fellowship of St Alban and St Sergius,[24] which eventually developed its own life independent of the SCM.

The mention of Zoë Fairfield makes it appropriate to continue her story into the 1920s, for in many of the Movement's new developments she was a leading spirit, inspiring others by her own vision. Always an advocate of the place of art in the Christian life, it was she who, just after the war, encouraged her colleague Leslie Hunter (later Bishop of Sheffield) to write a book called *The Artist and Religion*, and she was able to recruit such well-known public figures as William Rothenstein, G. K. Chesterton and Walford Davies as her speakers in a series of lectures on art, literature and music. From the foundation of the SCM's senior friends' Auxiliary Movement ('the Aux') in 1912 she was on its committee, and eventually in 1929 became its leader, with more than 3000 members and 80 centres.[25] With Bill Paton, who was to become famous in international mission and ecumenical circles, she worked to broaden the SCM's understanding of mission so that it would include international affairs, including politics; and international responsibility became one of the themes of the 1921 Glasgow Quadrennial, which she organized.

Zoë Fairfield had a great gift for friendship – friendship with an astringent quality to it – which made her very effective in finding and securing people to serve the Movement, even when they refused at the time of first asking. Robert Mackie[26] did just that; and Tatlow recounts how, at the Manchester Quadrennial of 1925, 'Miss Fairfield and I, and one or two others, sought to take him by assault' – and succeeded.[27] So too with Herbert Gray, a former army chaplain who in 1923 pioneered the SCM's first specific sortie into the area of sexuality with his book *Men, Women and God*. Zoë Fairfield epitomized a call to total commitment and ascetic self-denial which was very strong in the early days of the SCM as a missionary movement. Some of her friends and colleagues, like Joe Oldham, William Temple, Herbert Gray and Robert Mackie, would eventually lead the Movement towards a gentler understanding of the self. But none of her contemporaries was in any doubt about the integrity and effectiveness of her unsentimental, probing gift for friendship; nor of her creative intelligence, and her capacity to weld a group of people into a fellowship which in its turn became creative. Her contribution over 20 difficult years left the Movement immensely richer.

So what kind of person was her colleague Tissington Tatlow (1876–1957), commonly known as 'T squared' or simply 'T', whose name has featured so frequently in these pages? A Dubliner, and an engineering graduate of Trinity College Dublin, he signed the SVMU declaration in 1896; and although in the event he never served as an overseas missionary, his whole life was single-mindedly devoted to the mission of the Church.[28] At the age of 21 he was appointed travelling secretary of the SVMU in Britain (of which the south of Ireland was still a constituent part), and a year later became the first general secretary of the British College Christian Union, which would eventually become the SCM. His successor and friend Robert Mackie records that his greatest gift was administration: he turned the Movement, which otherwise might have been a passing student enthusiasm, into a continuing and growing organization. 'There are hundreds of people whose work for Christ is a little more effective because they saw a job once carried out supremely well in his name.' He saw possibilities for growth – for example in the SCM Press, which, starting with a few study outlines, with his encouragement soon developed into a significant religious publisher. He had a flair for finding the best people for the different tasks of the SCM: Bible-study secretaries, missionary secretaries, evangelistic secretaries and conference speakers. His working partnership with Zoë Fairfield was a remarkable one, and a disagreement between them on the general committee was always a battle of giants, but a battle which produced a host of new ideas. Mackie, in 1957, comments:

There are not yet too many men in public life willing to have associated with them women with abilities they do not possess. T was one of these. He took a great deal from Zoë Fairfield and used it with single-ness of heart.

It was he (together with H.-L. Henriod, Zoë Fairfield and George Cockin) who made Student Movement House possible. He was a friend of the Russian SCM in exile, and of the Theological Institute of St Sergius in Paris; and the Fellowship of St Alban and St Sergius would not have been possible without his 'imaginative love' of the Orthodox. It was he above all who gave the SCM its Church-centred character, so enabling it to move from its initial nondenominationalism into a fully ecumen-ical stance:

> T's steady insistence on complete loyalty to the churches as they were, and yet on the necessity of a common Christian witness in the universities, was one of the strongest influences in creating an ecumenical temper in Britain.

Starting from his base in the SCM, Tatlow was able to make an out-standing contribution to the early stages of modern ecumenism, not least through his part in making possible the Edinburgh conference of 1910. He had a passion for Christian unity, and a gift for getting alongside people of traditions other than his own, and for the whole of the period from Edinburgh 1910 until the formation of the WCC in 1948 he was a leader in the Faith and Order movement, of which, typically and unobtrusively, he was for many years treasurer. And, also typically, he arranged in 1929 that a small group of theological students should sit with the Faith and Order Committee whenever it met; he had an eye to the next generation of church leaders. When the time eventually came, in that same year, for him to hand over the general secretaryship to Robert Mackie, T's imaginative and creative instincts took a new initiative in the formation of the Institute of Christian Education. When Tatlow died in 1957, the Archbishop of Canterbury, Geoffrey Fisher, said of him, at a meeting of the British Council of Churches (BCC), that although he had never played a prominent part in the Council's life, he was one of its chief architects. And Robert Mackie, commenting on his singleness of heart, says simply that, though lacking some of the more obvious gifts of public leadership, he did more than anyone else, save William Temple, to make the ecumenical movement a reality in Britain. By 1935 the SCM in Britain had become, in Eric Fenn's words,

> a place where members of separated traditions could get to know one another so well that they could not only begin to laugh at themselves, but even at one another; and, if you have once done that when you are young, very few theological dissensions in after years can be fatal to fellowship.[29]

And on the other side of the Atlantic Charles West, coming from an atheistic humanist family and entering the undergraduate college of Columbia University in New York City in 1938, and asking, in a world of dictatorship and war, what power, what guiding truth could be worthy of complete trust and loyalty, found himself led to 'the place on campus where God was central, the Student Christian Movement'. He wrote:

> The SCM was a community that drew in people like me who were arguing, challenging, testing, and throwing their raw personalities against colleagues, against the church, and against God. We were accepted and welcomed, and we learned from people who knew something of the way Christ accepts, judges, and transforms us all . . . So I became, through the Student Christian Movement, an ecumenical Christian, a minister, and a missionary. It was all one conversion.[30]

3

Through depression, holocaust and war (*c.* 1935–45)

The two decades from about 1925 to 1945 witnessed great changes in the life of the student movement, reflecting the cataclysmic changes in the surrounding world, as it moved from the troubled peace of the early 1920s, through the economic gloom of the great Depression, into the period marked by the rise of Fascism and Nazism and the persecution of the Jews, and then into and through World War 2. In some countries, like Britain, the Movement pursued a fairly even course of development, even during the war: in others, like Germany, pressures amounted to persecution; while the Federation, from its Geneva base, sought to maintain the world fellowship in circumstances of great difficulty. In attempting to understand something of the variety and complexity of the life of the Movement as it developed through this period we shall occasionally need to look back to roots in the 20s, as well as to outcomes in postwar days.

Politics, industry and social ethics

The 1925 Stockholm conference on Life and Work was followed by the Oxford conference on Church, Community and State of 1937, the underlying preparation for which was largely done by J. H. Oldham. Because Oldham exercised such a powerful influence on the SCM, of which he himself was both a product and a pioneer, it is worth pausing here for a moment to recall some of the events and groups in which he was a moving spirit.[1] And it should be remembered that although he was in some ways an élitist, he never sought to be an authority figure; his method rather was to gather around him groups of people, experts in their own line, and encourage them to express a well-grounded view on the subject under discussion. We have seen how he served on the staff of the British SCM in its very early days. Next came a period in India with the YMCA, followed by the organization, with Mott, of the 1910 Edinburgh Missionary Conference – a vast undertaking. Then came his book *The World and the Gospel* (1916), and the inauguration (as the follow-up to Edinburgh) of the International Missionary Council. There followed, in the 1920s, a period of involvement in Africa, resulting in the creation of the International Institute of African Languages and Culture,[2] and the publication of *Christianity and the Race Problem* (1924).

From Stockholm in 1925 to Oxford in 1937 he was involved in Life and Work issues, and in the advance planning for the formation of the World Council of Churches. And then, in 1938, as the war clouds were gathering, came the first of many successful efforts in London to bring together, in unofficial but influential collaboration, a group of expert friends, both clerical and lay, drawn from the worlds of education, science, politics, business, the arts and theology. 'The Moot' was the first such group, beginning in 1937 and continuing until 1947, and including among its members not a few with an SCM background, like Eleonora Iredale, John Baillie, Eric Fenn, Kathleen Bliss and Marjorie Reeves, who described herself as 'a very junior member'.[3] Shortly after the outbreak of war in 1939 came the first issue of *The Christian News-Letter* (*CN-L*), which continued, at first weekly and later fortnightly, until 1949, with a circulation which eventually reached 10,000. Its collaborators included major figures like the Roman Catholic social philosopher Christopher Dawson, the New Testament scholar C. H. Dodd, the poet T. S. Eliot, detective writer and religious dramatist Dorothy Sayers, and radical Christian economist R. H. Tawney; and there were also people more closely connected with the SCM, like William Temple, Archie Craig of Scotland, Billy Greer (later general secretary of the Movement and eventually Bishop of Manchester), T. R. (Dick) Milford of Oxford, and Bill Paton of the International Missionary Council. The SCM influenced the group; and the group influenced the SCM. The *CN-L* and its collaborators also exerted considerable influence in senior academic, and even political and financial circles, as well as in the churches. We read of positive interaction with R. A. Butler, author of the 1944 Butler Education Act;[4] A. D. Lindsay, Master of Balliol and much involved in university reform; J. M. Keynes,[5] ground-breaking economist; and Sir William Beveridge,[6] originator of the Beveridge Report of 1942, foundation document of the British welfare state. Oldham gave a succinct definition of the aims of *The CN-L*: 'bridging the gulf which exists at present between organised religion and the general life of the community'.[7] *The CN-L* did not attempt to restate the faith of the Church: rather it *assumed* that faith, but sought to help Christians understand how they should *act* – individually, but more especially together – in their particular vocational situation. That was a very SCM way of looking at things, for *The CN-L* was strongly marked by 'the SCM tradition', and its readership included many staff and student members of the Movement.

The *CN-L* was followed in 1942, immediately after the inauguration of the British Council of Churches (BCC), by the formation, through Oldham's initiative, of the Christian Frontier Council.[8] The name 'Frontier' was chosen as signifying 'the borderland between the normal work of the church and the general life of society',[9] and Oldham and his colleague Walter Moberly saw it as a freer and less official body than the BCC. The Christian Frontier Council concerned itself with a variety of topics such as public health, where Daniel Jenkins (Birmingham SCM secretary 1942–44) wrote *The Doctor's Profession* (SCM Press, 1949); and education, where the Council produced two significant books, *Equality and Education* (SCM Press, 1961) and *The Educated Society* (Faber, 1966). Marjorie Reeves, pioneer and more recently historian of this period, has used the term 'conviction politics' to describe the outlook of Oldham's groups; and Duncan Forrester well describes this outlook, or rather tradition, as 'seeking a society in which freedom flourishes in the context of a special concern for the weak and the poor and the underprivileged'.[10]

Two years before the Oxford conference of 1937, and well before the beginning of the various Oldham-inspired groups we have been studying, Ronald Preston had in 1935 started work as industrial secretary of the SCM, working closely with Edwin Barker and Arnold Nash and strongly under the influence of Reinhold Niebuhr and his *Moral Man and Immoral Society*, which the SCM Press – still suspicious of such radical thinking – had refused to publish. Preston and Nash managed to persuade the press to publish Niebuhr's next book, *The Interpretation of Christian Ethics*.[11] Preston, who later became study secretary and also editor of the SCM's influential magazine *The Student Movement*, went on to become one of Britain's leading Christian social ethicists. And the industrial department of the SCM became a powerful force in enabling students destined for a life in industry and business to grapple with the Christian faith and with complex ethical issues, and to share their skill and understanding with students in other faculties along the lines foreshadowed in the 20s by Eric Scarlett. The department also helped the Movement as a whole to realize that mission went far beyond simple cross-cultural evangelism.

The development of the social justice arm of the SCM's approach to mission aroused suspicion from the leaders of the IVF. Oliver Barclay comments that

> by 1935 what the SCM was doing was open to criticism as being neither well based on the Bible nor dealing with actual questions for the student. It also distracted from evangelism. The SCM was led by older men who tried to run its programme as if it were a ministers' fraternal. Even the strong influence of William Temple in the central councils of the SCM meant that it was often talking about questions that were quite outside the experience of students.[12]

From time to time the SCM and the IVF tended to accuse each other of being run from the top, and by 'older men'; and no doubt Tatlow overstayed his period as general secretary, while Barclay's general secretaryship of the IVF from 1964 to 1980 is also open to question. But the engagement in social issues under people like Leslie Hunter in the 1920s and Ronald Preston in the 1930s and 40s was an engagement of *young* staff secretaries with students: and certainly under Preston, Bible study of the best kind was regarded as a necessity, not as something marginal. But even under Tatlow there was a difference in the way the two movements operated. SCM policy was never directed from above; it was always subject to full debate and decision in student councils, where senior advisers were in a small minority. In addition, the SCM was not governed, as was the IVF, by a Basis which enforced a more rigid doctrinal system than that of the mainline churches. The SCM encouraged its members to wrestle with the Bible personally, rather than simply to listen to, and accept, an interpretation handed down from an approved senior male speaker. As to the suggestion that the SCM was often dealing with questions 'quite outside the experience of students', what are students for if not to be educated, and encouraged to deal with the social and political issues which are already facing them, and for which, from the age of 18 (today if not in the 1920s) they are politically and officially responsible?

If we follow the history of the industrial department a little into our next historical period, a key figure is Leslie Hunter, who in 1939 became Bishop of Sheffield, after serving on the SCM staff from 1913 to 1921, successively as theological colleges secretary, Bible-study secretary and literary secretary.[13] A close associate of William Temple – Hastings describes him as 'perhaps as close to being Temple's heir as anyone'[14] – he established the Sheffield Industrial Mission in 1944, with Ted Wickham in charge. The SCM had been hoping to secure Wickham as industrial department secretary, but Hunter got in first.[15] Wickham's work – closely supported by the SCM, which helped to popularize it and make it known in churches other than the Anglican – proved to be 'the start of something important in the creation of a "missionary structure" for the Church's presence in a modern urban–industrial community'.[16]

The lasting contribution of the industrial department to the SCM tradition has at least three dimensions. First, it gave a clear focus to the field of industry as an essential area for the Church's mission, an area requiring professional and expert knowledge and experience. Second, working along with the theological college department it provided an opportunity for theological students to share in this specialized aspect of ministry and mission, with the result that many prospective ministers in different churches and different countries entered the specific field of industrial ministry, often with Ted Wickham in Sheffield, or Horst Symanowski of the Gossner House in Mainz-Kastel in West Germany.[17] Third, and especially through the work of Ronald Preston, Christian social ethics became a recognized and important part of the Church's life, and of its intersection with the industrial as well as the academic world.

Schools and teachers

The Schools Department of the British SCM was established in 1923,[18] with J. H. Grummitt as its secretary.[19] But already for 20 years before 1914 'The Universities' Camps for Public Schoolboys' had run annual camps, though these had dwindled by the time of World War 1; so in 1919 the SCM formed a committee 'to consider the relation of the Movement to the schools of the country and to any organization working among schoolboys'. This committee was able to widen the hitherto rather elitist catchment area through its co-operation with 'The Free Church Camps', later to be joined by a Welsh Camp movement, chaired by Prof. C. H. Dodd, and the camps were restarted in 1921, with the SCM eventually taking charge. Meantime some women members of SCM had started the Federation of University Women's 'Camps for Schoolgirls'.

Over the years the work in schools developed greatly, frequently with a general secretary based at Annandale and supported by other staff members in the regions. Robert Walton, for example, was general secretary from 1943 to 1949, and was assisted by Vernon Sproxton, who later became a well-known television commentator in the Religious Broadcasting department of the BBC. Walton produced a series of excellent textbooks, which were widely used in school departments of religious education. Other leaders included Ronnie Goodchild (general secretary 1949–53), Blodwin Lewis and Patricia Swain, and in Scotland Richard Baxter. 'SCM in Schools' was able to introduce a strong ecumenical element into the life of many schools based on a single church tradition. It also acted as a fruitful seed-bed of recruitment to the Movement for students who went on to the university. While the university, schools and training college departments of the Movement all had different clientèles, the fact that all were based at Annandale meant that the staffs were in constant communication with each other, in an atmosphere of mutual encouragement and interest.

There had been Christian Unions in teacher training colleges in Britain almost from the start of the Movement, but it was not until 1907 that the SCM began officially to organize its approach to this group of students, of whom in that year there were 8330, scattered over England and Wales in 64 colleges,[20] some church-related and some non-denominational, some residential and others for day students. Hitherto the Movement had been geared to work with university students only, but many travelling secretaries made a point of visiting the training colleges and establishing branches there, and in 1914 the first conference for training college students was held at Swanwick. Its leaders were an impressive group: William Temple; Winifred Mercier (later principal of Whitelands College); Winifred Sedgwick (one of the most redoubtable women leaders of the SCM in its early days, who had pioneered work for the Federation in Geneva and later in Russia in the early years of the century); S. H. Wood, subsequently a member of the government's Board of Education, and the indispensable Zoë Fairfield.

Already at this stage it was clear that in this area of the Movement's work, women would be the predominant partners, and so it was to remain. Winifred Sedgwick's contribution here was outstanding, and she produced a textbook for Bible study in training colleges entitled *Christ the Teacher*. Because she was a good musician, and also interested in art, she had a special appeal for music students and co-operated with the Art Students' Christian Union in founding SCM branches in music colleges.[21] And at general student conferences, in which training college students always took part in large numbers, it was she who first established the tradition that the standard of musical performance should be worthy of the occasion and the company.

The training college work grew, and by 1923 the total number of training college students in England and Wales had risen to 19,000. Yet always there was some tension in the Movement between those whose primary Christian concern was for the specific and professional questions of 'education', and those whose priority was the personal Christian life and witness of training college students. Davis McCaughey discusses the question as it affected the life of the Movement in the period from 1930 to 1950,[22] and regrets that the SCM was unable to do for the training colleges what it did for the universities through the work of Walter Moberly and others. He feels that perhaps the greatest contribution the Movement was able to make to teachers in training was through the work of former SCM members, university graduates who had risen to the top of the educational profession and its associated bodies – people like Tatlow himself (in the Institute of Christian Education), F. A. Cockin for the Church of England training colleges, J. W. D. Smith in Scotland, and the many former SCM members who had become principals of schools or heads of university education departments. Among such leaders the SCM itself was a major player,[23] since the Movement already possessed a large group of signed-up former members in its Auxiliary Movement ('the Aux'), a great many of whom were teachers. Through them, and once again under the influence of

William Temple, and with the guiding genius of Joe Oldham, a new organization was born, the Institute of Christian Education (ICE), founded in 1934, and with an influential journal, *Religion in Education*, published by the SCM Press. By 1945 the ICE had more than 3000 members. In this area the work of Marjorie Reeves and Roy Niblett was outstanding. Much later, in 1965, the Institute of Christian Education united with the SCM in Schools to form the Christian Education Movement, headed by Philip Lee-Woolf, himself a former SCM general secretary.

There are hundreds of teachers, past and present, who look back with gratitude to the work done through the SCM's education department, the ICE, and the Aux, and especially through the contribution of the many talented women who served as training colleges secretaries over the years – like Penelope Piercy, Margaret Thorpe (Jones), Joan Hardy (Burnett) and many others. The long-term effect of the SCM goes far beyond its work for university students: people with the SCM stamp upon them – whether that stamp was acquired at school, or university, or training college, or technical or theological college, or in a Dons' group, or as a senior friend – have served and are serving the Church throughout the world.

Biblical renewal

For the next major, indeed crucial, development in the Movement's understanding of the Christian faith, and its own responsibility, we move to continental Europe and especially to the Federation's headquarters in Geneva. Suzanne de Diétrich (1891–1981) was arguably the most important figure in the transformation of the SCM's biblical and theological outlook from a somewhat over-optimistic, somewhat naively 'liberal' one to a deeper, more critical, more existentially biblical interpretation of life, and especially of the power of evil.[24] She was aided and abetted by Pierre Maury of France and W. A. Visser 't Hooft of Holland, and all three were strongly influenced by the great Swiss Reformed theologian Karl Barth. Suzanne de Diétrich had first encountered the Movement as a student in 1914, and between the wars served on the staff of the French SCM ('the *Fédé*', as it was called – not to be confused with the wider international Federation) and later on the staff of the Federation itself. She was a pioneering and powerful expositor of the Bible, and was the author of *Le Renouveau Biblique* (Biblical Renewal), a book which, with its English version *The Rediscovery of the Bible*, was to prove very influential in the Movement.[25] M. M. Thomas of India has written about his first meeting with her in 1947 at the Bossey Ecumenical Institute:

One never remembered in her presence that she was a very handicapped person who needed crutches to walk about; she had overcome the handicap and established herself as a spiritual leader of youth, first in the Federation and later at Bossey. Her Bible study and the Bible sharing groups . . . brought not only a new understanding of the unity of the Bible around the history of a sojourning people of God, but also provided opportunities to make personal friendships with openness to each other in depth.[26]

Suzanne and her colleagues had been working to initiate a new kind of Bible study in the Federation. In the first two decades of the century, the SCM had encouraged students to read the Bible prayerfully, devotionally. Suzanne de Diétrich encouraged them to read it rigorously, grappling with the text, using every commentary, dictionary and concordance they could get hold of; and, in words popularly attributed to Karl Barth, 'with the Bible in one hand and the newspaper in the other'.[27] Whether her hand held a Bible or a newspaper or a steering-wheel – she passed her driving test at the age of 60 – students listened to her.

This changed attitude to the Bible had its origins in the interwar period. Many people would conveniently trace it back to Barth's 1919 commentary *Romans*. In the English-speaking countries, if not in continental Europe, the liberal era of the 1920s, in reaction to the war years, was in some ways a period of hopefulness, and of faith in humankind's ability to solve problems, even the problems left by World War 1. Barth had already repudiated that sort of optimism in 1919. The catastrophic events from the beginnings of Nazism in 1923 to the end of World War 2 in 1945 only confirmed his diagnosis. His was a new kind of biblical exegesis, soon to be mediated to the English-speaking world by Edwyn Hoskyns' translation of Barth's *Romans* (1933) and later by Hoskyns' and Davey's commentary *The Fourth Gospel* (1940). It was non-fundamentalist, historical-critical, but existential, and enabled people to face courageously the political situation posed by the rise of Nazism and its persecution of the Jews, and laying the basis for the Barmen Declaration of 1934 and for the German Church struggle.[28]

Writing in 1939 Eric Fenn said, somewhat apocalyptically,

> We have seen in these last years the collapse of the whole 'liberal' position in other countries, and the survival, as by fire, of those forms of Christianity which are fundamentally anti-liberal . . . Nothing but the recovery of the inmost essence of faith, coupled with the most realistic discipleship . . . will avail at all.[29]

Charles Raven of Cambridge, who as a thoroughgoing liberal had been a very popular speaker at SCM conferences in the 1920s and 30s, noticed – and regretted – a difference in his reception by the SCM after about 1934, when students began to turn to Niebuhr and Barth rather than to him.[30] There were painful confrontations in print with Alex Miller of New Zealand and Daniel Jenkins of the then Congregational Church, both with strong SCM connections; and Raven deplored the way in which, under Alan Richardson's editorship, the magazine *The Student Movement* had swung towards the neo-orthodox position. He even went so far as to propose, in 1943, that the Cambridge SCM should disaffiliate from the main SCM and set up its own more liberal organization.[31] That did not happen.

Yet traditional ivory-tower Protestant orthodoxy was equally under question, because the outbreak of war and the persecution of the Jews had raised acute questions of justice, to face which political involvement was essential. In Britain the 'return to the Bible' was led in the SCM by Fenn himself as study secretary, followed in turn by T. R. (Dick) Milford and Alan Richardson.[32] The Movement was indeed rediscovering not only the Bible, but the principle which had fired William Carey as he pioneered the English-speaking world's missionary movement at the end of the eighteenth century. He had convinced the doubters by his exegesis of Isaiah 54.2, 'Lengthen thy cords and strengthen thy stakes' (AV): if mission is to be taken to the ends of the world then the cables must be strengthened and the fixing posts planted more deeply. And that meant more and better Bible study: the Movement was learning the lesson, 'When in doubt, dig deeper'.

A glimpse of the seriousness with which students in the late 1930s were treating biblical and theological study can be seen in the study programme of the Oxford SCM for 1936–37. There were two student study secretaries, Penelope Piercy for social issues and Owen Lidwell for doctrine, each of whom produced substantial study-outlines, which were used in individual colleges by several hundred students. Lidwell was pleased when Joe Fison, who ran the evangelical group attached to St Aldate's Church, came to visit him at Balliol to express his entire approval of the outline.[33] Scholarly Bible study tends to produce a meeting of minds across divisions. The SCM, though providing its own printed study material, always encouraged serious and well-researched local initiatives: it was a 'movement from below'.

The student world of Great Britain and Ireland came rather gradually, perhaps even marginally, into the Barthian ambience. Students at a wartime SCM conference in Ireland in 1942 were addressed by Alan Richardson, who as SCM study secretary introduced them to the work of C. H. Dodd, especially *The Parables of the Kingdom* (1935), and *The Apostolic Preaching and its Development* (1936). They quickly realized that the SCM expected them to take the Bible seriously. The SCM Press, which under the editorship of Hugh Martin had in 1929 been formed into a limited company, was already producing excellent popular aids to

Bible study, and from 1937 came the Religious Book Club (RBC), which published six theological books a year, at a price which even students could afford. The RBC continued until 1979, and at its peak had over 20,000 members.[34] Hugh Martin continued as editor of the Press until 1950. When he died in 1963 Robert Mackie wrote of him,

> It was Hugh Martin who pioneered – I almost said in making theology readable – at any rate in bringing the knowledge of God through the written page to hosts of men and women, who would never have bought the grim-looking products of scholarship which were all that booksellers had to offer. It was a very great achievement.[35]

The Movement under the swastika

To understand the trajectory of the SCM within the history of the Church in the mid-twentieth century it is essential to follow the sequence of events in Europe from the advent of Hitler to power in Germany in 1933 to the end of World War 2. In the Soviet Union on the one hand, and in Nazi Germany on the other, absolute claims were being made – by Marxism and by National Socialism – on the loyalty of nations and individuals. In 1933 Pierre Maury of the French SCM wrote in the WSCF's quarterly journal *The Student World*: 'At this time, does not the true Christian duty to the nation consist in denouncing and refusing this absolutism? And is it not the Federation's mission to help its members to a better understanding and fulfilment of this duty?'[36] In the same issue, Hanns Lilje, general secretary of the German SCM (*Deutsche Christliche Studenten-Vereinigung* – DCSV) openly affirmed the Christian's duty to protest against the absolutization of nation and state. Soon the Nazi state decided to force the DCSV to apply the 'Aryan Paragraph' to its members, meaning the exclusion of all non-Aryans (in effect, Jews) from its activities. As a result, Lilje and Reinold von Thadden (chairperson of the DCSV) decided that they must step down as officers. The DCSV courageously reinstated them, with the result that in August 1938 the government banned the Movement. Already, since 1934, the DCSV had been closely linked with the outlawed Confessing Church (*Bekennende Kirche*), and it soon adopted the form of student congregations (*Studentengemeinden*), in which the student chaplains (*Studentenpfarrern*) played a key role. It was the first time in the history of the Federation that a Movement was placed in a situation of direct conflict with the state, and had to take a dangerous stand for the truth of the gospel.[37]

It was during the time of the German Movement's precarious existence, when government restrictions made it impossible for it to contribute anything to the finances of the Federation, that it began to produce the tiny metal lapel-crosses which were smuggled across the border to

Switzerland and sold by the Federation to the different national Movements, as a contribution from Germany. In countries all over the world these miniature 'Federation crosses', some of which still survive, were worn with pride, understanding and concern. Sometimes they were mistaken for a speck of dust on the lapel, and a friendly brushing off gesture might result in a scratched finger, and an explanatory conversation which could move rapidly from the makers of the cross to its ultimate meaning.

On 9 October 1938 (*Kristallnacht* – the night of shattering glass) came the destruction of 119 synagogues and the arrest of 20,000 German Jews. And in 1942 came the terrible implementation of what has come to be called the Holocaust – the wholesale destruction of the Jewish people within the territories controlled by Germany. The distinction between the forces of good and the forces of evil seemed for the moment to become terrifyingly clear, though it soon became clouded again with the Allied saturation bombing of German cities, and, in 1945, the atomic bombing of Hiroshima and Nagasaki in Japan.

The complexity of the ethical and theological issues between Germany and the Allies, and within Germany itself between the Confessing Church and the 'German Christians', as those who collaborated with the state were called, can be seen in the life of the best-known leader in the German Church struggle, Dietrich Bonhoeffer. Born in 1906, by 1929 he had become a teacher of theology in Berlin, attracted to Barth's dialectical theology and highly critical of the way the victorious Allies had treated Germany after World War 1.[38] At this point he did not associate himself with any student group – neither the Christian Socialists nor the SCM (DCSV) – but gradually there grew up around him what became known as 'the Bonhoeffer circle' of students, out of which arose strong links with the Movement. It was here that he began that experiment in life together in community which was later to find expression in his books *The Cost of Discipleship* and *Life Together*. After a year at Union Theological Seminary, New York (1930), he was appointed student chaplain to the Technical University at Charlottenburg, where he was not particularly successful, as this group was regarded as the weakest bastion in the Berlin SCM: yet through his chaplaincy he became known to a much wider circle of students in Berlin, and was much in demand in the German Movement for his leadership in Bible study and other discussions. It was in the SCM context also that he got to know Hanns Lilje, who was at that time its general secretary in Germany. In Holy Week 1932, the SCM invited him to address a large audience on the theme 'Thy Kingdom come', where he gave special attention to the earthly implication of Christ's message.

Bonhoeffer's first major ecumenical experience came in 1931 when he was a delegate at a conference in Cambridge of the World Alliance for Promoting International Friendship through the Churches.[39] This now largely forgotten body, founded in 1914, had quite a high profile in the period leading up to World War 2 and worked closely with the movement for Life and Work, with which it shared an office in Geneva and a general secretary, who at this time was H.-L. Henriod, an ecumenical stalwart of the WSCF. The World Alliance was a very 'liberal' body, devoted largely to the cause of peace, and including in its membership Roman Catholics as well as Protestants. Bonhoeffer at this time had come close to being a thoroughgoing pacifist, and found the World Alliance more congenial than the Faith and Order movement, as he felt it was the only ecumenical body trying to deal with the practical, earthy issues of peace and justice. It was at this Cambridge conference that he first met Visser 't Hooft, who later became a close friend. He also met C. F. Andrews, who stimulated his interest in Gandhi and his non-violent resistance, and aroused his desire – never to be carried into effect – of visiting India. The meeting appointed Bonhoeffer as honorary youth secretary of the World Alliance for Germany and Northern Europe; and so he became an international secretary in the ecumenical movement, with an official base. In January 1933 the executive committees of the World Alliance and Life and Work met together in Berlin, and Bonhoeffer for the first time met George Bell, who had just become Bishop of Chichester, and who was to become a close friend. Together they watched the vast flag-waving crowds rallying to support Hitler in his rise to power.

In October 1933 Bonhoeffer, by now aware of the divisive problems which the Church in Germany was beginning to face, arrived in London as pastor of two German Lutheran congregations. He carried an enthusiastic letter of commendation from Henriod, who described him as one of the most promising young men in Germany, who was 'prepared to accept any sufferings but cannot in conscience remain in the New Church' (the German Christians). Twelve years later that prophecy of suffering was to be fulfilled in Bonhoeffer's death. Meantime in Britain he was able to make useful contacts with Oldham and Moberly, which were to stand him in good stead later. Already he realized that there was going to be a struggle in Germany which would call for people prepared to go ahead of the Church and pioneer new and dangerous ways of Christian living. In a letter to Henriod at the Federation's Geneva headquarters in April 1934 he wrote:

'Allow me to go before', says the Gospel . . . and in this case it really is now or never . . . If there are none who are 'violent to take heaven by force' (Matt 11:12) then the ecumenical movement is no longer Church, but a useless association.[40]

49

They are words which both echo and proclaim the SCM tradition.

Later in 1934 Bonhoeffer was back in Germany teaching in an unofficial, and eventually illegal, theological seminary of the Confessing Church. His earlier Berlin experience of student community developed further in this setting, and resulted in the publication (in German) of *The Cost of Discipleship* (1937) and the writing, in 1938, of *Life Together*. It was in August 1938, as we have seen, that the German SCM was banned by the government, with the result that work among students became even more closely linked with the Confessing Church.

The story of the last 10 years of Bonhoeffer's life, ending with his execution at Flossenburg on 9 April 1945, is well known. The infamous Godesberg Declaration of 4 April 1939 asserted that National Socialism was a continuation of the work of Martin Luther, that the Christian faith was 'the unbridgeable religious contrast to Judaism', and that 'international churchism of a Roman Catholic or world-Protestant character [was] a political degeneration of Christianity'.[41] The provisional committee of the World Council of Churches, which though still 'in process of formation' was already assuming a strong identity, responded by issuing a manifesto of protest, drafted by Visser 't Hooft and signed by William Temple, Marc Boegner of the French Reformed Church, and William Paton – all four closely associated with the SCM. From now on Bonhoeffer was committed, as never before, to working for the destruction of Nazism, and also for the recognition by Britain, America, and the other Allied and neutral powers that there was a growing and organized German opposition to Hitler, that it needed support, and that planning for a post-war Europe should begin immediately. Through family connections Bonhoeffer was drawn into the conspiracy against the Nazi leadership, and became a double agent, working on the one hand (secretly but officially) for the German Defence Department (*Abwehr*), where he used his British contacts to try to avert the 'unconditional surrender' on which Churchill insisted; and on the other hand being involved in the plot by high-ranking military officers to assassinate Hitler.

In 1939, shortly before the start of hostilities, Bonhoeffer had a meeting with Visser 't Hooft at Paddington station in London. It was important for him to set up lines of communication which could be kept open after the war began; and in fact he was eventually able to make three wartime visits to Switzerland, as well as a memorable one to Sigtuna in Sweden in 1942 for a last meeting with George Bell. The network of 'the SCM tradition' was vital for these arrangements. In Geneva was Bill Paton, formerly a British SCM secretary, and now co-general secretary with Visser 't Hooft of the nascent WCC. In 1941 the SCM Press published Paton's book *The Church and the New Order*, of which Bonhoeffer received a copy via 'Wim' (as Visser 't Hooft was known to his colleagues) in Geneva. Bonhoeffer, who still had high hopes of the Confessing Church taking part in the post-war reconstruction of Europe, wrote a review of this book which Wim translated and Hugh Martin of the SCM Press circulated in Britain. An American SCM and YMCA staff member, Tracy Strong, acted as a courier from Geneva to George Bell in 1941. In all these ventures Bonhoeffer played a vital and dangerous role, constantly trying – especially through his contacts in Britain – to convince the Allies that a successful revolt would soon happen in Germany, urging them to support it, and simultaneously aware of and supporting the actual conspiracy against Hitler. The attempted assassination of Hitler in March 1943 was unsuccessful, and led to Bonhoeffer's arrest and imprisonment on 5 April. A further attempt on Hitler's life on 20 July 1944 also failed. Bonhoeffer, though much interrogated, never came to trial, but was hanged on 9 April 1945. In the meantime he had written the astonishing series of letters which were eventually published by his friend Eberhard Bethge as *Letters and Papers from Prison*, which brought a new vocabulary and a new wave of vitality to Christian theology and Christian life – a source of energy which continues to inspire the Church.

In this story of the SCM it is well to recall that in the English-speaking world it was the Movement, largely but by no means exclusively through the SCM Press, which brought Bonhoeffer's name before the public. Hugh Martin, as editor of the SCM Press, published an English translation of *The Cost of Discipleship* in 1948. I still possess a treasured proof copy of *Letters and Papers from Prison* (1953), passed on to me in that year by Davis McCaughey, who had received it from Ronald Gregor Smith, Martin's successor at the Press. The English version of *Life Together* followed in 1954. The influence of the SCM on Bonhoeffer was perhaps limited to providing him with his first student community (*Gemeinde*), and later surrounding him with an international circle of ecumenical friends who were able to give him some hope and comfort on his lonely journey. But Bonhoeffer's influence on the Movement was immense; and it is not without reason that Christine Ledger, in her account of the WSCF in the *Dictionary of the Ecumenical Movement*, is able to refer to him quite simply as a martyr of the WSCF.

From war to peace

The Movement survived World War 2 in remarkably good working order. In wartime Britain the Swanwick conferences had had to be abandoned (The Hayes at Swanwick had become a prisoner-of-war camp) yet many other activities had continued. Billy Greer, the general secretary, sent out an eagerly awaited and avidly read monthly letter to 'the SCM in

Dispersion' – members in the armed forces or other war work, as well as conscientious objectors – in which he shared with them news of the SCM and WSCF, and gave careful theological and pastoral responses to some of the many letters which came flowing back to him.[42] The international student community at Student Movement House continually produced surprises, as when Robert Mackie turned up mysteriously one day in 1944 (from Canada via Geneva) and gave a fascinating talk which enabled a group in London to share in what was happening to fellow Federation members in other countries, especially those in Germany and occupied Europe. There were even occasional meetings of theological students arranged by Anthony Hanson, who was theological college department secretary at the time: he and a prospective Presbyterian theological student on war service once read the Anglican office for evening prayer together as they rattled along in the Underground! The SCM went out of its way to keep in touch, and to promote ecumenical theology and worship.

Meantime the Federation – perhaps miraculously – held the different Movements together throughout the war, with Visser 't Hooft and Suzanne de Diétrich in charge in Geneva and Robert Mackie in Toronto, and with a system of communication often channelled through Switzerland and Sweden, which – with what was then the Irish Free State, now the Republic of Ireland – were among the few European countries able to maintain their neutrality. The fact that there was now an office in Toronto meant that the Federation was able to strengthen its relationship with the American Movement, and was even able to expand its operations in Latin America, in a remarkable *praeparatio evangelica* for the much later but not unconnected liberation theology, through the efforts of Robert Mackie and Helen Morton. From the Toronto base also the work in West Africa was expanded by Malcolm Adiseshiah (of India) and Miguel Ribiero.[43] *The Student World* and *Federation News-Sheet* continued to be published throughout the war, and from time to time staff members crossed the submarine-infested Atlantic.

As the war drew to an end, it was difficult for the old optimistic liberalism to survive. The biblical inheritance of the Church struggle in Germany was strong, as was the revulsion against what had happened in the concentration camps. Ronald Gregor Smith, who succeeded Hugh Martin as managing director and editor of the SCM Press in 1950, and whose German wife Käthe had suffered at the hands of the Gestapo, provided many of the tools for the SCM's study programme. Under his editorship many solid biblical books came from the SCM Press, including the excellent popular series of 'Torch' commentaries, already started in the 1940s but continuing into the 50s, whose general editors were now John Marsh, Alan Richardson and Gregor Smith himself.

'In process of formation': the SCM and the World Council of Churches

Before going on to the postwar period we need to go back and look at the development of what was taking shape as the 'official' ecumenical movement, a process in which many former members of the SCM were involved, and in which the Movement itself, at both national and Federation levels, would become significantly engaged.

A key figure in this process is William Temple (1881–1944), whose name has kept recurring in the story of the first 50 years of the SCM. The son of an Archbishop of Canterbury, he had grown up in the privileged world of public school and Oxford, and from early days had mingled on familiar terms with leaders in church, academic, professional and political circles. From philosophy he had gone on to theology, where his views became so radical that Hastings Rashdall was able, years later, to write to him, 'I used to be afraid that you would be too much of a heretic to be ordained.'[44] But he *was* ordained; and then came involvement in what then counted as very left-wing organizations like the WEA (Workers' Educational Association). He also became closely linked with the SCM, a partnership which was to remain strong to the end of his life. It was through the SCM that he had his first major ecumenical experience, at Edinburgh 1910, where he was a 'page' (Potter and Wieser describe this function as 'steward', while Mott's biographer C. H. Hopkins refers to it less politely as 'dogsbody'[45]). And it was at Edinburgh that Mott became so conscious of Temple's abilities and his commitment to the SCM that he sent him off immediately after the conference to Australia to consolidate the Australian SCM, especially in its relations with the somewhat unenthusiastic university authorities in that very secular continent. Throughout his life Temple gave high priority to his work with the SCM, being ready, when Bishop of Manchester, to give six hours of his time for preparation for each of the lectures he was to give at the 1925 Quadrennial conference, plus another three hours for the opening address, in place of another speaker who had been unable to come; and again in 1929 he insisted on keeping an appointment at an SCM conference almost on the eve of his enthronement at York.

His circle of friends included many whom we have already noted as SCM people, especially Joe Oldham (for whom he had an affectionate admiration), but also men like Mott, Tatlow, Hugh Martin and Charles Raven and women like Eleonora Iredale and Lucy Gardner. To these were added kindred spirits in the wider world of church and literature like the Swiss theologian Emil Brunner, the French Reformed Church's Marc Boegner, the Orthodox Archbishop Germanos of Thyatira, the German–American 'Christian realist' theologian Reinhold Niebuhr, and from Britain well-known writers like T. S. Eliot and Dorothy Sayers, distinguished figures from the world of politics and economics like R. H. Tawney, John Maynard Keynes and William Beveridge, and theologians like V. A. Demant, H. A. Hodges and Donald MacKinnon. Temple's way of working fitted in closely with Oldham's: indeed their work was really a shared work. His biographer F. A. Iremonger explains his approach, when Archbishop of Canterbury, as being that of 'a prophet in close and constant touch with expert advisers'.[46] That was the Oldham/SCM formula.

Temple's name is especially associated with the Conference on Christian Politics, Economics and Citizenship (Copec) held in Birmingham in 1924, which he claimed was the direct result of the SCM's Matlock conference of 1909 on Christianity and Social Problems. Copec was first mooted in 1919, with the important support of the Anglo-Catholic Bishop of Oxford, Charles Gore, and was given a forward impulse by the appeal for Christian unity made by the Lambeth conference of 1920. Temple himself chaired Copec, with Hugh Martin as chairman of the executive, and Lucy Gardner and Charles Raven as joint secretaries – a strongly SCM set-up. To begin with, the committee included Roman Catholic members, though they later withdrew.[47]

In a recent study of Temple and Christian social ethics, Alan Suggate notices that Temple's way of working was strongly influenced by the SCM, especially its use of small groups and larger conferences.[48] This method-ology, which goes back to Mott, Tatlow and Oldham, became the norm at the 1910 Edinburgh Conference, and in its ecumenical follow-up in the later Faith and Order and Life and Work conferences; and for many years it remained the accepted model for the WCC in its assemblies and other consultations.

Temple's background was a privileged one; but his obvious commit-ment to justice helped him to win the confidence and friendship of people right across the social spectrum. He stood effectively beside the strikers in the General Strike of 1926, and was a constant champion of the WEA. From the first he enjoyed working with laypeople, and gave them the kind of leadership which their professional expertise demanded. And so there grew up around him a body of men and women, young and old, rich and poor, lay and clerical, students and non-students, members of many churches – committed in their different ways to Christ, to the Church, to justice and peace, to mission and unity. The SCM was privileged to be not just a part of that large enterprise, but at times its pace-setter.

Basic to Temple's life and work was his commitment to the Bible and its exposition. Already in 1902, when he was at Balliol, he advocated what was then known as a 'Broad Church' approach to Christianity; but he insisted that it must draw its inspiration from the Scriptures, and affirmed that his own main interest was the interpretation of the Bible – an interest which many years later found its finest expression in his *Readings in St John's Gospel* (1940). His theology, like his churchmanship, starting off as 'Broad Church' combined with a fairly radical version of socialism, later became more 'central', and gradually his interest in the Church's liturgy, ministry and tradition increased; and his friendship with the ecumenical Archbishop Davidson was matched by that with the High Church Bishop Gore.

Mission loomed large on his agenda, but it was mission with a widening scope. In the depths of World War 1 he joined with others in advocating, and carrying out, the 'National Mission' of 1917: what he had in mind was 'not so much a [traditional] mission on a national scale as an effort directed to national life itself: not at the lives of individual people but . . . at the ordering of our national life'. His involvement with the SCM, with the WEA, with university missions (Oxford 1931, Indianapolis 1935, Dublin and others in between), with Oldham's *Christian News-Letter*, with the incipient WCC, and with his leadership of his own Anglican Church, was for him all a part of the one 'great historical movement characterised by a sense of divine mission'. In one of his last writings[49] he says,

> Our need is a new integration of life. Religion, Art, Science, Politics, Education, Industry, Commerce, Finance – all these need to be brought into a unity as agents of a single purpose . . . the divine purpose. The Kingdom of God is the goal of human history, but it is His Kingdom, not man's.

That is a good statement of 'the SCM tradition': and for Temple, as for the Movement, the underlying base was Scripture, interpreted with rigorous academic integrity.

Temple's devotion to the SCM, as well as his honesty, is illustrated by one of the few stories which speak of his failure. It was at a Swanwick conference, when he was speaking on 'Why I believe in God'; he was seen 'to hesitate, to fumble about words and lose his grip'. When someone dared to ask him what had happened, he replied, 'You see, I have never known what it is to doubt the existence of God, and I felt I had no right to be speaking to that audience of young people'. The story shows the humility of the man – and also his intimacy with the SCM. The 'SCM tradition' owes an immense debt to William Temple. And he would have been the first to admit that he owed much to the SCM.

Temple died at the height of his powers in 1944, and did not live to see the inauguration of the WCC four years later. But his support was strongly felt in the formative period of the late 1930s and early 1940s, to which we now return.

The year 1937 saw both the Oxford conference on Church and Society (Life and Work) and the Edinburgh conference on Faith and Order, meetings which resulted in active steps being taken for the coming together of these two bodies to constitute the World Council of Churches 'in process of formation'. An illuminating example of the close relationship between the SCM and the developing World Council of Churches can be seen in the career of Oliver Tomkins who, in 1938, as theological colleges' secretary, organized the winter theological students' conference at Swanwick. There were 200 students, 80 ministers and teachers, and a galaxy of distinguished speakers, most of whom we have already met: William Paton of the International Missionary Council, Walter Moberly (by now a senior figure in university education), John Baillie the Scottish theologian, Joe Oldham, Leslie Hunter and Visser 't Hooft, all of them glad to accept the invitation to address such an important and forward-looking gathering. In the words of Tomkins' biographer Adrian Hastings, 'If there was one moment in Oliver's life when he graduated into the ranks of senior ecumenical leadership, it was surely at Swanwick in January 1938 at the age of 29'.[50] It was a trajectory which would be followed by others, and not only in the British Movement. For Tomkins, the way had already been prepared through the international contacts he had made in the Federation, especially with people like Visser 't Hooft, Pierre Maury of the French Reformed Church, Leo Zander and Nicolas Zernov of the Russian Orthodox Church in exile in Paris, and Reinold von Thadden of Germany, already grappling with the rise of Nazism.[51]

The war put a temporary stop to the process of development towards a world council of churches. Yet behind the scenes much was happening, in which the Federation was deeply involved, for Visser 't Hooft, who was chairperson of the Federation in Geneva, was also the organizing secretary of the incipient World Council. It was in an atmosphere of much thanksgiving and rejoicing that the World Council of Churches was finally inaugurated in Amsterdam in 1948, with Visser 't Hooft at the helm as general secretary. In the years ahead many former members of the national SCMs and the Federation – Suzanne de Diétrich, Robert Mackie, Oliver Tomkins, Jean Fraser, M. M. Thomas, and Patrick Rodger among them – were to join him as colleagues.

4

The golden age (c. 1945-65)

The Federation re-assembles

The first postwar meeting of the general committee of the Federation (WSCF) was held at the Château de Bossey, Céligny, near Geneva, in August 1946 – the first conference to be held in what was to become the Bossey Ecumenical Centre.[1] Amid the gathering of ecumenical leaders who were present, Suzanne de Diétrich was for many the outstanding and memorable figure. At the same meeting was Visser 't Hooft – 'Wim' – who was about to give up his position as chairman of the WSCF in order to concentrate on his work as the first general secretary of the World Council of Churches in process of formation; and the Federation general secretary Robert Mackie of Scotland, about to be succeeded by Pierre Maury's son Philippe.

It was not an easy meeting at first. The encounter between French, Dutch and Norwegian students on the one hand – people who had suffered under and resisted the German occupation – and the handful of German students on the other – defeated, ill-clothed, pinched and apprehensive – was an experience fraught with tension. For people like Philippe Maury, who had been in the French Resistance, it was a difficult occasion.[2] But the spirit of reconciliation was there, and there were reminders too of unexpected acts of grace and forgiveness, for example in the presence of the veteran Reinold von Thadden, leader of the pre-war German Movement, who as wartime field commander of German-occupied Louvain in Belgium had won the respect and admiration of those whose lives he controlled, and was honoured by them after the war. It was a time for breaking down barriers, and picking up threads of communion, strained but unbroken.

This Bossey meeting incidentally gave a certain official *cachet* and even exegesis to the phrase which is the theme of this book about the SCM – that it was 'church ahead of the Church' – when the general committee described the Federation as 'an independent ecumenical Christian organisation, [intended] to be a pioneering and revolutionary force for and within the universal Church of Christ upon the earth'. It was a good definition.

Robert Mackie (1899–1984), who now took over from Visser 't Hooft as chairperson of the Federation, had seen a brief period of army service in France at the end of World War 1, followed by studies, including theology, at Glasgow University. There he joined the SCM, became student chairman of the national general committee in 1922, and then spent some time in India, working as chaplain at a coalfield in Jharia. In 1925 he became Scottish SCM secretary, moving on in 1929 to succeed Tatlow as general secretary, based at Annandale, where he remained until 1938, when he and his family moved to Geneva and he joined the WSCF staff. He is remembered above all for his sensitive understanding of people, his friendliness and his laughter; and that characteristic is reflected in Archbishop Randall Davidson's glowing tribute to the SCM at the time when he was in charge:

> Organisation is too rigid and prosaic a word to describe a movement which in its spontaneity and buoyancy, its international character and its quiet force seems to me one of the most remarkable movements which any part of Christendom at any place or time has seen.[3]

But Mackie was also – like T – an excellent administrator. Visser 't Hooft is quoted as saying, 'Robert says he doesn't like administration! That is absurd! It's like Rembrandt saying he doesn't like painting!'[4]

It was under Mackie's leadership in the British Movement that in 1937 two separate summer conferences began to be held at Swanwick, 'General Swanwick' continuing the traditional pattern. 'Study Swanwick' however was an innovation, which shared some of the features of the 'staff reading party' which was held each autumn, just before the opening of the academic year. For Study Swanwick a particular theme was chosen, a special library was assembled, reading lists were sent out in advance, preparation was required from everyone, and the occasional lecture by a distinguished authority in the chosen field was only incidental to the main work of wrestling – biblically, theologically and practically – with the subject. Politics, economics or literature, as well as theology, could be the theme: in a memorable statement on the relationship between Christianity and politics Mackie wrote:

> Let us freely admit that political discussion may be a way of escaping from the demands of Jesus Christ upon our lives. But so indeed may be worship and Bible study and evangelism. Any human activity may provide an excuse for avoiding a face-to-face encounter with our Lord . . . When we try to keep our politics separate from our religion . . . it usually means that our political opinions will not stand the full light of the Gospel upon them.[5]

Study Swanwick lasted for 10 days, and involved a real engagement of students with experts who considered it a privilege to share in such a gathering. It was a highly effective model for study conferences, from which the Movement later departed, to its loss, but which still survives in various institutions influenced by the SCM, like Cumberland Lodge, Windsor.

In 1938, when it became increasingly clear that the inauguration of the WCC would be delayed by the probable onset of war, Wim Visser 't Hooft, who had been general secretary of the WSCF since 1932 and had now been appointed general secretary of the WCC in process of formation, insisted that he would accept this new appointment only if Robert Mackie agreed to succeed him at the Federation. Mackie moved to Geneva, and immediately embarked on a rapid programme of international visits to Czechoslovakia, India, Singapore, China, Korea, Japan, Canada and the United States. He then carried out the final organization of the first World Conference of Christian Youth – a conference with a membership much wider than the Movement – which was held in Amsterdam in July 1939; and it was here that he set the precedent for what was to be the Movement's policy on intercommunion for many years. Each of the main traditions – which for the SCM did not as yet include the Roman Catholic Church – would hold a eucharistic service, Orthodox, Anglican, Lutheran or Reformed (including Methodist), at which all would be invited to attend, though only at the Reformed service would they be invited to communicate. At the introductory service he said, in memorable words, 'It is not our communion that is broken – it is the body of our Lord Jesus Christ that is broken . . . Whoever of *us* will be absent from any one of our communion services, Jesus Christ will be there'.[6]

When war came in 1939, Wim remained in Geneva, while Mackie and his family went to Toronto. From there he edited *The Student World*, with its memorable travel diaries and analyses of world events, and carried out pioneering visits to South America and the Caribbean, on which others were later able to build. After the war, as we have seen, Philippe Maury succeeded him at the Federation, and he moved to the WCC in Geneva, where he held the dual role of associate general secretary and director of the Department of Inter-Church Aid; in the latter capacity he earned the affection and gratitude of many of the Orthodox churches in Eastern Europe, which did not have overseas sister-churches to help them, and were in dire need.

In 1955 Mackie returned to his native Scotland, where for the next 30 years he gave distinguished, effective yet typically modest service to the cause of Christian unity. In 1957 he chaired the executive of the Tell Scotland evangelistic movement, and the planning committee of the Aberdeen Kirk Week (a Scottish version of the German *Kirchentag*). The Scottish Churches House in Dunblane (1960) might not have happened without his help. He was instrumental in the formation of a new Scottish Council of Churches in 1964. Perhaps one of the most perceptive tributes to his life and work was that of a friend who said:

You have served as a kind of ecumenical cement, to hold together the galaxy of primates and prima donnas who adorn the World Council fellowship. You have done much to humanize the rarefied atmosphere . . . your greatest contribution has been to help to provide the ecumenical movement with a heart.[7]

The ecumenical movement has indeed always had a heart, but Robert Mackie strangely warmed it, and enabled it to beat more strongly.

The golden age

For those who experienced it, the decade of the 1950s represents the golden age of the SCM. The Movement had a large and effective staff (internationally at the Federation headquarters in Geneva, and in many different countries) and also a very large student membership. The SCM had already, in 1948, given birth to its most famous child, the World Council of Churches. It exercised a considerable influence on the life of both the universities and the churches, where its voice commanded remarkable respect.[8] There were great issues to be reckoned with: atomic power, the creation of the welfare state, the break-up of the old imperial powers through independence movements in India, Indonesia, Central Africa and elsewhere. In all of these issues the SCM was actively involved – and was listened to, by both church and university. Within the churches there were schemes for organic union which actually came to fruition, in South India (1947) and eventually North India (1970), in many of which former SCM leaders played a significant part,[9] while in Australia the process which resulted in the formation of the Uniting Church began in earnest in 1956. Those were heady days whose characteristics need to be spelt out in some detail.

We shall look mainly at the SCM of Great Britain and Ireland (as its full title ran), on whose staff I was privileged to serve as secretary of the theological college department from 1951 to 1953. The national staff at this time numbered about 30, covering SCM work in universities, theological colleges, training colleges, schools and industry. The different regions had travelling secretaries, and the headquarters staff was based at Annandale in London. Philip Lee-Woolf had just taken over from Alan Booth as general secretary and there were two assistant general secretaries: Frances Paton (Australia), who had special responsibility for international relations, including what we now call cross-cultural mission, and Stephen Burnett. Ronald Preston and Davis McCaughey had recently moved on from being study secretaries, leaving a remarkable series of study outlines and a particularly good magazine, *The Student Movement*, behind them.[10] They had been succeeded by John Gibbs and Donald Mathers, who developed the somewhat controversial innovation of printing pictures by modern artists on the magazine's cover, some obviously Christian, and others not (like Edvard Munch's *The Scream*), but all significant for the discussion of issues of faith and life.

The pattern of life in most university or college branches was a weekly general meeting, usually with an outside speaker; a number of study groups – several of them perhaps on the Bible and others on political, social or personal ethical questions – usually meeting each week; and large annual conferences at Swanwick. Certain features of the Swanwick conferences remained virtually unchanged over the years, and Lesslie Newbigin's 1929 experience still held good for many students in the 1950s:

> That first Swanwick opened up a new world for me. It is hard to describe now how thrilling it was. I can only say that I was lifted up into the heights. The excitement of being able to share new ideas and insights with many different people of my own age but of different background; the sheer high spirits bubbling up in all kinds of fantastic performances . . . We saw Jesus in his glory, and like the disciples we just wanted to stay.[11]

In addition to General and Study Swanwick, national conferences were held each year in Ireland, Scotland and Wales. There were also opportunities for students to take part in Federation conferences in Europe, and large numbers of overseas students were welcomed to activities at every level of the Movement in Britain.

The SCM was a large and complex organization, run on a shoestring budget by young secretaries on minimal salaries, every penny of expense being accounted for in a little 'black book' (in later, more political days, to be known as a red book). It was also a true ecumenical community, with occasional problems and tensions no doubt, but mostly characterized by a great sense of joy and liveliness, and by a remarkably equal fellowship between men and women. Music was important, whether it was singing in worship – frequently using words and music from the multilingual Federation hymnbook *Cantate Domino* – or listening to and joining in a great variety of impromptu, and witty, topical songs, often led, at Swanwick, by Mary Trevelyan, and later by Reginald Barrett-Ayres, Geoffrey Beaumont, Margaret Falconer (later Webster) or Simon Phipps. A vivid picture of how a Federation secretary saw her responsibility in the Movement immediately after the war is given by Marie-Jeanne de Haller (Coleman) (1919–2006), who was on the WSCF staff from 1944 to 1953 and carried on and developed the work of Suzanne de Diétrich in making the Bible excitingly available and challenging to students. She was a person whose musical talents and warm gift for personal relations and pastoral concern put many a student in her debt;[12] she was also a very effective administrator, who on numerous occasions, especially during the prolonged illness of Philippe Maury, carried the full burden of acting general secretary of the Federation. From retirement in Canada she described how she, and the Federation, faced the post-war task:

> First, I had to establish contacts with the remains of those movements in different countries that had been isolated during the War, or had been forbidden and had gone underground. I then tried to initiate a mutual support system between these movements and encourage a rediscovery of the Bible; not as a source of pious exercise, but as a place to go for wisdom and strength in decision-making, and living in a tough world. Suzanne de Diétrich had been . . . instrumental in forming this Biblical revival. I also attempted to communicate the rediscovery of the Church Universal, the *Una Sancta* as we used to call it, as a living community; to stimulate theological thinking and education among non-theologians; to promote reconciliation and mutual understanding through honest and at times painful encounters between former enemies; to challenge students about their intellectual, professional, social, political, ecumenical responsibilities now and for the future; and to participate in relief and rehabilitation efforts.[13]

That large agenda was carried on – as it was by all SCM secretaries – through crowded and arduous journeys, in difficult and sometimes discouraging places, on a tiny budget. But it had all the excitement of apostolic days. Those who saw Marie-Jeanne de Haller and Suzanne de Diétrich in action at the 1946 general committee at Bossey know how challenging – and joyful – the student members of the Movement found such leadership.

Marie-Jeanne had great pastoral gifts, and she was not alone in exercising this very important ministry among both the Movement's staff and its student members. For a great deal of pastoral care went on in the Movement – secretaries caring for students in their many problems, students caring for each other, more senior members of staff caring for more junior ones; and senior friends, no longer members of the Movement but familiar with its life, listening, advising and helping. But mention should be made of a special kind of person – and they were mostly women – who served on the staff for longish periods, sometimes as office secretaries at headquarters, sometimes combining that work with being a travelling secretary. Many national Movements had such people. At the British SCM's base at Annandale, Dorothy Jackson filled the role for 28 years from 1929 to 1957, and successive generations of staff secretaries relied on her wisdom and calmness; it was to her that Davis McCaughey in 1958 dedicated his classic book *Christian Obedience in the University*. In Australia two names are remembered with affection and even awe. The awe is mainly for Margaret Holmes, a classics graduate who as executive secretary of the Australian Movement in the 1930s and

40s was gladly looked up to by travelling secretaries of the calibre of Frank Engel.[14] She is remembered especially for the work she did for the Jewish refugees who began to arrive in Australia in 1938, and particularly for 'the Dunera boys' – a large group of highly intelligent young Jewish men who had been interned in Britain, and deported to Australia as prisoners of war under appalling conditions on the troopship *Dunera*. The ASCM, on behalf of ISS (International Student Service), and largely through Margaret Holmes and VIREC (Victorian International Refugees Emergency Committee) which she was instrumental in creating, organized university courses for the men in their camps. They were wonderful students, and many of them went on to become leaders in professional and academic life in Australia and elsewhere; and they did not forget Margaret Holmes and the SCM. The other name is that of Rosalie McCutcheon, who is remembered as a person who radiated warmth and understanding; and many men and women who went on to make important contributions in academia, church and state testify to the way she helped them at times of critical decision-making. Charles Birch, later to become a world authority on ecology, wrote of her that 'she was the most saintly person I've ever met. Her heart was just in helping people and she had so many people to help'.[15] And David Gill (who would go on to be general secretary of the Uniting Church in Australia, serve on the WCC staff and edit *Gathered for Life*, the report of its 1983 Vancouver Assembly, and later become general secretary of the National Council of Churches in Australia) wrote that she was simply the kind of person you liked to be with, 'an extraordinarily magnetic personality and a great pastoral presence at the university. She drew a lot of us in simply by being Rosalie McCutcheon'.[16] The job of travelling secretaries, and headquarters staff too, could be very stressful; and national Movements which were blessed by people with the qualities of Rosalie McCutcheon, Margaret Holmes and Dorothy Jackson were fortunate indeed.

Worship

The SCM never claimed to be a church, and so did not attempt to provide a comprehensive liturgical life for its members: that was left to local churches and clergy, or to college chapels and chaplains. But worship was a vital part of the Movement's life, and prayer was central, right from the Morning Watch of the Movement's earliest days. Tatlow, indeed, writing in 1954 in the larger context of the whole ecumenical movement, speaks of prayer as 'its mainspring . . . without which ecumenical activities would be useless if not dangerous'.[17] In the 1950s most branches had a prayer secretary, and some, as in Trinity College Dublin, had a small room furnished as a chapel. At the Annandale headquarters, daily inter-cessions were held in the chapel; and a list of subjects for prayer, together with a Prayer Calendar, was published each month in *The Student Move-ment*. Occasional Schools of Prayer were held during the vacations, for which Olive Wyon, author of the popular RBC book *The School of Prayer*, was frequently sought after as a speaker. At conferences it was usual to have separate communion services celebrated by ordained clergy of the Anglican, Reformed (Presbyterian or Congregational) or Methodist traditions.

Prayer in the Movement was closely associated with the Bible. In 1915 *A Book of Prayers for Students* had been published, revised and enlarged in 1920 and again in 1923. J. H. Oldham followed this in 1925 with *A Devotional Diary*. By the 1940s it was felt that *A Book of Prayers for Students* was out of date, and Ronald Preston set about editing a new one, together with Dick Milford, and John Coleman of the WSCF staff. The result was *Student Prayer*, published in 1950. In listing four aims of the book, Davis McCaughey stresses its purpose of helping students to 'use the Bible in their prayers, or, more exactly, to "pray through" some of the great Biblical themes'.[18] Second, it differed from other books of prayers in that it was designed to give help about 'how we are to offer the obedience of our academic hearts'. Third, it was intended to encourage students to move beyond it to the sacramental worship of the churches. Finally, it provided a 'Treasury of Christian Prayer' taken from many sources ancient and modern, a feature later to be followed in the 'People's Version' of *Uniting in Worship* (1988), the first worship book of the Uniting Church in Australia. The emphasis throughout *Student Prayer* is on 'biblical praying'.

A tradition which seems to have been a speciality of the Australian SCM was that of the Quiet Time – a daily half hour at conferences, introduced perhaps by a Bible reading, after which people would go out for half an hour on their own, perhaps just sitting and thinking, perhaps walking around, after which they would come together again, perhaps sing a hymn – and that was it. There are echoes here of the Morning Watch of the early SCM, though it has also been attributed to Quaker influence, which was quite strong in the Australian SCM.

At Federation meetings, possibly even more than British ones, and no doubt because of the strong musical tradition in Germany and France, good music early became a characteristic mark of SCM worship (in-cluding sung grace before meals!). As early as 1924 the Federation had provided the student world with the multilingual and strongly bib-lical hymnbook *Cantate Domino*, which was largely the work of Suzanne Bidgrain of the French Movement.[19] It contained hymns from all the major traditions, including the French *À toi la gloire, O Ressuscité (Thine be the glory, risen, conquering Son)* by Edmond Louis Budry, which in effect became the anthem of the Federation. Each national Movement had its favourite hymns. To hear German students singing *Die Sach' ist dein, Herr Jesu Christ* (Samuel Preiswerk and Graf F. Zaremba), or *Lo, here is felawschipe* sung at an Australian SCM conference, could be a deeply moving experience. For many students the *Cantate* version of the ancient Greek *Phos hilaron*

> Jesus Christ! Joyous light, pure ray
> from the blazing splendour of the Father

sung to a tune of the Russian Church liturgy, was a first and stirring introduction to the wealth of Orthodox worship. The original edition, with 64 hymns, was followed by the second in 1930 with 82 hymns in 23 languages, and finally in 1951 by the third edition with 120 hymns, each edition being more representative of the worldwide membership of the Federation. For 50 years this, the WSCF's most widely used publication, was the hymnbook of the growing ecumenical movement, and from the time of the Amsterdam Assembly in 1948 it virtually became the hymnbook of the WCC. So it was no wonder that the WCC's Uppsala Assembly (1968) asked for a new edition, and entrusted its preparation to the Faith and Order Commission, with Erik Routley as editorial consultant to a committee which included Joseph Gelineau (of the Gelineau Psalms), Fred Kaan (author of many fine modern hymns like *Let us talents and tongues employ*), Konrad Raiser and Doreen Potter. This fourth edition, published in 1973, was really a new book, and 25,000 copies of it had been printed by 1983.

The music of the Taizé community springs from the tradition of the *Fédé* – the French SCM – and in later years it was cheering to see that already deeply ecumenical tradition being adopted and shared by Roman Catholics as well as Orthodox. In the words of a modern advocate of the Celtic tradition, Ian Bradley, 'hymnody has been one of the great successes and products of the ecumenical movement'.[20]

In 1934 the Federation published *Venite Adoremus I*, a collection of traditional non-eucharistic services from five of the main traditions represented in the Movement's membership, printed in English, French and German. The second edition of the book, published in 1951, marked a significant change of policy: in addition to four non-eucharistic services (Lutheran, Presbyterian, Anglican and Congregational) it printed four services of Holy Communion, with music: Church of Sweden (Lutheran), Reformed Church (Presbyterian), Church of England (1662), and Russian Orthodox (The Divine Liturgy of St John Chrysostom). The Preface to the book indicates the theological thinking behind this new departure:

> The Federation is not the Church nor a church. The Sacrament and pro-
> visions for its administration are wholly the province of the churches . . .
> The General Committee considers the Holy Communion to be of
> central importance in Christian faith and life. Consequently, in Federa-
> tion meetings opportunity should be provided for participation in Holy
> Communion by all present and no activities should interfere with such pro-
> vision . . . Therefore the Federation . . . cannot hold communion services
> of its own, and must avoid appearing to do so. In no circumstances can
> the Federation improvise services of Holy Communion which are not those
> of any church.

Yet at the same time the Preface affirms that 'our divisions are contrary
to the will of Christ and therefore radically sinful as well as tragic in
character. Hence members of the Federation must be challenged to see
beyond confessional limits and to study, pray and work for the unity of
the Church.' At every conference a great deal of discussion and heart-
searching went on as students wrestled with their consciences about how
to act in a way which was loyal to their church and at the same time
loyal to God's call to unity. And it was from such anguished discussion,
study and prayer that there emerged the leaders who helped, under God,
to bring the churches far closer in the years ahead than they had been
for centuries.

After *Venite Adoremus I* came *Venite Adoremus II*, which contained some
shorter, freely composed services (non-eucharistic), with prayers drawn
from the wide heritage of the universal Church. *Cantate Domino* and *Venite
Adoremus* marked the beginning of the fine tradition of ecumenical books
of worship, later continued and developed by the WCC. Worship at Federation conferences, led perhaps by Marie-Jeanne de Haller, was a stirring biblical and musical experience, foreshadowing the memorable tent
worship of World Council of Churches Assemblies in later decades.

Bible study and the SCM Press

A 1962 British SCM list of available Bible study outlines[21] mentions
no fewer than 23, including two written jointly by Ronald Preston and
Davis McCaughey (*Jesus' Farewell Discourses* on John 13—17, and *The
Living Community* on 1 Corinthians); and others by writers including
Alan Booth, Charles Cranfield, John Gibbs, and Anthony Hanson, on a
wide range of biblical books and subjects. Some of the outlines were
'self-contained', while most encouraged students to consult further
commentaries and reference books, and gave annotated bibliographies.
The SCM Press, under Ronald Gregor Smith, was constantly providing
fresh and accessible study material on biblical topics. It was also committed to publishing the work of serious academic biblical studies. David

Edwards, Gregor Smith's successor, gives a lively account of books on the Bible published in the period 1959–66:

> The SCM Press has now published 50 monographs in the series *Studies in Biblical Theology*, and more are in preparation. In my own time we have inaugurated *The Old Testament Library*, consisting mainly of commentaries, and *The New Testament Library*,[22] consisting mainly of specialist works . . . Biblical scholarship has, indeed, been the backbone of our publication programme. We owe our reputation chiefly to the fact that we have had the privilege of translating from the German the studies of the professors Aland, Bornkamm, Bultmann, Cullmann, Eichrodt, Fuchs, Harzberg, Jeremias, Käsemann, Kümmel, Noth, Schweizer, Tödt, Von Campenhausen, Von Rad, Weiser, – princes of research and interpretation.[23]

He had been assisted in his choice of titles by some of the leading British biblical scholars, like Alan Richardson, C. F. D. Moule, Peter Ackroyd and James Barr. Then, writing of the task of 'biblical popularization', he mentions the 25 Layman's Bible Commentaries from the USA, the continuation of the Torch series of commentaries, R. H. Fuller's *New Testament in Current Study*, J. N. Schofield's *Introducing Old Testament Theology*, many books by A. M. Hunter and the constant stream of popular commentaries and books by William Barclay – a veritable gold mine for the SCM Press. At the same time, the press was publishing major works on the Bible by continental scholars, including Oscar Cullmann, J. Jeremias and Martin Dibelius, as well as G. Ernest Wright, H. Wheeler Robinson and Alan Richardson from the English-speaking world. On the theological side came Alan Richardson's *Creeds in the Making* (1937), first produced as lectures at a Swanwick conference, which proved vastly popular and continued in print for many years.[21] Of special and lasting significance was Richardson's *Theological Wordbook of the Bible* (SCM Press, 1950), whose methodology drew on Kittel's famous *Theologisches Wörterbuch zum Neuen Testament*.[25] John Macquarrie's *Principles of Christian Theology* was published in 1966.

The editors of the SCM Press at this time – Ronald Gregor Smith followed by David Edwards – were in close touch with the leaders of the SCM and the Federation. Gregor Smith, for example, frequently took part in staff reading parties and student conferences, and was able to communicate his enthusiasm for continental biblical theology, especially from Germany. Steve Bruce, a stern critic of the SCM, is wide of the mark when he writes that 'commercial and market considerations were of the first importance and the apparent harmony between what the Press published and what the Movement thought in the forties and fifties was in large part coincidental'.[26] Gregor Smith was not only a remarkable theologian in his own right; he was also closely in touch with the

Movement, and his friendship with Davis McCaughey, Alan Richardson and others in the British Movement, and also with theologians like Barth, Bultmann and Bethge, enabled him to introduce German theologians, and especially Bonhoeffer, to the Anglophone world, just as, in his student days, he had introduced Martin Buber through his translation of *I and Thou*.[27]

Buber's understanding of the nature of personal relationships became at this time a significant influence on the SCM's theological outlook, reinforced by the work of the Edinburgh philosopher John Macmurray, who was a friend and collaborator of Joe Oldham.[28] Oldham himself wrote two popular and influential books along comparable lines, *Real Life is Meeting* (1941) and *Life is Commitment* (1953), both published by the SCM Press.

Mission: cross-cultural

The vocation to cross-cultural mission was still very much alive in the SCM of the 1950s, though tempered by the desire to work in partnership with the local church overseas rather than claiming a leadership role. In Davis McCaughey's revealing words, 'a Swanwick Conference without reference to that mission would be as odd as a conference without worship or Bible study'.[29] But in the period between 1948 and 1952 the issue of mission, and of commitment to it, was heavily debated in the general council of the British Movement, with the result that in 1952 the SVMU was disbanded.[30] The SCM had arisen out of the SVMU, and commitment to missionary service overseas had always had a high priority; by 1933, for example, 3600 members of the SVMU had actually gone abroad with British missionary societies, and the number from the SVM in America was far larger.[31] But there was concern about presenting the SVMU as 'the archetype of commitment': surely mission in the secular, industrial West was as important as 'overseas' mission; and surely it was possible – and desirable – for mission to be carried out by people in secular employment, whether at home or overseas? McCaughey writes:

> Rightly or wrongly the SVMU belonged with the older missionary outlook, and it had to go; but its disbandment was not simply a negative act, it was a decision taken in order to bring once more and vividly into the centre of the Movement's life the world-wide contact of the Church's life, and the universal significance of its gospel.[32]

Some of those who took part in these discussions, including some who were themselves student volunteers, argued for the retention of the SVMU. But probably the debate and the decision were essential in the development of the concept of mission, foreshadowing the much later Church debates on 'holistic' mission – mission which touches the 'whole' (Greek *holos*) life of human beings in their social and ecological environment. The SCM certainly did not move away from its commitment to mission in this wider sense, and the new Aim and Basis of 1951 reaffirmed unambiguously that the Movement sought 'the extension, unity and renewal of the Church throughout the world'.[33]

Through the missionary societies and church mission boards numerous requests for new recruits to work overseas as teachers, doctors, nurses, ministers, agriculturalists etc. continued to be channelled to the SCM. Each month *The Student Movement* printed a full page of advertisements for such jobs. And there was a significant response. In 1953, for example, there were more than 50 requests for college and school teachers in India and Pakistan. So arose The '53 Scheme, which sought to secure 53 recruits within the year – and succeeded in finding very nearly that number. Professor Chandran Devanesen, then of Madras Christian College, gave three months to the promotion of the scheme in Britain and Ireland.

In addition, a plan was worked out to encourage SCM members to take 'secular' jobs overseas, and to live in such situations as active Christians, sharing in the life of the local church, and commending the highest standards of ethical behaviour and social justice through their professional life. Here Frances Paton worked with Dr Harry Holland, secretary of Overseas Service, an organization set up jointly by the British Council of Churches and the Conference of British Missionary Societies. In what was still the colonial age, members of SCM were also encouraged to work overseas in the government's Colonial Service, taking with them their convictions on the need for justice and the development of local leadership. In the January 1952 edition of *The Student Movement*, for example, a full-page advertisement for Colonial Service educational appointments was published, and the same issue carried an article on the Colonial Education Service by W. E. F. Ward, Deputy Educational Adviser to the Colonial Office and a former SCM member. Co-operation with, recruitment for and advocacy within multinational companies was also suggested as a possibility, and the January 1953 Overseas Conference in Sheffield included among its resource people an oil company representative, Jack Lee of Shell.

At the same time, and within the same thought-frame, the Movement was involved in active protest against the proposed Central African Federation, which was to combine into a single territory what are now Zimbabwe (Southern Rhodesia), Zambia (Northern Rhodesia), and Malawi (Nyasaland). An article attacking the proposal by Julius Nyerere (later President of Tanzania) and J. Keto, both then at Edinburgh

University, was published in the May 1952 issue of *The Student Movement*.

Meantime, as usual, the Movement looked to the SCM Press to keep it – and the world – supplied with a stream of books on various aspects of cross-cultural mission, by authors like Walter Freitag, Lesslie Newbigin, D. T. Niles (of Ceylon/Sri Lanka) and, in an early approach to interfaith dialogue and inculturation, Paul Devanandan of India, whose book *The Gospel and Renascent Hinduism* appeared in 1959, and was followed by *Preparation for Dialogue* (1964), published in India.

Mission in industry and politics

Mission in the industrialized society of Britain was also a central concern. At the end of 1952 the Swanwick conference for theological students, with 145 attenders, had the theme of 'The Mission of the Church', and speakers included Ted Wickham (still at the Sheffield Industrial Mission) and Ernie Southcott (of the Parish and People movement) as well as cross-cultural experts like George Appleton (Burma), David Paton and Victor Hayward (China), theologians including Tom Torrance, John Robinson, David Cairns, J. K. S. Reid, and the New Testament scholar William Manson who, along with John Foster, spoke on the biblical doctrine of mission and unity.

An ecumenical pilgrimage for theological students in summer 1953 (of which more later) visited centres of the priest-worker movement in France, including the Abbé Michonneau's parish in Paris and a community of the Petits Frères de Jésus of Charles de Foucauld in Montbard. Here were young men working in industry and at the same time carrying on their vocation as priests in 'France Pagan' – their own *pays de mission*.[34]

The post-war decade was a time when many Christian students became involved in the attempt to break down the new East–West barriers which had arisen between the Soviet Union and China on the one hand and the western democracies on the other. At Christmas 1949 a group of students from British theological colleges went to a meeting of theological students in West Berlin, and had the opportunity (the Wall had not yet been built) of visiting the 'student congregation' (*Studentengemeinde*) in the Humboldt University in the East Zone, and to share in their stories. There was special interest in the witness of people like Professor Josef Hromádka in Czechoslovakia, whose political co-existence with the communist state, combined with a vigorous theological independence, was supported by Karl Barth, and by many church leaders in Britain and Europe, though it was heavily criticized in some parts of the Church as compromising with Marxism. At the Federation theological students' conference held alongside the Lund Faith and Order Conference of 1952 a stimulating evening was spent in conversation with Hromádka.

These were interesting encounters. But the steady ongoing work of making and sustaining contact with students behind 'the iron curtain' was undertaken, in the British Movement, by a small group of SCM staff and students led by Penry Jones. The International Union of Students (IUS), a purely secular body unconnected with the Federation, had been founded in Prague in 1945, and Penry Jones and his student colleagues like Walter Fyfe of Glasgow maintained a close association with it, and also with the Prague-based World Federation of Democratic Youth (WFDY). Already in 1947 Penry Jones and M. M. Thomas were arguing that the Federation should try to secure the appointment of a Christian to the WFDY secretariat.[35] And at Christmas 1947 MM did actually participate in an IUS 'Christmas University' in Prague, where he felt lonely because it was a Christmas celebration deprived of all Christian meaning; but at the same time he regretted that there were so few convinced Christians prepared to take part in such gatherings.[36] In a letter to his wife he wrote, 'I feel that I have real opportunities of taking evangelism seriously in Europe today! And I find the contacts with atheists and others challenging; that is, challenging me to take my faith seriously and be a thorough-going evangelist.'[37] SCM students in many countries – Britain, Europe, India and Australia for a start – eagerly read the reports in *The Student World*, and admired and supported Christian students and church leaders in Eastern Europe who persisted in remaining in dialogue with their Marxist colleagues, refusing to compromise their faith while at the same time refusing to retreat into a ghetto type of underground existence which withdrew the Church from public life and witness.

Mission in the university

From time to time the British movement organized a direct evangelical approach to students through 'missions to the university', with at least one major mission a year happening somewhere in Britain and Ireland. These were large, well-advertised events in a particular university, to which every student was invited. They usually lasted a week, and featured a leading figure as 'missioner' – D. T. Niles, the world Methodist leader, was probably William Temple's most popular successor in this role – supported by SCM headquarters staff and others, who acted as leaders of worship, study-group leaders, and counsellors. The aim was definitely to win to the gospel – and hopefully also to membership in the SCM and in a church – students who hitherto had not been so committed.

In December 1953, for example, a university mission was held in St Andrews: the missioner was Archie Craig, well known in Scotland as a church leader and ecumenist, and closely associated with the Iona Community, who gave the main addresses on the theme 'A Faith for Life and Death'. Frances Paton of the SCM staff was woman missioner, the Anglican Franciscan Michael Fisher was chaplain, and Penry Jones (much in demand through his involvement in radical student politics) spoke on 'The Political Student'.

At longer intervals great national Quadrennial conferences were held to which students came from all over the country, and from overseas. The original four-year sequence had been broken by the war, but a large and successful one was held in the Central Hall, Westminster, in January 1948, with the theme of 'Christian Obedience' and with speakers including Reinhold Niebuhr from the USA and M. M. Thomas from India. David Edwards wrote:

> The conference was a closely argued and detailed summons to accept the fact of God's sovereignty and to obey him here and now . . . Perhaps no larger student gathering has ever had its nose rubbed so firmly in politics and economics. And its main attention was fixed on Britain itself.[38]

But the most thorough and scholarly of all the SCM's ventures in mission in these years was its ground-breaking work on Christian obedience in the university itself – the SCM's own particular *pays de mission*. The story is told in detail in Davis McCaughey's *Christian Obedience in the University*, which in turn followed on David Paton's pioneering and stirring *Blind Guides?* (1939), with its telling subtitle *A Student Looks at the University*, Arnold Nash's *The University and the Modern World*, published in the USA in 1943, and *The Crisis in the University* (1949) by Sir Walter Moberly, friend of the SCM and head of the University Grants Commission in Britain. As part of this study process the SCM in 1946 printed 12 'University Pamphlets', edited by Ronald Preston, by writers including John Baillie, H. A. Hodges, Dorothy Emmett, Alec Vidler and Daniel Jenkins. Internationally, the Federation had already in 1944 initiated a study on 'The Task of the Christian in the University'.[39]

The medieval European universities had been *Christian* enterprises. The nineteenth-century British 'redbrick' universities were often secular institutions, whose orientation Cardinal Newman had challenged in his *Idea of a University* (1852). The SCM's university project was probably the most significant attempt since Newman to consider the purpose of a university, and the possibility for Christian life and witness within it, not only by students but also by staff. For the SCM had now extended its sphere of interest beyond the student body to the staff, and to the very structure of the university itself, and in 1951 a Dons' Advisory Group was set up.[40] The SCM was indeed acquiring a new reputation for being not only 'church ahead of the Church' but also 'university ahead of the University'.

The main task of the SCM, in these years as from the beginning, was to witness to the gospel in the unique 'culture' – a word just beginning to be used in this sense – of the university. McCaughey quotes Bonhoeffer: 'I should like to speak of God not on the borders of life but at its centre'.[41] For the SCM the 'centre' was the university; and McCaughey comments that 'the attempt by men and women in the universities to see their work in the light of faith is an attempt to do just that'.[42] Today such language may sound like a quaint and nostalgic recall of the days before university education became a market-controlled industry; but does it not rather record an exciting venture into the contextualization of theology – and into cross-cultural mission? And might it not be, once again, a call to the universities to recover their true, and widely abandoned, vocation?

For this was indeed mission. McCaughey tells how he had originally included in his book a separate section on evangelism, but then had decided that 'the whole book has either been about evangelism, or about nothing at all. And in the last analysis that is the question which the Movement must face: does its multifarious activity impress upon students the claims, and make known to them the grace, of Jesus Christ?'[43] And he ends with the words, 'Where the Movement has made that possible for men and women it has fulfilled the end of its existence'.[44]

Mission: the widening scope

Increasingly in the 1950s the definition of mission was being widened to include what in the 20s and 30s would have been seen as belonging to the 'Life and Work' strand of the Church's witness rather than to the narrower 'home' and 'overseas' evangelistic mission. It was difficult to draw a line of separation between the different aspects of mission which we have been discussing – cross-cultural, socio-political and university-centred – for these were the objectives which Oldham had been advocating ever since Edinburgh 1910: and the costly testimony of members of the European Movement during the war, both in Germany and in 'the Resistance', had put political witness firmly on the Movement's agenda. Philippe Maury, the young WSCF general secretary with his experience in the French Resistance, was joined in Geneva in 1947 by M. M. Thomas of India, who had participated in a lively political dialogue between the Indian and British SCMs in the period leading up to Indian independence in 1947. In that same year the WSCF set up a commission on 'The SCM in the World Struggle', which eventually produced a

'Federation Grey Book' entitled *The Christian in the World Struggle* by M. M. Thomas and Davis McCaughey.[45] Thomas described the scope of the book by affirming that

> the world struggle was the result of the awakening of hitherto submerged nations, races and classes, seeking a revolution of social justice which would bring them human dignity; and that every revolutionary situation was created by the relation between three aspects of the revolution, viz. its power-political expression towards justice, the opposition of the counter-revolutionary force of the established order and the misdirection and corruption of it, leading to the betrayal of the ends of justice by the revolutionary forces.[46]

From now on the political agenda was firmly part of the SCM programme, where it would remain. It would remain also, for the foreseeable future, on the programme of the WCC. And the time would come when it would be seen as inseparably linked not only with the mission of the Church, but also with its very faith and order.[47]

A person who attractively represents the widening scope of the SCM tradition of mission – in philosophy, history and theology, in education generally and the university in particular, and in Christian involvement in politics and social ethics – is Marjorie Reeves (1905–2003).[48] Although she never served on the SCM staff, she is a distinguished example of 'the SCM tradition', and of the way in which people involved in the Movement in their student days went on in later years to live out that tradition in their professional lives. In the 1920s at Oxford and later London University (where she did her doctoral studies on heretical mystics of the Middle Ages) she was an active member of the SCM, and her association with the Movement, which had begun long before the golden age of the 1950s, continued long after it. In the 1930s she spent time in Germany, where she established contacts with the German Movement (DCSV) during the struggle with the Nazis. Returning to Oxford in 1938 as a history tutor in what later, and to a considerable extent through her efforts, became St Anne's College, she remained in Oxford for the rest of her long life. She was especially interested in the Christian engagement with ethics and politics, but also with the arts and spirituality, so that although she did not become a professional theologian she did become, like her friends Joe Oldham and John Macmurray, a significant lay theologian. During the war she became a member of Oldham's Moot, and felt much at home in the atmosphere of 'persons-in-relationship' which pervaded it. Her historical, literary, iconographic and theological skills were of the highest order, and she became an authority on the twelfth-century Italian theologian Joachim of Fiore.

In the 1940s Marjorie Reeves was an important figure in the SCM's study project on the university, serving on the University Commission set up in 1944 'to consider the fundamental presuppositions of university education and their implications for the work of the SCM in the post-war University',[49] and again in 1951 on the Dons' Advisory Group (later renamed the University Teachers' Group). Her talents were recognized in public life, and in 1947 she became a member of the Schools Broadcasting Council of the BBC, and later sat on the government's 1964 Robbins Committee on higher education, whose recommendations resulted in the post-war wave of new universities in England. During the difficult period of the student revolt of the late 1960s (and here we anticipate) she showed an understanding of the student mind which was both more radical and more sensitive than that of most senior university figures. In later years her Oxford history tutorials were challenging and popular, as were the 'fresh and combative seminars she ran under the aegis of the Student Christian Movement'.[50] She was 98 when she died; yet in the decade before that she had published books on higher education (*The Crisis in Higher Education: Competence, Delight and the Common Good*, 1988), and on conviction politics (*Christian Thinking and Social Order: Conviction Politics from the 1930s to the Present Day*, 1999). 'Conviction politics' was a concept in which Marjorie Reeves delighted, and which she put in practice. Her life was a vivid illustration of how the SCM tradition could, under God, transform the lives and communities of those it touched, and especially the university community.

Christian unity

The inauguration of the WCC in 1948 to some extent changed the ecumenical role of the SCM. The coming together of the mainline churches (with the major exception of the Roman Catholic Church) in a single fellowship, so long advocated by the SCM, had been achieved. And already the WCC had begun to produce a stream of theological reports defining its position in relation to the churches, and outlining possible lines for future action towards closer unity. Foremost among these was the 1950 Toronto Statement *The Church, the Churches and the World Council of Churches*, drafted by the SCM veterans Oliver Tomkins and Wim Visser 't Hooft; it is a seminal document which for more than half a century has provided a theological basis enabling the Orthodox churches and – in a more limited way – the Roman Catholic Church, to be the WCC's partners in the ecumenical enterprise.[51] Adrian Hastings comments:

> Their draft stressed a number of crucial points – that 'The World Council
> exists in order to deal in a provisional way with an abnormal situation',

that it is not based on any one ecclesiology, that no church need alter its own ecclesiology in order to enter the Council and hence that it is acceptable for members of the Council not to recognise one another as 'true and pure churches' so long as they share a common belief in the Lordship of Christ and in the need, through the Council or otherwise, to seek the unity of Christians within and without their own church.[52]

This reflects the practical ecclesiology already pioneered in the SCM and WSCF. To those points should be added the fact – so prominent in the life of the SCM – that when members of different churches meet together with this intention, a new kind of forward-looking community (the Greek word *koinonia* has come to be used more and more in this connection) is the result. Hastings, as a Roman Catholic (albeit a very liberal one), suggests that the WCC approach 'did in a way necessarily consecrate denominations'.[53] That is hardly fair to the WCC, and is not true of the ecumenical approach of the SCM which, although it honoured denominations, tended to regard them as provisional expedients, and certainly never consecrated them.

It was into this new and exciting world that I entered in September 1951 as theological college department (TCD) secretary of the British Movement. So much had been happening – the inauguration of the WCC in Amsterdam, the Toronto Statement, and now the preparatory reports for the 1952 Lund conference on Faith and Order. How was all this to be communicated to the churches, and how were they to be caught up in the enthusiasm for unity which so many of us felt? While the whole life of the SCM was bound up with seeking and demonstrating Christian unity, and while the Movement was proud of the prominence within it of the witness of laypeople, there was always an awareness – a slightly uncomfortable awareness – that the task of actually achieving unity involves a massive biblical and theological enterprise, and that theological students have a special responsibility in this enterprise. The men and women who would eventually carry out much of the technical part of this task were the current generation of theological students; and so the SCM's commitment to promoting ecumenism in theological colleges had a crucial role.

The TCD secretary's contribution to this 1951 environment was to visit the 79 affiliated theological colleges in Britain and Ireland (Roman Catholic seminaries were not at this stage on the agenda) and encourage more active ecumenical commitment, especially on both the evangelical and the Anglo-Catholic sides, where enthusiasm was minimal, and hostility was sometimes apparent. A report to the British Council of Churches in April 1953 spelt out what the department was trying to do:

to make students aware of the developments of ecumenical theology and practice, and above all to bring them out of the theological isolation of their own tradition into lively encounter with students of other churches, in the belief that ecumenical work is impossible without the basis of mutual knowledge and mutual trust which is gained, not from books or speeches, but from meeting *people.*

The clearly expressed aim was not simply the improvement of relations between the churches: it was organic unity. The report goes on to define the kind of ordained ministry which the SCM hoped would emerge from these colleges: it was to be 'a ministry which believes in the ultimate unity of the Church, and is committed to full co-operation in the work of the ecumenical movement in its various manifestations'. In practice much of my advocacy on visits to the colleges was in defence of the recently inaugurated Church of South India. The SCM as a whole – though not all its members – defended the CSI, which for the first time had secured a union of Anglicans with Reformed and Methodist churches. There was concern that Anglican objections to the ministry of that church should be sympathetically met, and that further theological work, like that going on in North India, should ensure that in future such problems would not arise.

An essential part of my task as TCD secretary was encouraging theological students to meet together locally, in places like Oxford, Cambridge, London, Birmingham and Manchester, where there were many different denominational colleges; and also to organize local conferences and, every second year, a national conference at Swanwick – in the depth of winter! Theological students were also urged to take part in university SCM meetings wherever that was possible. There was a TCD committee of students to advise and help in the work, including people who later became well known in the life of the churches and the ecumenical movement, like Mary Lusk (Levison) (pioneer of women's ordination in the Church of Scotland), John Martin (later general secretary of the British SCM), Harry Morton (later ~~general secretary~~ president of the British Methodist Conference), and John J. Vincent (later of the Sheffield Inner City Ecumenical Mission and the Urban Theology Unit and author of many books including *Secular Christ: A Contemporary Interpretation of Jesus* (1968), *Alternative Church* (1976), and *Hope for the City* (2000). The contacts established and maintained with students and staff of theological colleges of different traditions were a vital part of the Movement's theological life and witness, and also a fruitful source of recruitment for staff. In the councils of the Movement, and in its conferences – especially Study Swanwick – it was important to have a lively mix of lay and theological minds grappling with one another.

There were other ventures, including the annual 'Anglican, Orthodox, Presbyterian' conference, held in Paris in 1951 and again in 1953, and in 1952 on the island of Iona. The Iona event, with a two-day pilgrimage across the Isle of Mull in pouring rain with George MacLeod, was a memorable experience of which Donald (A. M.) Allchin (later to become a leading historian of religious communities) wrote, in a report to *The Student Movement* – 'The divisions of Christendom as seen from Iona take on a different aspect from their appearance in the more familiar perspectives of Geneva, Canterbury and Rome'.[54]

The inclusion of the Orthodox tradition within the fellowship of the Movement was highly significant, and contributed strongly to the emphasis, during this period, on ecclesiology and liturgy, as well as on the classical doctrines of the incarnation, the Holy Spirit, and the Trinity. The Federation normally adhered to the ecumenical principle that in each country there should be only one Student Christian Movement. Most of the national Movements were thoroughly interdenominational, though some, for historic and demographic reasons, were virtually 'monochrome' – like that of Greece. The one exception, for many years, to this principle of 'one country, one Movement', was the Russian Orthodox Movement, which, in a favourite expression of Professor Leo Zander (1893–1964), its beloved theologian-photographer leader, was 'a glorious paradox'. The pre-war Russian SCM had been broken up by the expulsions following the 1917 Revolution; but a group of exiles who had known Baron Paul Nicolay and Ruth Rouse, or had some experience of the YMCA or WSCF, came together in Pscrov, Czechoslovakia, in 1923 to form 'the Russian SCM in Exile', which soon became centred in Paris.[55] It was closely linked with the Orthodox Theological Faculty of St Sergius, founded in 1925, and over the years provided many ecumenical leaders, including Nicolas Zernov, Alexander Schmemann and Boris Bobrinskoy. A wider Orthodox youth movement (not limited to students), which according to one of its leaders, Nikos Nissiotis, was founded as an idea in 1949 and a concrete reality in 1952, was Syndesmos (the Greek word for the 'bond' of Ephesians 4.13, 'maintaining the unity of the Spirit in the bond of peace', RSV), which has continued to maintain relationships with the WSCF to the present day, and in whose foundation other members of the Russian SCM, like Leo Zander and Kyril Eltchaninoff, took part.

In that same summer of 1952 an international WSCF theological students' conference was held in Lund, Sweden, with access, as accredited visitors, to the WCC's Faith and Order Conference; and it proved possible to attract church leaders like Michael Ramsey, Josef Hromádka, Martin Niemöller, Tom Torrance, Visser 't Hooft, Georges Florovsky and

Donald MacKinnon to join the students and give of their wisdom. It did the cause no harm that the students were housed in a brand new student hostel which had hot showers on offer, while many of the theologians were in billets with no such comforts! Adrian Hastings points out that Lund was, supremely if unobtrusively, Oliver Tomkins' conference.[56] What later became famous as 'the Lund Principle' was in fact part of Tomkins' opening sermon as organizing secretary of the conference. In its developed form it reads:

> Should not our churches ask themselves whether they are showing sufficient eagerness to enter into conversation with other churches, and whether they should not act together in all matters except those in which deep differences of conviction compel them to act separately?

It was D. T. Niles who insisted that this sentence should become part of the Conference Message, where it reads simply, 'Should not our churches ask themselves whether . . . they should not act together in all matters except those in which deep differences of conviction compel them to act separately?'[57] In their centenary history of the WSCF, Philip Potter and Thomas Wieser have no hesitation in describing this principle as one 'forged in the life and mission of the Federation'.[58]

In the following summer, 1953, a group of seven theological students – all men, sad to say – embarked on an ecumenical pilgrimage through France, with the help of a four-seater Ford Prefect in which five travelled in turn, while the other two went by train. They had three objectives: first to take part in the SCM's Anglican, Orthodox, Presbyterian conference in Paris; secondly to see something of the priest-worker movement in the French Roman Catholic Church; and finally to visit what was then the relatively new, and still very much French Reformed, community at Taizé. This was probably one of the earliest occasions on which an official activity of the British SCM, at the student level, crossed the barrier which still separated it from the Roman Catholic Church, even though the WSCF – as far back as Constantinople in 1911 – had adopted a resolution effectively permitting Roman Catholics to be members of national SCM bodies. In Lyon the group stood around the grave of the Abbé, Paul Couturier (pioneer of the Week of Prayer for Christian Unity) who had died only a few months earlier, and heard their Dominican host Père Biot say, 'Though our churches do not encourage it, I think we might say the Lord's Prayer together'. And they did. It was, for them all, the opening of a door which has never since shut.

The Federation, as we have seen from the preface to the 1951 edition of *Venite Adoremus I*, adhered conscientiously to the rules of the different churches on intercommunion, and the national Movements followed suit. But there was no censorship of opinion, and the 'TCD Column' in the October 1951 *The Student Movement* says, 'The Churches have perforce to be cautious, but the SCM has sometimes a duty to be rash, and theological students are in a position to give a sound theological lead to the Movement's thought'. By June 1952 the column was saying that well-informed people should 'put their mutual recognition to the proof by limited intercommunion' – which was already permitted in certain ecumenical circumstances, but seldom practised. The SCM believed in pushing the boundaries.

Meantime the SCM Press continued to provide the churches with a rich diet of ecumenical literature, particularly in relation to the Lund Faith and Order Conference, for which all the preparatory volumes – *The Nature of the Church, Ways of Worship,* and *Intercommunion,* as well as *Social and Cultural Factors in Church Division* – were published by SCM, as was the conference report, edited by Oliver Tomkins. Davis McCaughey and Richard Hanson wrote a six-study outline as preparation for Lund on *The Churches' Unity,* designed to be read in conjunction with Tomkins' *The Church in the Purpose of God*; and two years later the Press published the report of the WCC's second Assembly at Evanston in 1954.

These were exciting years for all those involved, with moments of pain, as when – on visits to Anglican colleges – Methodists, Presbyterians, Congregationalists and Baptists had to stay in their seats while everyone else went forward to communion. But there were also moments of great joy, when, for example, staff and students shared (so far as they could) in the Russian Orthodox liturgy in Paris, or were pedalled along a French country road on the cross-bars of young worker-priests' bicycles! Vatican II was still almost a decade in the future, but things were already moving.

5

Documents, developments, donations (*c.* 1945–65)

After our survey of some of the many activities of the SCM in the golden age of the 1950s, we shall in this chapter look at some other features of the Movement's life, at both national and Federation levels, during the same period – questions about its Aim and Basis, its rules for membership, its relations with the IVF, its growing commitment to inter-action with Roman Catholic students, and its financial arrangements.

Revising the Aim and Basis

The debate in the British SCM's general council which led to the disbandment of the SVMU in 1952 was part of a renewed discussion of the Aim and Basis which continued for several years, and was largely focused on the question of 'open membership' – whether membership should be open to all students, or should be limited to those who personally accepted the Aim and Basis. It is worth quoting the resulting 1950 Aim and Basis in full, as it is very brief:

Aim
The Student Christian Movement is a fellowship of students which seeks to acknowledge and to lead others to acknowledge God through Jesus Christ in the power of the Holy Spirit. It works for the understanding and acceptance, in the thought and life of College and University, of the Lordship of Christ over the whole of mankind. It seeks the extension, unity and renewal of the Church throughout the world, and calls students to bear witness as responsible members of a particular church, in personal commitment to Jesus Christ as their Saviour and Lord.

Basis
The basis of the Movement is the Word of God witnessed to by prophets and apostles in Holy Scripture and affirmed by the Church in its worship and creeds.

Membership
Membership is open to all members of the College/University.

The Movement in addition adopted a Declaratory Statement as 'a basis for responsible discussion and examination'. This is a remarkable document, described as 'an attempt to make articulate the concerns which God is laying upon the Movement at this time'. It is not a 'confession' which members are required to sign, but rather an indication of how the SCM understands both its identity and its mission. Through the distinctly non-inclusive language of the time, we can hear the authentic and inclusive ring of the SCM tradition. In typical SCM style, members and branches are encouraged to keep questioning, and especially to question their life and examine their programmes until their fellowship manifests five distinguishing marks:

1 Significantly the first mark is *Prayer* and the whole life of worship, since the SCM's 'first duty and its chief end is to worship and glorify God'. And the question is asked, 'Is the Movement pointing its members to the rich inheritance of worship made available in the Christian Church?'

2 The second mark (because the SCM is called to serve God particularly in the student community) is *Study*, and above all Bible study. And here comes a classic SCM affirmation, based on Romans 12.1: 'The reasonable service of the student as such is the liturgy of the mind'. And then: '. . . Jesus Christ as witnessed to in Holy Scripture is the truth. He is the utterly reliable messenger of God . . . Are members learning not merely to read but to study their Bibles, as full-grown men, giving the response of the committed mind?' And study is to be corporate, not solitary, and linked with witness: 'No truth is to be received, understood or used privately, but corporately and (if it may be) publicly'. And again, 'It is not given to man to possess the truth, but only to believe it and love it . . . The Movement will therefore ask itself, do we welcome in our study those who differ from us, whether or not they call themselves Christian?'

3 The third mark is *Evangelism*, and the SCM is 'called to make known to men the name of their Redeemer, Jesus Christ . . . Evangelism is a human, and conversion a divine responsibility. We must make known as intelligently and intelligibly as possible the name of God in Jesus Christ.' And then – following the SCM's long tradition in cross-cultural evangelism – 'Not only is the Movement's own life a place of evangelism, but it also has a responsibility for calling its members individually and in groups to commit themselves to the Church's work of evangelism throughout the world.' And finally 'God presses in upon us, through those who acknowledge, those who deny, and those who blaspheme the divine name. The Movement will therefore ask itself: is its life so ordered that its members are continually being challenged by those who think they stand outside the faith?'

4 *Ecumenical Churchmanship* is the fourth mark. The SCM 'believes that its fellowship is part of the life of the Church'. It is also a fellowship 'in

which believers and non-believers can meet to the benefit of both parties'. And it asks the question: 'Is the SCM really *in* the intellectual world of our day? If it is not, it is not truly a part of the Church; for the Church is in the world when she is the Church of the Lord Jesus Christ.' The SCM is especially indebted to the 'wider fellowship' of the WSCF, and seeks from the Federation, as a gift, the correction and enrichment which come from 'an ecumenical imagination'. ('Ecumenical imagination' is a concept very much illuminative of the SCM tradition; and many years later, when Davis McCaughey retired in 1980, the Festschrift published in his honour bore the title *Imagination and the Future*.)

5 The fifth mark is the intriguingly Lutheran and unmistakably future-orientated one of *Citizenship of Two Kingdoms*. The SCM lives in the world – starting with the university but also including the family and the wider communities of the State and society. 'It shares and exemplifies the world's failures; and it looks beyond the world to the world's Redeemer.' And it asks the question, 'Is it preparing men and women to live in this world as those who have had the mark of Christian studentship laid upon them? Does it know what it is doing when it prays: *Thy Kingdom come?*'

The SCM never produced a doctrinal statement along the lines of the IVF Basis: it left the task of doctrinal definition to the Church. Membership of the Movement is open to all members of the university, but each branch is expected to run its activities along the lines laid down in the Aim and Basis, and the Declaratory Statement is a set of guidelines about how members and branches should tackle their task. Echoes of Barth and Bonhoeffer can be clearly heard in the language of these two documents of 1950, which are probably the most complete theological statement the SCM, at least in Britain, ever made.

IVF and SCM: the attempt to understand

Christian unity is not simply an *inter*church matter: *intra*church divisions – the divisions within the churches themselves – require healing, and of these perhaps the most intractable one is that between evangelicals and liberals – to use two highly unsatisfactory but widely prevalent terms. We have seen the origins of the division between the two student movements in Britain, culminating in the foundation of the IVF in 1927. At various times since then, efforts at overcoming the division have been made. And there have always been individuals who have worked for co-operation, even to the extent of becoming members of both bodies, though this was very problematical on account of the IVF's conditions of membership, and its virtual prohibition of shared activities.

WSCF and IFES

By 1947 the IVF had become established in many countries, and the different national movements became organized as the International Fellowship of Evangelical Students (IFES). The WSCF sought to give guidance to its national Movements on how they should relate to the IFES, and after a long consultation process in which Philippe Maury and Robert Mackie took a leading part, it produced a 47-page mimeographed document entitled *The Relationships of the WSCF and SCMs with the International Fellowship of Evangelical Students and Inter-varsity Fellowships: A Symposium for the Use of SCMs and their Leaders.*[1] Philippe Maury first of all makes clear the SCM's commitment to Bible study and evangelism: 'To my mind . . . the only important thing in the life of the Federation is that the Bible study remains its cornerstone',[2] and goes on, 'Our basic purpose, our *raison d'être*, our vocation as student Christian Movements, is and can only be evangelistic . . . a particular instrument to evangelise universities and schools'.[3] He fears that the IFES is in danger of substituting itself for the Church by insisting on the acceptance of a narrower confession than those of the churches, and writes,

> I personally would never accept to be a member of a Christian body which closes its doors to anybody who bears the name of our Lord and witnesses to Him.

And he goes on:

> Indeed there are in the Federation people with whose faith I myself do not agree, and whom I consider as heretics, but at the same time I shall immediately add that I am not afraid of this because the Church is not the gathering of people who agree with each other theologically. The Church is the body of Christ brought together by his redeeming action.[4]

Yet he longs for the two movements to come together, and concedes that the British IVF arose at a time when, in his (no doubt Barthian) view, 'the SCM was at a particularly low ebb'. But he insists that neither the IVF nor the SCM has a right to a separate existence: they should be witnessing as a single body in the universities, recognizing that 'the confession of faith is properly one of the marks of the Church' – not of a student movement.

London summit, 1950

In the British Movement – almost immediately after the adoption of the new Aim and Basis – the general secretary Alan Booth made a renewed attempt to improve relationships with the IVF, and after considerable negotiation a one-day meeting of leaders was arranged for 1 March 1950, under the agreed chairmanship of Dr Nathaniel Micklem, principal of

Mansfield College, Oxford, who had been a member of the Movement in the days before it divided. Both groups fielded a strong team. On the IVF side was Dr Martyn Lloyd-Jones – also a pre-division member of the Movement – supported by Oliver Barclay and Douglas Johnson from the IVF staff, and several student representatives including John Sertin, president of CICCU. The SCM side included Alan Booth, Davis McCaughey and John Gibbs from the staff, as well as David Jenkins (later a radical Bishop of Durham) and James Blackie (later professor of Christian ethics at New College, Edinburgh) among the student representatives. A stenographer was present, and a transcript was carefully recorded.[5] The SCM team hoped that the meeting might result in better mutual relationships at the top level, which might be reflected in shared activities in the colleges, such as joint Bible study, prayer and missions to the university.

The meeting, though courteous, was not an easy one. The IVF rejected the possibility of joint study groups, even at the top level of both movements, and also made it clear that for them it was not sufficient to leave questions of belief to the churches. To the chairman's question, 'If a person . . . accepted genuinely the Apostles' and Nicene Creed, would that be satisfactory?', Lloyd-Jones replied, 'No, I would have to ask particular questions'. And when Davis McCaughey protested that 'it was not a series of propositions [the apostles] taught; it was the news about a new relationship . . . After all, they begin: "I believe in . . .",' Lloyd-Jones completed the sentence with the words, 'a number of propositions'. When McCaughey went on, 'I think that the healing [between our movements] will begin much more at the point at which we can worship together and discover those things which we can say together to God in prayer and worship, because then we will be in this new relationship which is prior to the propositional statement', Lloyd-Jones replied, 'I disagree entirely with that because . . . the whole position of the heretics is bypassed.' The SCM was in effect being regarded as a heretical body, which could be approached only in proclamation of the gospel, not by sharing in Bible study.

Some of the IVF's questions indicated that they were hoping that the SCM would express repentance for what they saw as its earlier liberal vagueness of belief; but when Alan Booth agreed that it 'is part of Christian life that you ought to be finding opportunities for repentance', and expressed the hope that 'any body that is constantly reforming itself according to the Holy Scriptures will be changing', they did not find that convincing, and the SCM's new Aim and Basis left them unimpressed. Sadly, no arrangements were made for future meetings, and the sole recorded agreement was the hope that if they ever met again it would be under the same chairman, Nat Micklem. The SCM leaders, especially Alan

Booth who had worked hard to bring the meeting about, were greatly discouraged.

A Scottish initiative, 1951–53

It would not be long, however, until events at the local level raised the issue again. A significant development within the IVF-affiliated Edinburgh University Christian Union (EUCU) – and with virtually no initiative from the SCM, though it was indeed a co-operating partner – occurred in the early 1950s, and is worth recounting in some detail.

The student situation in Scotland at this time, so far as Christian students were concerned, was considerably different from the English one.[6] The Scottish university system had more in common with continental European than with English models, and students for the ministry were mostly taught theology in university faculties rather than in separate residential theological colleges. In New College, Edinburgh, for example, students of both the SCM and CU traditions found it natural to work together as they prepared to enter the ministry of the Church of Scotland. They were all members of the same university faculty; they shared the same Reformation history, with its strong critical tradition – the tradition of the critical Word – and they shared links with continental theology and biblical criticism. Many of the leaders in both movements were theological students, and so the CU members tended to be somewhat less dogmatic, less abstractly theological, less individualistic and more engaged with practical issues of social justice than their English counterparts. As a result the evangelical/liberal tension was more successfully held together in Scotland than in most other places.

In January 1951 the EUCU, which was a large, active and outward-looking society, held a wide-ranging six-day student conference at New College on 'Christ and the World', at which the speakers included Tom Torrance (then teaching in Aberdeen), Norman Goodall (secretary of the International Missionary Council) and a gathering of well-known missionary leaders from Asia and Africa. That autumn, at the beginning of the new academic year, the EUCU and the Edinburgh University SCM began to hold a weekly joint prayer meeting. The student leaders of both organizations knew each other well, and were anxious to co-operate as far as possible in Christian witness to the university. There was also interest and encouragement from staff members of the university faculty of divinity, including Tom Torrance, who had by now joined the Edinburgh faculty, and James S. Stewart, professor of New Testament and a well-known preacher, who was honorary president of the EUCU.

The joint prayer meeting continued successfully for a year, but in November 1952 the EUCU committee, which was divided over the issue of co-operation, decided, on a majority vote, to discontinue it. A special business meeting of the whole membership of the Union was called, and it became clear that there was a large majority against the committee's decision and in favour of 'a broader policy including joint CU–SCM prayers'.[7] A vote of 'no confidence' in the committee was passed (by 92 against 58), and the committee resigned. The majority group, led by David Philpot as president, continued to function as the EUCU, while the minority group, with the support of the national IVF head-quarters, made clear their minimum requirements for co-operation, which were that:

- The basis of the Union's witness to the Lord Jesus Christ is the full scriptural revelation and in particular those fundamental truths indicated in the eight clauses of the IVF Doctrinal Basis.
- The whole committee shall agree in its invitations to speakers, only those men being considered who are known to uphold those fundamental scriptural truths indicated in the IVF Doctrinal Basis.
- The committee shall not involve the Union in a joint witness with any body which does not substantially uphold those truths.[8]

There followed frequent correspondence and discussion between the EUCU and the national IVF headquarters in London. Eventually the national chairman, John Bendor-Samuel, voiced his regret that 'it has been impossible to obtain definite assurance as to the future policy of the Union with regard to joint witness (and even with regard to eventual assimilation) with other religious bodies not having a similar doctrinal basis'.[9] The situation remained unresolved for a year, with the IVF assuring the CU that its members were free to pray with other Christians provided they did not do it *officially*, as that would involve 'compromising the witness of the CU as a body'.[10] By June 1953 the issue had become more focused, with the EUCU asking why the IVF felt that the SCM – as seen in its new (1950) Aim and Basis – came under the heading of a proscribed body with whom no joint activity could be held. The IVF's somewhat bleak response was, 'We have not accused the SCM's Aim and Basis of actively upholding any major heresy, but neither does it uphold the truth and this is the point at issue: do the SCM Aim and Basis substantially *uphold* the truths stated in the Doctrinal Basis of the IVF or not? We cannot see how they do.'[11]

By now the EUCU was pointing out that the national IVF's interpretation of its own Clause 17 (forbidding joint activities) demonstrated 'an approach which is clearly contrary to that of the Reformers in such matters, and [is] one which does not appear to be based on a balanced theological estimate of the SCM Aim and Basis'.[12] This reflects the suspicion that the approach indicated considerable ignorance or misunderstanding of the tradition of the Scottish Reformation, and also of the

Scottish university tradition, so different from that of England. There is also the fear that the IVF is 'asking us to place our fully inter-denominational Union upon an *un*-denominational basis'.[13]

The EUCU had consistently maintained its desire to remain within the fellowship of the IVF. At no time had there been any suggestion of integration or even 'reconciliation' with the SCM: the desire was rather to co-operate in prayer and, where possible, in working together in evangelism, particularly through missions to the university. Despite repeated appeals from the EUCU that there should be further consultation before an irrevocable step was taken, the final response of the national IVF to the EUCU came in their letter of 15 September 1953:

> The differences between us are fundamental and the Executive Committee have unanimously decided that they must withdraw the name of the Inter-Varsity Fellowship from the Edinburgh University Christian Union with immediate effect.[14]

Despite the disaffiliation the EUCU continued its life and witness in the university, with the firm support of its whole honorary committee, whose distinguished members included James S. Stewart, Geoffrey W. Bromiley and Tom Torrance, and which affirmed its conviction that the EUCU was 'not acting in disloyalty to the IVF Basis or compromising its distinctive witness to Jesus Christ in the University'.[15] Within a year the co-operation with the SCM, encouraged by the university chaplain David Read, took significant shape in a major 'Mission to the University', held from 21 October to 3 November 1954. The purpose of the Mission, as stated in its final report, was 'to present the Gospel of Jesus Christ, with all its implications, to the whole University'.[16] The theme was 'One Christ, One World', and the executive committee – representative of both staff and students – was headed by David Read as chairman, Patrick Rodger[17] (chaplain to Anglican students and a former SCM secretary) as vice-chairman and David Philpot (outgoing president of the EUCU) as secretary. The missioner was D. T. Niles, who was then chairman of the WSCF. Coming as it did just after the second Assembly of the WCC at Evanston, it was a thoroughly ecumenical as well as a thoroughly missionary occasion, and student audiences of about 1,000 regularly came to hear 'DT' speak in the vast McEwan Hall.

One important outcome of the Mission – an outcome strongly advocated by D. T. Niles – was the emergence of an ecumenical Christian community, 'the Edinburgh University Christian Community', gathered around David Read as university chaplain and committed, in the spirit of the recent Lund Faith and Order Conference, to 'doing together everything except that which theological principles prevented'. The community took as its aim 'to express the unity Christ has given us, to worship, work and witness'; and as its basis, 'a belief in God, Father, Son and Holy Spirit, and acceptance of Jesus Christ as Saviour and Lord'.[18] It was a community which extended right across the university, regardless of membership in any other student body. The community, begun in the time of David Read as university chaplain, continued with his successors James Blackie and Andrew Morton: the chaplain acted as a focus, but the community, which involved members of both SCM and EUCU as well as the continuing IVF-affiliated group and the denominational societies, was thoroughly 'conciliar' (i.e. operating through councils rather than by a line of command from above) as well as ecumenical, and fully encouraged student initiative.

This ecumenical community, while setting a remarkable precedent, and one which well deserves revisiting in the future, was not without its effect on the SCM. It removed from the SCM its role as the only ecumenical forum in the university; and this diminution was increased by the positive way in which relations between the chaplain and the university staff developed. And it also – perhaps because of this lessening of the ecumenical role – pushed the SCM in the direction of the greater political radicalism which was soon to become so prominent.

The interesting chain of events which had begun in the Edinburgh University Christian Union in 1951 had, sadly, resulted in its being disaffiliated by the IVF. But it had also, in the 1954 University Mission, made possible a massive and effective act of common witness to the university by a large group of university students from both the evangelical and ecumenical traditions, in which the primary initiative had come from the evangelical side. And in the following year, 1955, its influence spread even wider than the regular university missions when a student team was invited to share in the national evangelistic campaign of the 'Tell Scotland' movement – a large and popular interchurch enterprise led by the Church of Scotland's Tom Allan. Under the chairmanship of David Philpot a committee was formed with representatives from St Andrews, Glasgow, Aberdeen and Edinburgh universities, with the particular task of running a mission in the city of Perth in autumn 1955. As usual, there was a distinguished sponsoring committee, including George MacLeod of the Iona Community. The combined Christian students were taking the message of the gospel right outside the bounds of the university, and were doing it together.

Over the years countless former members of both IVF and SCM – including the author of this book – have found themselves, within their various churches in many different countries, and away from the hot-house atmosphere of the university, in situations where they were more than happy to work closely, as members of a single team, with former members of the other movement.

The Federation in the golden age: Christians in the world struggle

A penetrating insight into the inner workings of the WSCF, as it sprang into renewed life after World War 2, is given by M. M. Thomas (1916–96) of India in his book *My Ecumenical Journey* (1990). 'MM', as he was always called, was a member of the MarThoma Church, of which he wrote a history, and was strongly marked by its combination of the Syrian tradition of Orthodoxy with the personal evangelicalism of the (Anglican) Church Missionary Society (CMS) which had greatly influenced its independent development in the mid-19th century. In later years, when he joined the staff of the Federation in Geneva in 1947, it was he who introduced the Syrian 'kiss of peace' into the worship of the Movement,[19] from where it spread throughout the world, aided by its use in the liturgy of the Church of South India. As a student in Trivandrum in his native Kerala State he first joined the SCM in 1931, and became involved at national level when for a year he edited *The Student Outlook*. Though he seriously considered training for the priesthood he remained a life-long layman; and indeed for many people he was the model of what the laity should be like – deeply and intelligently committed to Christ, to the Church, to social and political justice, to Christian unity, and ultimately to the unity of the whole human race.

In 1946 he was invited to join the WSCF staff in Geneva, where he arrived in 1947 to find himself involved in WCC affairs as well as Federation ones, as preparations for the inauguration of the WCC the following year were under way; and he was in frequent contact with Visser 't Hooft and Robert Mackie, as well as with people like Joe Oldham and Reinhold Niebuhr. Incredible as it may seem today, at that stage WCC events went on virtually without the participation of non-Westerners,[20] so his role was a significant one, and he had to fight his corner, which he did with a combination of well-based criticism and disarming friendliness. The situation was quite different in the Federation, where women like Mohini Maya Das and Lilavati Singh (India) and Michi Kawai (Japan) and men like S. K. Datta (India) and T. Z. Koo (China) had served with distinction long before World War 2. Arriving in Europe shortly before India achieved its independence on 15 August 1947, MM soon found himself appointed to the Federation's Political Commission; and it was in the arena of political witness that his greatest contribution to the life of the Movement, and ultimately to the life of the world Church, was to be made.

His theology was always biblical; and after a lifetime of speaking and writing in English it gave him great pleasure, when he retired, to have time to write a series of biblical commentaries in his own Malayalam language. Although he never had formal theological training he was a widely and deeply read theologian – a lay theologian in the best sense, since he thought and wrote like a layman, and never felt the least temptation to clericalism. He was deeply committed to Indian nationalism, and had shared in the war-time dialogue between the British and Indian Movements on such matters as Gandhi's imprisonment. He had a truly Gandhian simplicity of living, utterly free from the temptations of jet-set ecumenical travel; and many colleagues have treasured memories of walking along Miller's Road, Bangalore, long after most people had gone to bed, and seeing him sitting at his desk at an open ground-floor window, dressed in a white lungi and T-shirt, writing – late into the night.

Starting from his evangelical Mar Thoma background – Emil Brunner once detected in him a combination of Lutheran theology with communist politics, of which he himself was totally unaware![21] – he moved through Brunner and Barth to Reinhold Niebuhr. But he was first and foremost an Indian, and of these three theologians only Barth seemed to him to deal at all adequately with the problems of poverty and oppression: it was the Marxists who appeared to be doing that, and so he found himself drawn, in Federation circles, to the witness of Hromàdka, in his efforts to co-operate with the Marxist government while never forsaking his Christian allegiance. Though he appreciated Niebuhr's theological understanding of human nature and society, MM could not accept his justification of the cold war in defence of the capitalist West against Soviet communism, nor his ignoring of the 'third world' (then becoming a current phrase) and its problems. He also criticized Niebuhr's failure to accept, over against the American 'free society', the ideal of 'the *responsible* society', the phrase which, at Visser 't Hooft's suggestion and with Oldham's and MM's approval, was adopted in the volume on 'The Church and the Disorder of Society' prepared for the inaugural assembly of the WCC in 1948. MM, with his background of Asia's national struggle against European colonialism, and as the only non-westerner in the WCC preparatory process, found himself in sharp theological debate not only with Niebuhr, but also with the new Europeanism which was emerging from the Resistance movement against Fascism, seen in his French colleague Philippe Maury.[22]

During his years on the WSCF staff (1947–53), MM took a leading part in the first World Conference of Christian Youth (Oslo, 1947) (which gave so many young people their first and unforgettable experience of the reality of the world Church) and also in the second one at Kottayam in India in 1952. In *The Christian in the World Struggle* (1951), the Federation Grey Book which, as we have seen, he wrote with Davis McCaughey, he put political issues well and truly on to the Federation agenda. Many years later he and McCaughey, along with their SCM friend and

colleague Chandran Devanesen of Madras, were to be given the opportunity of putting their ideas into practice on wider national stages: MM
and Chandran as governors of Indian states and Davis McCaughey as
governor of the Australian state of Victoria.

Back in India once more, MM worked with his friend P. D.
Devanandan and the NCC (National Christian Council, later National
Council of Churches) to co-ordinate the council's work on social
justice issues into a single agency, the Christian Institute for the Study
of Religion and Society (CISRS), with which he continued to be associated for many years. CISRS (or 'Scissors' as it was popularly known)
became a veritable power-house of theological reflection on issues of
political and social ethics, and MM himself wrote numerous articles and
books, like *The Christian Response to the Asian Revolution* (1966), which
were widely read not only in India but in the world-wide missionary
and ecumenical community. In these and the following years he also
became a leading encourager and practitioner – and I write as one so
encouraged – in the emergence of the specialized study of Indian
Christian theology, notably through his book *The Acknowledged Christ of
the Indian Renaissance* (1969).

'The Life and Mission of the Church', 1958–63

The use of the term 'golden age' for the SCM of the early 1950s has
no doubt idealized the period of the author's own direct involvement
in the Movement. But new and exciting things continued to happen,
notably the Federation's massive project on 'The Life and Mission of the
Church' (LMC) which ran from 1958 to 1963, not unsurprisingly under
the inspiration of the chairman, D. T. Niles.[23] The 1956 general committee at Tutzing (Bavaria) had noted widespread disquiet among students
about the mission of the Church: was it still necessary to proclaim the
gospel with a view to converting others? The committee gave a positive answer to this question, and decided on 'a long-range programme
of systematic teaching, study and meetings, as well as prayer', leading
to a major world teaching conference in Strasbourg in 1960. Students
were to be challenged to discover together the missionary message of
reconciliation, in a world marked by the rising expectations of newly
independent nations in 'the third world'. The treatment of the subject
was to be biblical, theological and historical – in the well-tried SCM
tradition of academic integrity.

The programme proved to be the biggest the Federation had ever undertaken, and involved students from Movements all over the world,
including Latin America, the USA, Africa and Asia, in all of which student groups were already being radically politicized. The first stage of

the project was the production of study materials, which were given a trial run at the British SCM's Edinburgh conference on 'Life for the World' in 1958, attended by 2000 students from 42 countries. The second stage, organized by Charles Long, an American SCM leader, was a pilot conference in Rangoon, Burma (winter 1958–9) on 'God's People in God's World'. This conference significantly looked at the Lordship of Christ in the political context of the Asian revolution, and also took seriously the faiths of people other than Christians: the whole world, in all its suffering and injustice, was seen as standing under the judgment of Christ. The third stage produced a great deal of study material, including the book *History's Lessons for Tomorrow's Mission* (Geneva, WSCF, 1960), and more than 15 Bible and other study outlines. In the meantime, the different national movements were following up the project: in the British SCM, for example, this was done at Study Swanwick in 1961 and 1962, and at the large Bristol Congress in January 1963. The special LMC conference at Graz in 1962 also helped British students to understand their European neighbours.

The fourth stage of the project was the world teaching conference at Strasbourg in 1960, to which we shall return in the next chapter. Everything seemed to be falling into place for a significant step forward in the life of the Movement.

Breaking the Rome barrier

Meanwhile, in another part of the *oikoumene* exciting things were happening through that unlikely saint, Pope John XXIII. Vatican II marked the acceptance by the Roman Catholic Church of the movement for biblical renewal in which its scriptural scholars had increasingly been sharing with their colleagues of other traditions. Suddenly the Bible became, for Roman Catholics, as exciting and essential as it had been for SCM students in the period from 1890 to 1960; and ever since, in the Church at large, Bible studies have been a shared ecumenical discipline. There was no bar on the SCM side to the development of closer relationships with the Roman Catholic student body, for as far back as the 1911 Federation conference in Constantinople it had been resolved to accept as members Christians from *any* church, provided that they accepted the Movement's Basis.

As early as 1932 the Federation had held an ecumenical retreat with Roman Catholic participation, and in doing so had begun to open up a road which had been effectively closed by the 1928 encyclical *Mortalium Animos*.[24] Then in 1937 Tomkins – on the Federation staff – had taken part in a highly confidential conference at Bièvres, in which he and Visser 't Hooft, among others, were involved in ecumenical discussions with Yves Congar and other Roman Catholic theologians.[25] A further meeting was held in 1939, which included Jacques Maritain and Gabriel Marcel, Tomkins' place on this occasion being taken by Francis House, another former SCM secretary.[26] Theological discussion, reinforced by personal friendships, had already begun to break down the barriers which had been firmly in place since the Reformation. This pioneering role was continued by Tomkins and Visser 't Hooft when in 1950 they drew up the WCC's Toronto Statement *The Church, the Churches and the World Council of Churches*, which opened up the possibility of some sort of future communion with both the Orthodox and Roman Catholic churches.

The Roman Catholic Church was not officially represented at the inauguration of the WCC in Amsterdam in 1948. However, a great deal of discussion was going on behind the scenes, especially between World Council staff members like Visser 't Hooft and Tomkins on the one hand and French Roman Catholic theologians like Congar, Pierre Dumont and M.-D. Chenu on the other.[27] Things began to develop rapidly after the beginning of Vatican II, and especially after the publication of the Constitution on the Church (*Lumen Gentium*), and the Decree on Ecumenism (*Unitatis Redintegratio*) in 1964. The Joint Working Group was set up between the WCC and the Secretariat for Unity; and from that time the Roman Catholic Church has been a full partner in the ecumenical enterprise.

At the student level, there had been cordial relations between the Federation and Pax Romana, the Roman Catholic student organization, since 1955, when a consultation had been held at Bossey on 'University, Culture and Human Community', followed by a second one in Louvain on 'Science and Technology in the Purpose of God' in 1961, and a third in 1964 at Taizé on the Christian community in the academic world. The development of reciprocal relations was, however, very gradual and tentative. Before Vatican II, such contacts as there were – and they were considerable, as we have seen – were kept secret, though one hears of pleasant incidents like that of a Federation leader saying of the American Roman Catholic ecumenist Fr Tom Stransky, at that time secretary to Cardinal Bea, 'He's really one of us'! The events of Vatican II produced great excitement in the Federation, especially after Lukas Vischer (later to serve for many years on the WCC staff) reported on it to his WSCF colleagues. *The Student World* in 1965, commenting on the new atmosphere created by the Council, spoke of

> a more vital awareness of belonging one and all to the same community
> in Christ through baptism . . . It has led to a more profound discovery of
> our common vocation in the university, and of ecumenism as an essential
> dimension of our life as Christians.[28]

In 1965 a meeting was held at Taizé, at which members of the WSCF, YMCA and other organizations met with colleagues from Pax Romana and other Catholic movements,[29] among the leaders on the Federation side being Brother Roger Schutz of the Taizé community. For some time a strong bond developed between these movements, but eventually pressure from Rome was applied on the Roman Catholic groups, warning them not to risk abandoning their own separate existence. At the same time Visser 't Hooft – somewhat sternly as was his wont – rebuked the Federation representatives, warning them that they were 'playing with fire': he was cautious of any move to get closer to Rome, no doubt reflecting the fear at the time that 'return to Rome' was the only option which the Vatican, despite all appearances to the contrary, was ready to offer. Talks between Pax Romana and the Federation continued throughout the 1960s and 70s, but little came of them. We shall look in the next chapter at how the situation developed in Britain and Ireland.

Although the Movement was never afraid to move ahead of the churches, it is perhaps important at this point to raise the question of whether the new possibilities opened up by the entry of the Roman Catholic Church into the ecumenical enterprise acted as a brake or even a deterrent in the progress of the already strong movement for unity among the churches stemming from the Reformation. For at just this time in Britain the movement towards the actual organic reunion of separated churches had gathered new momentum; and the BCC's 1964 Nottingham conference on Faith and Order, in inviting its member churches – who at that stage did not include Roman Catholics, Orthodox or Pentecostals – 'to covenant together to work and pray for the inauguration of union' by a date agreed among them, affirmed that 'we dare to hope that this date should be not later than Easter 1980'.[30] Oliver Tomkins, by now Bishop of Bristol, strongly supported this proposal, which was destined to meet with a stern rebuff when in 1969 and again in 1972 the Church of England rejected the scheme of union with the Methodist Church. It is interesting to see how Tomkins, with his SCM background, felt that the approach to unity must be multilateral – including, for Anglicans, unity with the Reformed and Methodist traditions as well as the Roman Catholic one – rather than bilateral, the concern simply of Anglicans and Roman Catholics.[31] In this he differed from his colleague John Moorman, Bishop of Ripon, who felt that Anglicans should concentrate primarily on their relationship with Rome. It is significant, if not surprising, that in all these schemes for church union – the 1960s proposals for Church of England/Methodist union and the Covenant proposals of the late 1970s, for example – a leading part was taken by SCM people like John Huxtable of the Congregational Union, whose

95

paperback *New Hope for Christian Unity* (1977) conveys something of the widespread enthusiasm for the Covenant scheme.

Money matters

It may seem strange to move from such a high theme as Christian unity to the question of finance. But the SCM, like any movement, needed money to survive, and this chapter on documents, developments and donations gives the opportunity to address it, albeit briefly.

In national Movements all over the world the SCM ran on shoestring budgets; travelling secretaries worked for what was in effect little more than free accommodation and some pocket money, while headquarters and married staff received salaries far less than they could have commanded in the professions for which they were qualified. We shall take the British Movement as a case study of how the Federation in general financed its operations.

So far as the students were concerned, and also the travelling secretaries, finance was an issue rarely discussed, though everyone knew that there was not much money around, and that expenses had to be kept to a minimum. Each branch was not only expected to be self-supporting, but was encouraged to raise money for the Movement at large through fund-raising events like the occasional party or dance, as well as by personal giving. All conferences were budgeted so as to be self-supporting, and there was usually a 'fares-pool', so that students travelling from distant locations were not penalized. Each year during 'Federation Week' in February students visited sympathetic local churches, by invitation, and sought to raise funds by sharing stories of the life and work of the worldwide Movement. In the branches, 'Federation boxes' were distributed, and students collected money from their friends and relations, for it was well known that the work of the Federation depended largely on contributions from the national SCMs.

In the early days of the British Movement – right back, in fact, to the days of Henry Drummond in Scotland – financial help was sought for and given by many well-to-do families who supported the work among students; and gradually a substantial donor-base was built up, later augmented by legacies and by contributions from charitable foundations and trusts. In 1921 Tatlow and others founded the SCM Trust Association, whose objects were:

- to promote the spiritual, moral and physical well-being of past and present Students of Universities, Colleges, Schools and of similar Institutions, and
- to form and maintain a fellowship among those of them who desire to understand the Christian Faith and to live the Christian life.

The Movement, under Tatlow's guidance, gradually acquired property, notably Annandale, which became the SCM's very pleasant and welcoming headquarters, and of which freehold was eventually secured. The Hayes at Swanwick (First Conference Estates) was another major asset which served the Movement well over many years. The Trust Association was responsible for the buying and selling of property, and for making investments on behalf of the SCM. In the golden age of the 1950s the day-to-day finances of the movement were supervised by S. R. Hepper, accountant and business secretary from 1944 to 1957, and later by Gilbert Ferrier. Kenneth Darke became secretary of the Trust Association in 1957, and for some years also acted, part-time, as accountant and business secretary.[32] A 1968 report, written at a time of considerable financial difficulty and heart-searching (for example over investments in apartheid South Africa, which the Movement sold after a two-year 'usury debate') indicates that at that time only 4 per cent of income came as donations from the churches: the remainder came from trusts, investments, the SCM Press (a handsome £5000 per annum), senior friends' donations and from student subscriptions and fund-raising efforts.

All over the world – in peace time and under normal conditions, which in some countries rarely applied – national Movements operated along comparable lines. It was a precarious system, but for many years it worked.

6

'Story of a Storm' (c. 1965–80)

Gathering clouds

We return now to the Federation's ambitious project, led by D. T. Niles, on 'The Life and Mission of the Church', the final stage of which was to be a world teaching conference at Strasbourg in 1960. Detailed preparations were made, and an array of distinguished theologians was invited as speakers. What happened, however, was not what the planners had expected. For some time a mood of unrest had been growing among university students, especially in Europe and America: it was directed against authority of any kind, including university and church authorities, and was in fact the beginning of a student revolution which had already gone further than many people realized. Lesslie Newbigin was at Strasbourg, and noted the change in student attitudes towards both Church and mission. He tells how there was 'great indifference to the theological issues and ecumenical achievements of an earlier generation', and how the ideas expressed by people like D. T. Niles, Visser 't Hooft, Philippe Maury and Newbigin himself were dismissed as 'pious talk and Geneva ideology'. He found it difficult to accept the critique of Hans Hoekendijk of the Netherlands – a well-known WSCF leader – who called for the radical desacralization of the Church; and he was especially hurt by 'the contempt in which missions were held'. 'The secular decade had arrived', he writes. 'The SCM would not again in my lifetime be, as it had been, the most powerful source of new life for the ecumenical movement'.[1]

Karl Barth, however, was given a pin-drop hearing, by an audience bigger than that which came to hear Jean-Paul Sartre;[2] and the very good Bible studies were well attended. Visser 't Hooft was on the whole sympathetic to what he called 'the new orientation'. 'But', he added,

> If the Church is the Church of Jesus Christ, it knows only one destination: the Kingdom of God. And all human goals must be critically analysed in the light of the information we have received about the nature of that Kingdom and of the road that leads to it . . . We must not forget that at the heart of the definition of 'the Responsible Society' . . . there is the responsibility to God. All other responsibilities depend on that original one.[3]

Secularization was in the air. Paul van Buren's *The Secular Meaning of the Gospel* was published by the SCM Press in 1963, and the advocacy of the secular was widely seen as something positive. The SCM in India, for example – like the Indian Christian community as a whole – saw the 'secular state', advocated by Nehru, as an essential bulwark against the development of a theocratic Hindu state, and this point of view was well argued in Federation circles by M. M. Thomas. There was the growing influence of Bonhoeffer's 'religionless Christianity', and of the Dutch theologian Cornelis van Peursen's interpretation of the Old Testament as showing God's concern for Israel to be focused precisely on its *secular* life – an interpretation strongly advocated at the 1962 Federation conference in Graz, at which van Peursen was a speaker.[4] At its 1964 general committee, the Federation, under the influence of Hans Hoekendijk in its commission on the theme 'Called to be Human', had affirmed that

> Priority in our day rests upon what has traditionally been called 'prophetic witness'; to call the realities of injustice and inhumanity by their real names, without the veneer of rationalisations and ideologies; to side with the exploited against the exploiters . . . and to announce the possibility of new beginnings in a world in which a just and loving God is at work.[5]

To begin with at least, the secularizing effect was not so much within the Movement as in the general secularizing of society, which meant that the wider student body – the recruitment pool for SCM membership – was less church-minded than it had traditionally been, and so more ignorant of the basics of the Christian faith, and often simply agnostic.[6] Within the Movement, the 'secular Christianity' of which Bonhoeffer had spoken tended (certainly at the Federation level, or in Scotland) to be the Christocentric and biblical secularity of Bonhoeffer and Gregor Smith. Elsewhere, however, through a somewhat slanted interpretation of Bonhoeffer by theologians like Paul van Buren and John Robinson, and through a popularized version of Bultmann's 'demythologizing', there developed a tendency to move away from the Bible and from the church community of Word and sacrament. The SCM was entering a period in which – both nationally and internationally, and for a variety of reasons, theological, political and social – it would experience rapid change.

That change began to be apparent in the British Movement when in 1962 Bishop Ambrose Reeves was appointed general secretary. Reeves, originally from England, where he had served on the SCM staff as theological college department secretary from 1927 to 1931, had become one of apartheid's most doughty opponents in South Africa, from which he had recently been expelled because of his public criticism of the Sharpeville shootings. Political witness, especially against apartheid, was naturally at the top of his agenda. A crucial decision was taken, under Reeves' leadership, at a meeting of the general council in April 1963, when the branch delegates and staff decided to promote a 'radical change in both our attitude towards and also our activity in the Student Christian Movement'.[7] 'It may well be', wrote Reeves in a memorandum to the general council, 'that we can best serve the Churches by ceasing to be a "religious" society, and moving out to where so many students now are, even if it means giving up a great deal that was once most valuable in the life of the SCM.'[8] A contemporary letter from a concerned friend of the Movement refers to reported moves 'to abandon the whole existing structure of the SCM. Even the "Christian" in the title may go, leaving the denominational societies to provide that element, while the SCM gets to grips with the secular life of the universities.'[9]

Reeves had come into a difficult situation, and his tenure of the post of general secretary (1962–65) marks perhaps the critical point in the history of the British SCM. Aged 63, he was decades older than any previous general secretary had been at the beginning of his tenure; and it was generally believed, probably rightly, that Archbishop Fisher was no more eager than was Prime Minister Harold Macmillan to have such a turbulent priest as an English diocesan bishop. His biographer, who gives a mere three pages to the SCM stage in Reeves' career, remarks that it was hoped that he would 'give the movement an impetus and direction which it badly needed', and goes on to say that the SCM 'was flagging, having lost its enthusiasm, and its *raison d'être* was fast disappearing'.[10] This statement does not reflect the actual state of the Movement at the time, under the leadership of John Martin, the energetic and effective general secretary whom Reeves' arrival displaced,[11] and whose five-year appointment (1958–63) still had a year to run. Despite increasing if unintentional competition from the chaplains, John Martin had actually continued and strengthened the SCM's special ecumenical ministry, together with its concentration on understanding the Christian faith and its imperatives. Reeves, however, was an exciting figure, and the Movement (including John Martin, who with great dignity accepted a move to a Manchester parish) welcomed his dedication to justice. Eventually, however, both staff and members became divided over what to many appeared his concentration on the 'single issue' of witness to political and social justice, and also over his interpretation of 'openness' (open membership, without actual Christian commitment, both for ordinary members and for office-bearers), which seemed to go far towards eliminating the witness of the SCM as a specifically Christian organization. Symbolic of the departure from traditional and tried SCM activities was the abandonment of the Swanwick summer conferences, though indeed a major reason for this decision was the fact that SCM members, like their IVF contemporaries, had to pay their own way at conferences, while the denominational societies, with their far greater resources, ran highly subsidized events. The American Bruce Douglass of the WSCF staff, after a visit to the British Movement in June 1966, wrote:

> In many branches the openness policy has been interpreted to mean that the SCM must rid its programme of all the activities traditionally associated with the Christian religion, such as prayer, worship, theological and Bible study . . . in order to focus exclusively on secular concerns. The question has then arisen: if the SCM is going to perform only the same kind of functions that are already being performed by other, secular societies, then what reason is there for the SCM to exist?[12]

Reeves' strong Christian faith – biblical, spiritual and Church-focused – was not in doubt, and he rightly distinguished between 'faithfulness' – Christ-centred and always issuing in action – which was his passion, and 'religiousness', which he abhorred. He was an uncomfortable prophet, who drove himself, and expected others to match his own standards, and saw the disputed 'openness' policy as simply an effective means of mission in the highly secular world of the university. And the fact that he had a high public profile, and was much in demand as a speaker and consultant on apartheid, even at the United Nations, had a great appeal to students. But the policy was divisive. In addition, there was a feeling that Reeves' strong Anglo-Catholicism was tending to keep in position traditional barriers between Anglican and other students, especially in connection with intercommunion. At a time when Canterbury and York were moving towards the acceptance of intercommunion at conferences focused on Christian unity, Reeves made it clear that he himself could not share in this way, and this created problems for his colleagues. The churches, it seemed, were for once advancing ahead of the SCM.

There were also problems with Reeves' relations with staff and students and with his style of leadership, since his 'decisions were made *internally* after consultation rather than *externally* during consultation'.[13] He resigned in 1965. A man of great dedication and courage, he had a passion for justice, and total commitment to the Church; yet the question must be asked whether he was the right person for the job in 1962, and whether the impetus and direction he gave the Movement were the right ones. He was succeeded by David Head, a minister of the Methodist Church, who had served on the SCM's theological college department (TCD) committee, spent some years in West Africa and published several books on prayer, including the well-known *Shout for Joy* (1960). His arrival in 1966 was greeted warmly. Meanwhile the Movement had agreed on the wording of its new 'open membership' Basis:

> The SCM, being based on Jesus Christ the Lord, is open to all members of universities and colleges who are willing to enter its life and work. It shares the aims of the WSCF to which it is affiliated.

101

The storm clouds which were gathering in Britain were piling up in other national Movements, and especially in the Federation. A detailed account of what happened in the critical period between 1968 and 1973 has been provided by Risto Lehtonen of Finland, who was himself a member of the WSCF staff at the time, and is fittingly entitled *Story of a Storm* (1998).[14] A much briefer, and considerably less critical account is given in the centenary history of the Federation, *Seeking and Serving the Truth* (1997) by Philip Potter and Thomas Wieser.[15] In what follows I attempt to be fair to both these accounts, though it will be obvious that for much of the detail I am dependent on Lehtonen.

The late 1960s were a time of revolutionary student unrest, especially in Europe but also in America, Australia and other countries. Decolonization had been proceeding rapidly and often bitterly; the 'third world' had begun to make its identity and its presence felt, along with its poverty and its radical protest. The Cold War had set up a barrier of armed distrust between East and West, and there was a sense of anger and helplessness in face of the arms race, as well as dissatisfaction with the defects of both capitalism and communism. And over everything hung the cloud of possible nuclear war. The Civil Rights movement in the USA was violently reflected in many places, including South Africa and Northern Ireland. In Latin America, under the influence of Paulo Freire, 'conscientization' opened the way for 'base communities' and the activism of liberation theology, a movement in which the Federation, notably in the person of the American Richard Shaull, played a considerable role. Shaull makes the comment, highly interesting in view of the development of the base communities' methods of Bible study, that it was a visit from Suzanne de Diétrich as early as 1959 which helped him and others to develop a new type of Bible study leading to action – the interpretation of the Bible from the perspective of the poor.[16] The Vietnam war (1965–73) provoked anti-war protest in combatant Australia as well as the USA. Student protest took to the streets, and became more and more radical politically. In the USA in 1959 the National Student Christian Federation had been formed out of three earlier organizations, including the Student Volunteer Movement with its strong emphasis on mission.[17] In 1966, however, it virtually dissolved itself and was replaced by the University Christian Movement (UCM), 'a radical form of participatory ecumenism' – 'anti-academia, anti-intellectual, and anti-institutional'.[18] Students were looking for 'liberation from paternalism and authoritarian and hierarchical structures'.[19] In 1969, however, the UCM in turn voted itself out of existence. There had been an abrupt change in the American political climate, with the assassinations of Martin Luther King and Robert Kennedy, the violent suppression of the protest movement, and the election of a Republican President, Richard Nixon.

There were hopes that a new and different, but still radically politically-minded Christian student movement might arise, but in the event these hopes did not materialize.[20]

Writing about the state of the British SCM in 1968, Alistair Kee says:

> There is no doubt that the running was being made by the proliferation of Marxist groups, notably International Socialists, as they were then called . . . Humanist Marxism raised the value questions . . . Young Christians who would normally have been involved in SCM meetings were attending political meetings which functioned in a broadly Marxist framework.[21]

1968 was the critical year, the year when Martin Luther King was murdered. In Czechoslovakia there was the Prague Spring, with Dubček's attempt to affirm 'socialism with a human face'. It was also the year of the May Revolution in France, causing the departure of President de Gaulle. There was a move away from university life towards a unity of students and workers, and revolutionary students, with the highest of motives, nurtured 'a utopian vision of total democracy, freedom, justice, participation; the fulfilment of a new humanity'.[22] Soon afterwards, however, with the Gaullist victory in the elections, the student revolt collapsed. But the character of the French SCM had changed, and in particular its ties with the Church had been severed.[23]

Honest to God

During the early 1960s David Edwards, aware that the SCM Press had come to be regarded by well-meaning senior friends as over-academic, began to encourage the publication of a wide range of paperbacks, of which the best known was John Robinson's *Honest to God* of 1963, which led to a discussion of the Christian faith more widespread than anything in the previous half century: the SCM's 1963–64 annual report told of 700,000 copies being in print. Robinson was not really saying anything unfamiliar to most theological students in 1963 – certainly to those who had read authors like Bultmann, Bonhoeffer and James Barr. But the book had a vast impact, not so much because of what it was saying as because the standing and integrity of its author meant that ordinary people had to take seriously information which the churches had not succeeded in conveying to their members. *Honest to God* had two very distinct effects. A medical friend of mine responded to it by saying that it had at last bridged the gap between his desire to be Christian and his desire to be honest, and so had brought him back to faith; and in Scotland, for example, where Christian students of both SCM and IVF backgrounds were familiar with Bultmann, Bonhoeffer and Tillich (and less inclined to conflate them than did John Robinson!) there was little panic or frenzy.[24] Others, however, saw it as an irresponsible attack on the Church, deliberately intended to separate people from the faith which until then had nourished them. Certainly the controversy came at a time when the SCM, for a variety of reasons, was going through turmoil. At no time, however, did the Press print anything which was not backed by scholars of the highest integrity: it simply took the courageous step of making available, in a form which laypeople could understand, the findings of the best academic biblical scholarship. The Movement was not prepared to be accused of withholding the truth from its members: at its conferences, whether for university students in general or for theological students, it had always sought to invite speakers of the highest scholarly integrity in biblical and theological studies, and had encouraged students to seek out the truth for themselves, in the company of others committed to this search. The encouragement was to engage in deeper and more careful Bible study, and to treat the Bible and the great tradition of the Church with the seriousness and respect they deserved. To those who, perhaps following a Barthian line of biblical theology, now found some of their exegesis challenged, this was a challenge to dig deeper in the same quarry, not to abandon the search. As the acuteness of the debate began to relax somewhat, the diversity and questioning found in the text of the Bible came to be better understood, and to be seen as an enrichment rather than a threat.

Different kinds of controversy followed the 1966 British Council of Churches' report *Sex and Morality*, published by the SCM Press – by now under the editorship of John Bowden – and the 1977 publication of *The Myth of God Incarnate*, to say nothing of Don Cupitt's *Taking Leave of God* and *The World to Come*. Yet these controversial publications were scholarly; and in the event they elicited comparable scholarly responses from those who opposed them. The Press also produced John Bright's much consulted *History of Israel*, as well as books in the established SCM tradition of biblical exegesis linked with commitment to mission and justice, like John V. Taylor's *Enough is Enough* and *The Go-Between God*. And under both David Edwards and John Bowden a new trail was blazed by popularizing, for English-speaking readers, the work of such modern Roman Catholic theologians as Edward Schillebeeckx, Hans Küng, Rosemary Ruether and Gustavo Gutiérrez.

Changes at the WCC

Meantime the same winds of change were having their effect on the WCC, which could still be regarded in some ways as the SCM's child – by now an adult child but still susceptible to the radicalism of its parent, and still strongly marked by the family tradition. The fourth

WCC Assembly at Uppsala (Sweden) in 1968 saw a move away from what was pejoratively described as the 'low-profile servicing of member churches' towards 'prophetic' leadership. There was praiseworthy concentration on 'the plight of the underprivileged, the homeless and starving', and advocacy of 'the most radical contemporary rebellions against all "establishment", civil and religious'.[25] Yet for Newbigin, who was there, it was in many ways a shattering experience, not least because the change of mood was considerably influenced by the student presence, many if not most of whom had SCM connections:

> The mood was one of anger. The well-drilled phalanx of students in the gallery ensured that the emotional temperature was kept high. It was a terrifying enunciation of the law, with all its (proper) accompaniments of threat and wrath. We were corporately shaken over the pit of hell. The word of the Gospel was hardly heard.[26]

M. M. Thomas, however, took a more positive view:

> Some criticise Uppsala as the beginning of ecumenical withdrawal from world mission. Some criticise that the activism it led was carried to excess, destroying the capacity to do fundamental study of new social problems . . . In spite of it all, I for one consider that the new turning the ecumenical movement made at Uppsala was on the whole for the good. In any case it was probably inevitable.[27]

He continues:

> The new Division of World Mission with its study on 'the Church for Others' and the beginnings of the urban industrial mission and interfaith dialogue sought to relate world mission and evangelism to the search of all religious cultures and peoples for the humanisation of structures of social and international life. The student revolt of France and the black revolts against white racism in America and Southern Africa symbolised the world-wide awakening of peoples. In such an atmosphere the emergence of a new theological climate in the ecumenical movement with a central emphasis on the humanum was inevitable. The Uppsala Assembly reflected that emergence.[28]

Under its new general secretary, Eugene Carson Blake, the WCC responded sympathetically to Uppsala's radical call for justice. It was a call which had recently been heard and responded to by Vatican II, leading to the setting up of the ecumenical SODEPAX (Joint Committee on Society, Development and Peace). And it was a call which came most strongly from the churches of 'the South' – from Africa, Asia and Latin America – whose voices were at last beginning to be heard on the world stage, in protest not only against political injustice and oppression, but also against the fact that hitherto their views had commanded little attention in the debates and decisions of the WCC itself. In response the WCC set up its Programme to Combat Racism (PCR), and took steps to rid itself of all signs of western dominance.[29]

This thoroughly laudable and Christian emphasis on peace and justice had, however, some questionable results, in the WCC as in the SCM. A lack of interest in the discipline of biblical and classical theology seemed to develop, and to some it appeared that 'a preference for an ideologically predetermined approach in matters of social and economic development crept in'.[30] Critics noticed a trend towards an oversimplification which discouraged informed and detailed discussion. Instead of the traditional method of working through careful biblical exegesis and theological grounding, coupled with detailed and critical social ethical analysis, a tendency seemed to be emerging of simply issuing 'prophetic' public statements. Lehtonen, a somewhat bitter critic, writes that 'inclusiveness overtook competence as a priority'.[31] This is going too far. The leaders of the WCC rightly felt that they must listen to the voice of the voiceless, and respond in a way which challenged not only powerful western churches but also powerful western governments. Yet at the same time (and here the WCC was wiser than the SCM) the Faith and Order Commission and the Commission on World Mission and Evangelism (CWME) were able to maintain their strongly biblical and theological emphasis, without being diverted from their agenda by the much more public political and economic pronouncements made at Assembly level.[32] Despite the fact that its political debates and decisions invariably attracted an undue share of media attention, the WCC always ensured that at its Assemblies a full day was given to issues of Faith and Order. At the Vancouver Assembly in 1983 Bill Lazareth, then director of Faith and Order, was concerned that political issues were going to crowd out what he believed to be the vital debate on the *Baptism, Eucharist and Ministry* document. But in the event the document was thoroughly debated, and effectively endorsed, and the Assembly convincingly demonstrated that when it came to essential issues of Christian faith and unity, the Council was prepared to make responsible and well-informed decisions. A delighted and relieved Bill Lazareth gladly admitted that his fears had been misplaced.[33]

One WCC action, after Uppsala 1968, with a direct impact on the student world was the drastic diminution, through restructuring, of its Youth Department, which in the past had brought together young people, many of them SCM members, to ecumenical work-camps all over the world, and that on a large scale – 10,000 young people from over 60 countries in 387 camps up to the end of the 1950s. There were several reasons for this decision, one of them being financial pressure. The main justification, however, was that young people were now full participants in the general work of the Council. After Uppsala the Youth

Department staff was reduced from seven to one, and youth work diminished accordingly. True, nine per cent of the official delegates at Uppsala were aged between 18 and 30. But in practice an excellent enterprise for young people, and one which helped to win many of them to the cause of world-wide Christian fellowship and unity, was lost.

The Federation

1968 was a critical year for the Federation, as it was for the national SCMs. The WSCF held a student conference at Turku, followed by its Assembly at Otaniemi, both in Finland. At the conference, the plans carefully made in advance for what seemed a radical enough study of Christian presence and of secular theology were jettisoned by the students. What was described as 'pure' or 'transcendentalist' theology was repudiated as being 'part of the ideological system which justifies oppression'.[34]

There was opposition also to the planned conference worship, and we are told that 'African delegates were perplexed by participants who did not want to worship'.[35] Bill Corzine, who was the organizing secretary at Turku, wrote, 'One sensed that delegates had come with their own priorities, anxious to achieve clarity and win support for "their own thing". They exhibited no particular interest in the causes of theologians, WSCF personnel, statesmen or the conference planners.' He asks,

> Should we have retained theological reflection at all costs? Should we have added a period of Bible study each day? Should we have insisted upon worship by incorporating it into plenary sessions? I think not – at least not in a student conference of this kind. We have finally realised that we must begin where people are in their faith struggles – not where we think they are or where we think they should be.[36]

The question, 'Should we have added a period of Bible study each day?' is a strange one to ask within the SCM tradition. And it marks a watershed in the journey: it was not *bad* exegesis which led the Movement, for a time, into 'the far country': it was the rejection of exegesis.

The Otaniemi Federation Assembly, in a discussion of the theological foundations of the WSCF, demonstrated the division which had arisen. It affirmed the theory of 'Christian presence' in two distinct ways: (1) 'the affirmation of the presence of Christ as God's supreme gift to the world', to be discovered through the study of the scriptures and the Christian traditions; and (2) 'concrete and effective action in the struggle for the creation of a new society and a new man' [sic].[37] These two ways were not, however, accorded equal status. In Lehtonen's ironic words, 'traditional theological categories had lost their usefulness . . . Only theology which played an iconoclastic role was considered helpful.'[38] As a result, 'the articulation of the meaning of Christian faith became increasingly difficult', and the 'politicization of the membership of the WSCF' was advocated.[39] Richard Shaull, the newly elected chairman of the Federation, deeply involved in the beginnings of Latin American liberation theology, found much to encourage in the situation. 'We find ourselves on the road to a new theology, a new university, authentic politics of social reconstruction', he wrote, 'and in this situation, authentic ecumenicity is the relationship which we share along the road to the future'.[40] The veteran Marjorie Reeves was at both Turku and Otaniemi, and she too was understanding of the 'openness' to the world which the students were demonstrating.[41] Interesting, also – and ecumenically challenging – was the fact that the customary shared eucharist at the end of the conference was on this occasion celebrated by a Roman Catholic priest from the then oppressed and divided South Africa.[42]

The debate continued for some time between the radical, revolutionary and neo-Marxist group on the one hand, and the 'reformist', democratic Christian Left on the other. The latter, well represented by the veteran French SCM leader André Dumas, were keen to 'work out concrete goals for a more humanised society'.[43] In the event, both points of view were, at this stage, approved as 'valid framework for the Federation's future'.[44]

In 1970 Risto Lehtonen, by then Federation general secretary, wrote a circular letter to the national SCMs and some senior friends, outlining the situation, and listing the alternatives before the Federation. It was a choice between global revolution, in which Christian students would join forces with the working class, on the one hand; and on the other a WSCF seen primarily as 'an expression of the Christian community – the Church – in the academic world' and encouraging 'a diversity of expressions of faith and patterns of witness in the political sphere'.[45] Lehtonen asked for responses to his letter.

The response of André Dumas is significant, and appears to me to express the authentic voice of the best tradition of the SCM:

> I am definitely in favour of an explicit Christian confession, and this in the interests of politics itself. In my opinion, there are certain irreplaceable contributions which cannot be made without the Christian faith: its witness to God makes the worship of an ideology impossible . . . its practice of justification by faith makes impossible sectarian self-justification. Finally, in seeking reconciliation, which is the opposite of separation, Christian faith brings freedom from the negativism of terrorists.[46]

The importance of this debate is confirmed by some of the other responses. Inga-Brita Castren (Finland and Africa) expressed a concern that explicit 'Christian faith and biblical theology' should remain the foundation of the Federation's involvement in political and social matters.[47]

And the Norwegian SCM said that it was 'not satisfied with references only to Christian "tradition", "heritage", or "background". Faith in the suffering and living Christ belongs not only to the past, but to the present and the future.'[48]

There was no response from the German SCM, which was at the time torn apart by conflicts and by strains between the churches and the students. However, one distinguished German senior friend of the Movement, Jürgen Moltmann, did respond. Stressing the importance of biblical theology, which alone could point to the liberating character of the Kingdom of God, he regretted the diminished interest in contextual Bible study among theologians, and advocated the reading of the Bible with a new perception.[49] He continued:

> In my opinion, the Bible is the book of the poor, the oppressed and hopeless. It is not the book of priests and lords. It is not a book of laws for the just, but of promises, and of the Gospel of God to sinners . . . We must read this book with the eyes of the poor.[50]

Charles West, who had exercised a prophetic ministry in the revolutionary China of 1947–50, then in East Germany, and later at the Bossey Ecumenical Institute, and was now teaching social ethics at Princeton, replied in terms which are equally in the classic SCM tradition:

> The WSCF had better decide whether there is a God who has come into this world in Christ or not, and if not, it had better go out of business so as not to deceive people. For years . . . the WSCF functioned as the Church ahead of the Church, as the seed-bed for the theological and social insights which later became the garden which fed the ecumenical movement.[51]

And he affirmed a principle with which SCM members had long been familiar, and which the Movement had hitherto always tried to put into practice, when he said that the SCM should at all costs resist Church control, while at the same time believing that responsibility towards the Church is one of the basic reasons for the Movement's existence.[52] He also recalled the Movement to its primary responsibility for the university as its field of mission – a responsibility which had been so eagerly and fruitfully accepted in the 1950s, but had now been almost totally neglected: 'what is needed is to find the form of the Christian mission to the university, and to focus the responsibility of the academic community for the whole community of the nation and the world'.[53]

The majority of students and student leaders in the European and American Movements were, however, reluctant to listen to the counselling of senior friends, no matter how distinguished or radical they might be. More surprisingly they also seemed deaf to the views of students from Africa and Asia, and from the Orthodox churches. We have noted the perplexity of African students over the marginalization of worship at the Turku Federation conference. M. M. Thomas, while acknowledging that the Movement was dealing 'with the meaning of the totality of human existence', insisted that 'no ecumenical organisation can justify itself as Christian unless it is all the time involved in exploring further, as a matter of imperative, the truth and meaning of the person of Jesus Christ'.[54] Chandran Devanesen, also of India, affirmed that 'the WSCF and the SCM would be relevant only as far as they were explicitly Christian. [The] SCM of India can't opt for one particular political position. Instead its task is to raise the level of political interest among Christian students.'[55] Devanesen's rejection of the 'single issue' politicization of the WSCF is significant.

The response to Lehtonen's letter from the Orthodox student Movements of the Middle East stresses the need for a strengthening of theology rather than a weakening:

> The Christian life is new with the newness of the world which is to come. It is this eschatological reality which we express in professing that 'Christ has risen again' . . . Our faith as it is lived out is . . . experience of the resurrection of Christ; it is the essential liberation of man . . . No social form can be dogmatised, and the gospel does not provide a new political program.[56]

Lehtonen sees the Federation Assembly held in Addis Ababa in December 1972–January 1973 as marking a final rupture in the life of the WSCF, and quotes Visser 't Hooft as going so far as to say that this Assembly marked the most drastic break which had ever occurred in the ecumenical movement.[57] For the first time the members of the Federation did not join together in a communion service. Lehtonen gives a highly critical summary of the results of this Assembly, asserting that in it the Federation

- rejected the ecumenical vision;
- turned away from the missionary vocation;
- sacrificed Christian respect for intellectual and academic work in favour of a doctrinaire anti-institutionalism;
- left untouched problems of 'third world' poverty and oppression;
- rejected the Church.

It is a serious indictment. The more radical leaders in the Federation had been hoping to revolutionize both university and society. But by the early 1970s it was becoming clear that this change was not going to happen; and in his opening statement to the Addis Ababa WSCF assembly Richard Shaull admitted that the forces of the established order were not going to yield so easily: 'We are now aware that this same order is moving towards increasing and more effective repression'.[58]

Lehtonen's first criticism above refers to the rejection of the ecumenical vision; and this had particularly disappointing results, as we shall see, for the relationship between the SCM and the Roman Catholic student community. Vatican II should have provided an opportunity for increasingly significant contacts between students of that church and the SCM; if it had come a decade earlier, it is not unreasonable to say that an extraordinary enrichment of the student ecumenical *koinonia* would have occurred. But the Movement had been deflected from its ecumenical task.

7

Living under 'the Storm' (*c.* 1965–80)

Britain

Events in the British SCM – Britain under Prime Minister Harold Wilson had avoided involvement in the Vietnam war – were less traumatic than in the USA, continental Europe and the Federation, but they led towards a similar decline which some friendly critics (Ronald Preston, for example) did not hesitate to call 'the collapse of the SCM'.[1] The politicization which we have seen at work under Ambrose Reeves in 1962 continued, and Lehtonen states simply that leaders of the British Movement, including its general secretary David Head, 'expressed their unambiguous commitment to Marxist socialism',[2] with the result that, in the period around 1969, SCM branches in Britain were gradually extinguished, as the Movement adopted a 'neo-Marxist counter-culture style'.[3]

Steve Bruce, a scholarly but negative sociological critic of the SCM, has asserted that 'the Catholic Marxists and the alternative life-style cohorts'[4] caused the decline of the British SCM. It is worth looking at the background of this charge, linked as it is with what for the SCM should have been the promising ecumenical developments of Vatican II. One gets the impression that the Movement, weakened as it had been by its concentration on the single issue of politics, was unable to benefit from this new ecumenical awakening as it might have done if its traditional marks of Bible study, worship, mission commitment and unity had been adhered to. At a time when many Roman Catholic students were ready to enter the *koinonia* of the Movement, the leaders of the SCM were moving away from the theological understanding which was needed in order to draw out the significance of this new ecumenical relationship.

In 1966 Fr Laurence Bright, a radical and brilliant Dominican friar who had a doctorate in nuclear physics and was theological adviser to the publishers Sheed and Ward, became the SCM's first Roman Catholic staff member.[5] Widely read in Latin American liberation theology, he believed that Marxist social analysis was one of the most effective tools for understanding the world situation and acting effectively in it. His coming – with the blessing of Cardinal Heenan and the Dominican Order – was widely welcomed, and regarded as a significant ecumenical breakthrough; and even though it was challenged by no less a figure than George MacLeod of the Iona Community, it was stoutly defended by David Head.[6] A major conference was held that year with the title 'The Unmasking of Man: Marx and Freud', with two well-known radical Roman Catholic speakers, Herbert McCabe, then editor of *New Blackfriars*, and the youthful Terry Eagleton of *Slant* magazine, later a leading Marxist literary critic. Laurence Bright became a valued member of the University Teachers' Group, with which the SCM was still much involved; and his influence virtually dominated the headquarters thinking of the Movement for some years. Not unnaturally, in the freedom provided by the SCM, he encouraged his colleagues on the staff to take up a variety of political causes, starting with apartheid – which very rightly appealed to the membership. But their discourse became increasingly Marxist-theological rather than theological in the biblical, ecumenical and mission-orientated tradition of the Movement. In 1969 Bright produced a radical document, *The Political Stance of the SCM*, which rapidly assumed a central position in SCM policy, seeming indeed to marginalize all the Movement's other concerns, including Bible study, theology, prayer and evangelism. Reading its 11 points today one realizes that most of its aims have in fact been achieved – not least perhaps because the SCM was instrumental in their becoming the common cause of thousands of students in the late 60s and early 70s. They include opposition to discrimination based on race, age, gender or income; opposition to the control of the media by advertising interests; opposition to the support of unjust regimes in places like South Africa and Rhodesia; to the Vietnam war and to oppression in Latin America – and also in Eastern Europe (where the Soviet Union had recently invaded Czechoslovakia); advocacy of comprehensive education; of increased overseas aid, of fair trade for all; and support of the United Nations. Two further points were more controversial: workers' control of industry and the justification of 'revolutionary movements all over the world'.

The necessity of biblical and theological grounding for Christian political action was affirmed at the large and successful Student Congress, attended by 1500 students, which was organized by the SCM in Manchester in April 1969, with the theme of 'Response to Crisis', and with Visser 't Hooft and Dom Helder Camara as speakers.[7] Helder Camara listed seven deadly sins of modern society – racism, colonialism, war, paternalism, pharisaism, estrangement and fear – and in urging students to fight these sins reminded them in simple words that they needed 'the greatest friend of all young people . . . Jesus Christ'. Visser 't Hooft, preaching on Matthew 6.33 – 'Set your minds on God's Kingdom and his justice, and the rest will come to you as well' – and encouraging students to take seriously the WCC Uppsala Assembly's programme of social justice, told them that 'in order to give we must first receive – Jesus and his Kingdom: the Archimedean fixed point'. The problem was that by making the pursuit of justice a single issue, and by limiting the significance of Jesus to the political struggle, students were being effectively detached from the channels of Christian faith in Scripture and Church.

The critique of social and political structures in the outside world was matched by a critique of the Movement's own structures. In 1970 the traditional general council, with members elected by the regions, was replaced by a general assembly with an executive committee. David Head resigned in 1972, and the post of general secretary was abolished. Parity of salary for all staff was established. In the annual report for 1972–73 Laurence Bright writes, with some enthusiasm, of

> the general perception that those engaged in a struggle for democracy must reflect it by changes in their own structures. The dynasty of General Secretaries has come to a close, and a team now gloriously reigns at Annandale . . . We are, however, beginning to realise that the next step is to recover a Christianity, a theology within complete faithfulness to the secular . . . A theology appropriate to our struggle for socialism can only be born out of it.

Instead of recovering such a theology, however, further radical changes in the structure of the Movement itself were proposed, including the setting up of a series of issue-related 'colleges', each with a resident staff member, and with the Annandale headquarters acting simply as the central service agency. Another proposal was for a 'Free University for Black Studies', a project which was in fact commenced in 1970 but, despite its praiseworthy ideals, proved to be financially and practically irresponsible, and failed to attract black students. The Movement had become overstretched; and the inevitable ensuing fragmentation of its life provoked the alienation of many influential senior friends, including Oliver Tomkins and Kenneth Grayston, head of theology at Bristol University.

These developments did not go unchallenged by the student membership of the Movement. A group of students which met after the last general council meeting at Swanwick in January 1970[8] produced a Declaration which said:

> 1. We want to learn about Jesus, how we are to live with him and how we are to speak of him. Hence we are determined to study, and to ask, 'Who is Jesus Christ for us today?' We need aids for this study, and invite Executive to advise us.
> 2. We believe that there must be SCM branches, in which people can learn together, worship together, and help one another to grow. National projects – and we support them – are no substitutes for a lively network of local groups.[9]

In 1973–74 the radical leaders took the financially very risky step of selling Annandale, the Movement's historic London headquarters, and – in order 'to run the movement along lines which were not on the civil service model'[10] – bought a large rural property at Wick Court, near Bristol, where a non-authoritarian commune was set up. This British departure was in keeping with the direction in which the wider Federation was moving. It no longer wanted to think of itself as a 'movement' with a centralized organization and universal claims, but increasingly preferred to be a *community* of believers, a community of small communities. In the later words of Emidio Campi, Federation general secretary 1977–84, it wanted to be a relevant minority with a pluralistic approach.[11]

Huddersfield, 1973

An illuminating insight into the life and thought of the British SCM at the time of the move to Wick Court is provided by an account of a four-day gathering in Huddersfield in January 1973, published by the SCM Press under the title *Seeds of Liberation: Spiritual Dimensions to Political Struggle*.[12] It was a large gathering – 350 people, many but not all of them students – and it was very much a *community* event, much less formal than the traditional Swanwick conferences. The speakers included the American Jesuit Daniel Berrigan, recently released on parole from prison, where he had been serving a three-year sentence for burning draft records in an active protest against the Vietnam war; Bishop Colin Winter, who had just been deported from Namibia by the South African government; and Jim Forest, a founder-member (with Dorothy Day and Thomas Merton) of the Catholic Peace Fellowship, who had also, in 1968, taken part in the burning of draft records. Also present were Basil Moore, a Methodist theologian from South Africa, who had resigned as general secretary of the South African SCM (University Christian Movement), had come to England to escape a banning order and was now 'co-ordinating secretary' of the British SCM; and Alistair Kee from Scotland who had lectured in theology in Southern Rhodesia, and was now at the University of Hull and actively involved in radical student politics.

The British SCM had by now been undergoing a process of 'politicization' for most of a decade; and Alistair Kee, in introducing the book about the meeting, recalls how a great many radical Christians had left the churches 'for the sake of their souls'.[13] They did not regret their flight into political struggle, yet by now there was a feeling of 'hollowness at the centre of political life'. A reaction had set in, though it by no means heralded a movement back to the churches, which indeed seemed to provide 'no alternative to the conventional wisdom of the culture'.

Meanwhile a new, and disturbingly ambiguous, term had entered the radical Christian vocabulary – 'spirituality' – and the Huddersfield meeting represented a lively attempt to reconnect with 'the biblical tradition which is concerned with the spiritual depths of our social and political lives'.

Significantly, the term 'spirituality' does not occur all that frequently in the account of the Huddersfield meeting, and much more stress is laid on Bible and eucharist. Dan Berrigan tells how the most subversive thing he and his friends could do in prison was to celebrate the eucharist and read the scripture: 'it held us together, it kept us ready, it kept us hopeful'.[14] Their experience was that it is in reading and meditating on the Word that Christians, especially radical Christians, become clear on what action they are to take – 'where they are to go'.[15] And the report notes that over the years the only radical groups which had continued and gone on (when secular ones had faded away) were not only Christian, but eucharistic.[16]

There is no softening here of the political commitment. Colin Winter's contribution is a passionate call to maintain the struggle against apartheid; and Berrigan, in an interesting exegesis of Revelation 13, launches a sustained attack against 'the Beast', which he identifies (in terms foreshadowing Walter Wink's 1984 'naming the powers' of the 'Evil Empire') with all domination, both capitalist and Marxist, which use physical and economic violence to enhance their own wealth and suppress the poor. His anger, at this time of the Vietnam war, is turned especially on the United States, and on the churches which so uncritically support an aggressively imperialistic government. Viv Broughton, the main organizer of the meeting, writes, 'It must . . . be an absolute pre-condition of all else we do, that we extricate ourselves from the community that exists by the subjugation of others, and consciously opt to be part of a community whose very survival is daily threatened'.[17] The experience of the previous years had shown that this was no easy thing to do, especially for relatively elitist university students, and Alistair Kee is both more modest and more practical when he describes what he calls 'the resistance community':

> Its life does not depend on dealing with a particular issue . . . The life of the group has a deep spiritual centre, and it is nourished not by tactical sessions, but by eucharistic occasions and by study of the Bible . . . The life of the spirit is sustained from its spiritual depths.[18]

In a development which marked a change from the SCM's 1960s tendency to become identified with, and ultimately indistinguishable from, the prevailing Marxist activism, two clear new notes are sounded. First, Christian activists recognize that they themselves are part of the enemy in the struggle.[19] They are self-critical, seeing their own involvement in the evil they oppose; and of course they are critical also of the churches, but now in a way which draws its spiritual strength from the Bible and the eucharist. And second, they embody and exemplify the kind of lifestyle which they proclaim.[20] 'In our Christian tradition . . . we are promised an earnest, a first instalment now, of the life of the gospel. This suggests why the political groups in America have collapsed, while the eucharistic groups have continued.'

There is even a call to return to 'the great tradition' of the Church, provided, as Berrigan says, that tradition is understood as 'the links that bind a believing community today to a community of believers at the time the gospels were written'.[21] For he had found in his prison experience that 'the best thing we could do to communicate in, or to exist in . . . this secular culture, was to return to our roots, and try to be faithful to them'.[22]

Summarizing the Huddersfield experience, Viv Broughton writes, 'For a brief period, this event flashed a number of extraordinary images at us, allowing us a fleeting glimpse of a truly alternative Christian community'.[23] Huddersfield indicated a new and impressive development – a continuing political commitment to justice and peace, yet marked by a return to the Christian sources of Bible, eucharist and tradition. It is a stance which today – over 30 years later – exercises a strong attraction, at a time when once again the 'Evil Empire' seems to be in the ascendant, and when Christians are again being summoned by the gospel to be a community of resistance.

Abandoning the university: Wick Court, 1973–77

The move to Wick Court in 1973[24] was an experiment in creating a community which in practice fell short of the 'resistance community' suggested at Huddersfield, with its emphasis on Bible and eucharist. Lehtonen – laconically if somewhat unkindly – suggests that after the move to Wick Court the British Movement 'fell into a deep sleep for at least a decade'.[25] But it was certainly not an undisturbed sleep, even though the life of the scattered branches in universities and colleges quietly disintegrated. The developments of the early 1970s not unnaturally led to considerable, and sometimes acrimonious, differences between the SCM Trust Association and the Movement itself.[26] The Trust Association, as we have seen, had been founded by Tatlow in 1921, and was composed largely of senior friends of the Movement. Some of the SCM's activities appeared to the trustees to be purely political rather than specifically Christian; and the sale of Annandale, accompanied by the move – at considerable expense – to Wick Court, had greatly perturbed many friends, both senior and not so senior, who expressed the fear that the SCM was no longer fulfilling its proper function, and was in danger of disintegrating. The situation was complicated when the matter was reported to the Charity Commissioners, so risking the SCM's charitable status. The SCM itself, or a majority of its members, saw things differently, and their viewpoint is expressed in the 1975 annual report, edited by Richard Zipfel:

> They see the decisions of the last few years as forming a coherent and creative direction for the movement: community houses, the move to Wick and a different style of headquarters, a modest parity wage for all staff, a collective rather than hierarchical staff structure, the reduction of central bureaucracy combined with regionalisation and decentralisation. Behind this pattern of decision lies the broader decision to translate SCM's Christian values into a new way of operating and into some form of Christian commitment to politics. This whole development has been anything but haphazard or sudden. It has been a long process, discussed by many generations of SCM students and staff.

The anxieties of the Trust Association were, however, not relieved; and they had additional concerns about the membership of the Wick community, which by now included people with no direct SCM connection. To the students, the Trust Association epitomized paternalism: to the Trust Association the SCM was being irresponsible. On 15 October 1975 the executive committee of the Trust Association resolved to cease payments to the SCM from 30 November. The decision was not in fact implemented, and the situation gradually began to improve, so that by March 1977 the Trust Association Executive was able to say that it regarded the dispute between itself and the SCM as being in the past.[27]

Robert Mackie, who had successively been general secretary of both the British SCM and of the Federation, writing in 1976 on the occasion of a visit to the Wick commune, where he had been invited to open the Tatlow Centre, speaks appreciatively of the small community, where he was made very welcome.[28] 'There was a simplicity and openness about it all . . . The great question is whether this kind of group, and this kind of method, can build up a national movement', he wrote. Already the Movement had greatly diminished; public support, including financial support, had dwindled, and the Movement's influence in the universities was very small.

Mackie's explanation for the decline of the SCM is clearly stated. Referring to the way in which, for very good reasons, apartheid in South Africa had become the major concern in the 1960s, he describes the problem as 'the impact of a legitimate and powerful expression of public conscience tending to use the SCM as an auxiliary'. Apartheid, on this occasion, had become a single issue, in which the SCM was *used* by other organizations. He reflects on how at this period 'legitimate concern with politics seemed to get out of hand', and this concern was 'hard to integrate with the basic task of helping students . . . to find Christian roots'. He concluded that 'external problems of conscience – e.g. in South Africa, South America, Vietnam, Ireland . . . have loosened, though by no means destroyed, its traditional functions'.

Though impressed by 'the complete natural ecumenism' of the Wick commune, and by its members' clear interest in spiritual experience, he is unable to make a judgement on their attitude to the Christian faith, though he has 'no sense of sinister influences at work'. In his address he commends the members of the commune for their concern for 'the uncommitted areas of relationships, personal and social, on the limited and on the world scale', but he adds, 'All your discussion will only be of value if you relate it to Jesus Christ, if it can be taken up into Christ's purpose, and moved by the power of his Spirit'.

Talking, after his visit, with several of his former SCM staff colleagues, Mackie voices two sources of their disquiet. One is the question of the suitability of Wick, in its isolation, as a base for what should be a *national* Movement. The other is what they feel to be the need for 'greater theological clarity'. Interestingly, too, they feel that the contemporary IVF is 'wearing more of the old SCM mantle these days'. This is an issue to which we shall return.

In a letter written to Davis McCaughey in 1979, comparing the 1960s and 70s with the 1930s and 40s covered in McCaughey's book, Mackie gives another penetrating insight into what had happened: 'For myself I feel that the SCM [at Wick] reflected the lack of leadership in the churches' meetings and conferences, which was the great asset of the period you wrote about'.[29] At all earlier periods of its life the SCM had looked to church leaders and theologians for inspiration and guidance, even if it tended to be very selective about what advisers it chose and what advice was taken. And in a strange way – the Spirit works in strange ways – its corporate decisions enabled it to be seen and widely acknowledged as 'church ahead of the Church'. Why was it then that in this period no very inspiring or positive leadership came from the churches, so that the Movement turned instead to secular political activists, whose voices seemed more nearly to reflect the biblical imperative to justice?

In the event, the Wick experiment proved short-lived. In 1977 Wick Court was sold, and the SCM transferred its headquarters to Selly Oak, Birmingham. Since then the Movement has remained financially viable, but only on a greatly reduced scale.

The developments which we have been discussing, following as they did the 1972–73 Federation Assembly in Addis Ababa, did not go unchallenged by long-standing British friends of the Movement. Martin Conway, who had served on the staff of the British SCM, the Federation and the WCC, wrote, 'I cannot for the life of me understand how a body claiming the inheritance of the WSCF, let alone its name, can be anything else than based on explicitly Christian affirmations. If the WSCF simply slides away from its earlier basis, than I am sure that in a few years time there will be as good as nothing left.'[30]

Australia

On the other side of the world, in Australia, events similar to those in Britain were taking place, and the process is briefly charted by Frank Engel[31] whose name looms gently and large[32] in the story of the Australian SCM (ASCM). Born in Korea, the son of Presbyterian missionary parents, he was inspired to join the Movement by the impressive and effective Chinese WSCF secretary T. Z. Koo, whose visit to Melbourne in 1931 gave a new vision of the world Church and its mission to many university students. After graduating, Engel became a travelling secretary for four years, and went on to become the general secretary of the ASCM in the golden age of 1949–58. (He also – typically, for he had wide horizons – served for a period as general secretary of the New Zealand Movement.) In 1951 he wrote an article for the British SCM's *The Student Movement* magazine entitled 'Australia faces North', signalling Australia's new-found identity with Asia, rather than as an outpost of the British Empire (Indonesia, with the world's largest Muslim population, is after all a mere 300 kilometres north of Queensland). In the 1950s, when Asian students first began to arrive in Australia under the Colombo Plan, he and the formidable Margaret Holmes, with others like Jean Waller and Una Ross, led the Australian Movement in providing a welcome and hospitality for the students as they arrived. They went on, in the 1960s, to help in the setting up of the Overseas Service Bureau, under which Australian volunteers, including many SCM members, gave service overseas through AVA (Australian Volunteers Abroad). From 1959 to 1961 Engel was SE Asian secretary of the WSCF (with a field covering the Philippines, Hong Kong, Korea, Japan and Indonesia, as well as Australia and New Zealand), and greatly strengthened the links between the Movements in this vast area. After that he went on to be general secretary of the Australian Council of Churches (ACC: it later became the National Council of Churches), which, largely through his advocacy, became a very effective instrument in opposing the government's long-standing 'White Australia' policy. Equally important was the courageous and painstaking work he did in support of Aboriginal land rights in the 1960s and 70s, both through the ACC and through his own church (Presbyterian until the union of 1977 and thereafter Uniting Church). And after retirement he went on to put all the Australian churches in his debt by writing a two-volume history of ecumenism in

Australia from 1788 to 1978,[33] as well as his personal recollections of the East Asian region of the Federation from 1931 to 1961.[34]

It is from his standpoint within such a massive sweep of ecumenical and missionary history and geography that Frank Engel briefly and penetratingly describes what happened to the Australian Movement in 'the storm'. The change and decline was, he says laconically, 'an accelerating movement from Bible study to action, from "churchiness" to "causes", from doctrine to street demonstrations.'[35] In Australia as in Britain the SCM moved physically out of its headquarters, even out of the university, into small communities. The Bible ceased to interest students, even Christian students. They had other things to engross them – important things like the Vietnam war, Aboriginal rights, uranium mining, the right to protest. For an account of what happened under the storm we turn to Sandy Yule, who was there.

Sandy Yule,[36] who was ~~at the time of writing~~ secretary of the ᵗⁱⁿ 2006 Christian Unity working group of the Uniting Church in Australia, was closely in touch with the Australian Movement through much of the 1960s and 70s, first as a student, then as general secretary of the ASCM, and later as a senior friend. Going to Melbourne University in 1959 to study philosophy and history, he joined the ASCM branch, which was still quite large, with more than 100 members, while the national conference at the end of his first year had over 400 people. He was impressed by the informal relationship between students and academic staff which the Movement was able to provide: well-known professors were glad to attend conferences, and were thoroughly approachable when they did. Relations with the Evangelical Union (EU) were difficult, but a fruitful relationship was developing with the Newman Society, which greatly helped to break down the still traditional Australian hostility – even at student level – between Catholics and Protestants, in what Yule does not hesitate to call the beginning of a historic healing.

The years from 1959 to 1966 saw the growth of political involvement in the Australian Movement, under the pressures of the Cold War, the nuclear threat, the campaign against capital punishment, and in particular the highly controversial Australian involvement, as allies of the Americans, in the Vietnam war of 1965–73. The ASCM, like the mainline churches, was vigorously opposed to the war; and many of its members came to feel that their voice would be more effective if it simply united with what Yule calls 'the broad student movement', with its demonstrations and street marches. There were also several particularly Australian issues, notably the 'White Australia' policy, which was directed not only at excluding non-white immigrants but also at marginalizing the original inhabitants of the land; and which was not effectively bypassed until the granting of the right to vote to

Aboriginals in 1962, and their long overdue admission to full citizenship in 1967.

After several years of study in America (at Princeton) during which he shared actively in the student protest against the Vietnam war (guiltily aware of his own country's heavy implication in it), Yule returned to Australia in 1970, to become general secretary of the ASCM. He found a Movement greatly reduced in size and influence since he had first joined it 10 years earlier, and with much diminished senior support. Aboriginal land rights had become a major issue, as had the protest against uranium mining, which in turn led to an increased interest in ecological questions. Yet it was not easy to develop effective relations with the Aboriginal community, and an effort to secure an Aboriginal delegation to attend a Federation conference in Fiji in 1974 proved an embarrassing failure.

The ASCM had already moved out of its original city headquarters in Melbourne, and now moved into some Presbyterian church buildings in the inner urban suburb of Fitzroy. Brian Howe, who with his wife Renate Morris had been a co-president of the ASCM in 1960, was now Methodist missioner there, and in 1972 Yule joined the resident team as general secretary of the ASCM. The parish was already a united Methodist–Presbyterian one, formed under arrangements anticipating the 1977 union of Methodist, Presbyterian and Congregational churches. The community was soon joined by nine students. It was a move in some ways comparable with the British SCM's move to Wick Court at about the same time, but had the merit of remaining in the city, not very far from the university, and of providing a group of students with the opportunity of living in a Christian community and becoming involved in a difficult inner urban situation without abandoning their role as students. Brian Howe, with his experience of inner-city problems in an area where many immigrants were being settled in high-rise flats, later entered national politics and, while still remaining a minister of the Uniting Church, became a very effective government minister – first for Defence Support, then Social Security, Health, Urban and Regional Development and Housing, and finally Deputy Prime Minister (1991–95) in the Hawke and Keating Labor Governments.

Meantime Yule, as ASCM general secretary, was in 1970 virtually the sole staff person for a vast continent, in contrast to the situation in the 1950s when there had been a staff of 14. Through the WSCF, as well as through his own Presbyterian Church, he became involved with South Korea, for this was a time of severe political and industrial repression there, when many Christians, including church ministers and students, were imprisoned on the charge of being agents of the North Korean communist government. In 1974 Yule went to South Korea as part of a WSCF delegation to do what they could to secure the release of these political prisoners. They met with considerable success; most of the prisoners were released within ten months, and testified that the WSCF intervention had helped the democratic forces to maintain their voice of protest. Yule and the Federation delegation were strongly aware of the bed-rock support of the churches in this work. And, in contrast to what was happening in many areas of student protest all over the world, they were convinced that a society cannot recover from a traumatic situation unless there is forgiveness. Whether in relation to Vietnam or Korea, or to the treatment of Aboriginals in Australia, Yule came more and more to believe that his contribution – and that of the SCM – ought to be the encouragement of 'a spirituality to support political causes', which would include confession of the sins of one's own side, and the search for mutual forgiveness. It was not enough to be mesmerized by the pain of the world: genuine confession and forgiveness must be part of protest.

Ireland: a lost opportunity?

In Ireland also there was a great need for mutual forgiveness. Here the alienation was between the Roman Catholic[37] and Protestant communities, who were divided from each other politically and sociologically as well as religiously; and beginning from 1969 lethal violence had entered the situation. Like the Irish churches, the Irish SCM, as part of 'the SCM of Great Britain and Ireland', had, even after the partition of Ireland in 1922, always operated throughout the whole island. Up to the 1960s it had been almost exclusively Protestant in membership (as indeed it had been in most countries) though it always included people with strong Irish nationalist views, like Lionel Booth, an officer in the Irish Army (whose brother Alan Booth was general secretary of the British Movement from 1944 to 1951 and later director of Christian Aid) and Risteard O Glaisne (a well known exponent of Irish language and culture). The Irish contribution to the British Movement as a whole had been considerable, providing, for example, the leadership of Tissington Tatlow, Billy Greer, Alan Booth, Anthony Hanson, Davis McCaughey, Carlisle Patterson and many others. In the critical period of Irish history after 1969 commonly referred to as 'the Troubles', the SCM undoubtedly did make valiant efforts at reconciliation between Catholics and Protestants. Yet because of the prevailing 'storm' in the life of the whole Movement, its numbers and influence eventually declined dramatically.

Despite the traditional division between Roman Catholics and Protestants, things in the university arena had begun to change for the better as early as the late 1940s, to no small extent because of personal friendship between Ray Davey, the first Presbyterian chaplain at Queen's University Belfast (QUB), and Fr Cahal Daly, who was then teaching moral philosophy in the university and later became a cordially if cautiously ecumenical archbishop and cardinal. They were both involved, together with the Irish SCM, in a lively ecumenical mission to the university in 1951, with J. V. Langmead Casserley as chief missioner. Occasionally, however, the Movement's relations with the churches proved more difficult, and when in the early 1960s Salters Sterling (Irish secretary 1961–64) sought the permission of the registrar of University College Dublin (UCD), where the great majority of students were Catholics, to introduce the SCM to the college, he was asked to leave the office!

The Movement's new Aim and Basis of 1965 encouraged the SCM to regard itself as a fellowship open to all members of the university, no matter what church they belonged to, and in 1965 the Queen's University branch elected its first Roman Catholic chairperson, Don Phillips. It was a move which received encouragement from many senior friends of the Irish SCM, like the veteran Tom Barker, who had been Irish secretary in 1911–13 and again in 1931–32, and later as a missionary prisoner in Japan had survived the Nagasaki atomic bomb. But, with some such notable exceptions, few leaders in the Protestant churches were prepared to give the SCM the support it needed when it took this courageous step: it was regarded as rocking the boat too violently. The natural nervousness of many people in the Protestant churches was increased by the Revd Ian Paisley's constant denunciation of the imagined 'Romeward trend' of the Presbyterian Church, whose 1966 General Assembly he blockaded. (He had never himself been a member of that church, and had Baptist not Presbyterian antecedents.) The specific object of his wrath was the WCC, but he extended it to any effort to promote better relations between Catholics and Protestants. The Irish Theological Colleges' Union (ITCU) was a case in point. Set up, like similar unions in Britain, under the theological college department of SCM, for many years it had organized useful ecumenical meetings between Church of Ireland, Presbyterian and Methodist students. But when the SCM became fully ecumenical through the inclusion of Roman Catholics in its membership, tensions arose between it and the ITCU. Nevertheless (and with the interesting inclusion in the planning committee of the local IVF secretary) an ITCU meeting in 1967 did raise the possibility of including the Roman Catholic seminaries in its membership. Before that could happen, however, the British SCM in 1969 decided to abolish the whole theological college department, which had been an essential part of the Movement almost from the first, on the grounds that it was unnecessary to separate theological from other types of students. And so the ITCU also ceased to operate – a victim not of Irish sectarianism but of British anti-clericalism – and what might have remained a very useful branch of the ecumenical and missionary movement in Ireland withered away.[38]

Meanwhile, however, more positive things were happening in the Irish universities. Queen's University Belfast by now had many hundreds of Roman Catholic students, as also had Trinity College Dublin, an Anglican foundation which Roman Catholic students were forbidden to enter (by their own church, not by the university) until 1970. By 1966 things had changed also at University College Dublin, so that where Salters Sterling had been rebuffed, Foster Murphy was able to set up an SCM branch. It proved extremely popular, attracting many Roman Catholic seminarians and religious sisters, even though the meetings – sometimes attended by as many as 600 people – were at first banned from college buildings, and had to be held in a nearby Methodist church. There was strong support from Fr Brian Power, chaplain of the Catholic student society (closely linked with Pax Romana), and two years later the college Pax Romana and SCM combined to form a distinct group under the name 'Logos/SCM'. A new world had opened up for these students, a world of openness not only to other Christians, but also to issues of politics and social justice, for which, in *Mater et Magistra* (Pope John XXIII's encyclical on 'Christianity and Social Progress') of 1961, their own church had now provided a new and exciting vocabulary.

So by 1966 the Irish SCM was expanding spectacularly into a new and successful field of work which brought together Catholics and Protestants in a spirit of friendship and shared exploration. For the first time in its history the Irish Movement was 'fully ecumenical'. In Martin Rowan's words, the SCM was 'in a position to lead students in Britain and Ireland to a Gospel-based response to the challenging religious and political situation in Ireland'.[39] Yet that did not happen. For at precisely the same time the Movement in Britain (in which the Irish SCM was still a constituent member) was, as we have seen, becoming involved in deep trouble, and was rapidly losing the support of its senior friends. Sadly, the promising revival of life in the Irish Movement was soon to run into its own difficulties, some of them – though not all – relating directly to the deteriorating political situation in Northern Ireland.

For one thing, there was strong competition among Christian student organizations. In the North this was mainly from the IVF. In the South the increasing openness of the Roman Catholic colleges following Vatican II, and the remarkable influx of Irish Catholic students into the SCM, led in the 1970s to a receptiveness to many different new kinds of 'spirituality', both Christian and non-Christian, not all of them as intellectually challenging or as politically involved as the SCM. Foremost of these was the charismatic renewal movement, spreading from Duquesne University in America in 1967 and reaching Ireland in 1971 through a special meeting of the Logos/SCM in UCD, where the speaker was Fr Joseph McGeady, and the chairperson of Logos/SCM was Alan Mitchell, a Presbyterian student who would later become director of the Presbyterian Church's Irish Mission. The charismatic movement spread rapidly in Ireland, bringing many Catholics and Protestants into close fellowship with each other, and in its early days exerting a strong influence among university students. Cecil Kerr, at that time Anglican dean of residence at QUB and later to be the founder of a well-known charismatic retreat centre at Rostrevor, spoke of 'Roman Catholics and Protestants finding a unity in the Lord Jesus'.[40] Gradually, however, official pressure was applied on Catholic members of the groups to ensure the presence of a priest who could centre the meetings on the eucharist, and this meant that Protestants felt excluded. The movement became more and more focused on the parishes, and its influence in the universities faded. Interestingly, however, the new international language of the charismatic movement had introduced many Irish Catholic students to the vocabulary of evangelical fundamentalism, and this made it easier for movements like Campus Crusade to find an opening in Ireland. Beginning with UCD in 1975, Campus Crusade spread rapidly, and by 1980 it had 15 full-time staff members working in Irish colleges – far more than the SCM or IVF had ever had. But the radical Christian voice of the SCM, speaking a language which had many resonances with that of Vatican II, found it harder to gain a hearing in an atmosphere of reinforced conservatism.

Through the 1960s the SCM, in both Britain and Ireland, had frequently talked about Christian presence – like the silent witness of the Petits Frères de Jésus of Charles de Foucauld. In the 1970s the focus shifted to the parallel theme of community. More and more the emphasis was changing from the SCM as a Movement to the SCM as a community. And the kind of community that was meant was inevitably a *small* community, a small-scale experiment in communal living. The Irish SCM was a pioneer here, when in 1972 it bought a house in the suburb of Rathmines, which became the Dublin Community House, headquarters of the first Roman Catholic Irish secretary Mari Fitzpatrick,[41] and the centre for the Resources Study Group set up by UCD and Trinity College students. This Dublin house became the model for many similar, and at times somewhat Bohemian, community houses in England, Scotland and Wales, including the community at Wick Court.

But the shared participation of Catholic and Protestant students in the life of the Irish SCM was very limited, and undoubtedly the greatest obstacle to it was the political conflict in Northern Ireland. The SCM of Great Britain and Ireland had adopted the *Political Stance* document in 1969, and so was ready to apply categories of Christian faith and commitment to current political issues; and the growing violent conflict in Ireland was obviously such an issue. It was also a very divisive one. In Britain it was easier for the Movement to make policy decisions about South Africa than about Northern Ireland, though in 1969 the general council recommended the abolition of the Northern Ireland Parliament at Stormont, and also gave support to the nascent Civil Rights movement. The Irish SCM took up the political question, difficult as it was, and the initiative came largely from Stranmillis Teacher Training College in Belfast, whose students were nearly all Protestants, but with radical and courageous leadership in the SCM. From 1971 to 1973 they published a fortnightly *Despatch from Ireland*, which attempted to give a clearer picture of the political situation than was being provided by the media. In keeping with the SCM thinking of the time it tended to give a Marxist analysis, implying that both the Catholic and Protestant working classes were the victims of a small and selfish ruling class. Not unnaturally this approach upset the largely middle class Protestant supporters of the SCM, including many though not all leaders of the churches, who felt that the SCM had moved in a republican and Marxist direction which they could not support. Throughout this time relations between the British and Irish regions of the Movement, both of which were now 'fully ecumenical', remained both radical and cordial. And indeed in 1975 the editorship of *Movement* magazine (the words *The* and *Student* had long since been dropped from its title) was moved from Wick Court to Dublin.

Strangely, between 1970 and 1975 no SCM secretary was resident in Northern Ireland, the traditional stronghold of the Movement, though for much of the period two secretaries (both of them Catholics) were based in Dublin, where the work was expanding. Finally in 1975 a secretary for Belfast was appointed – Rob Mitchell (later Fairmichael) – and during the next three years a series of programmes was organized, including five joint meetings with the Corrymeela Community on 'The Meaning of Peace'. But it was uphill work, and the SCM in the North of Ireland shrank. Rob Mitchell blamed the shrinkage on student apathy resulting from the Troubles, and that no doubt was true. Yet at the same time it is hard to avoid the conclusion that the Movement paid insufficient attention to the views of the many Protestant students who, while anxious to secure justice for all and reconciliation between the divided communities, and repelled by hard-line Paisleyite Unionism, did not feel that they could support the republican cause. Mari Fitzpatrick, herself a Catholic, recognized this point when in 1970, after affirming the SCM as a place where Catholics and Protestants really could meet, she went on – sensitively but realistically – to comment that although they could not co-operate in working for a united Ireland, they *could* worship together, and could work together in practical activities like housing projects and playgrounds for children.

Some of the more radical members of SCM in the North marched with the Civil Rights movement, while many found their spiritual home in Corrymeela; a few, indeed, did both. Other Christian students were happier in the IVF, and in an apolitical quietism. The default position was tacit acceptance of sectarianism, with the curious result, which became typical of Northern Ireland, that while a substantial proportion of the older generation of university graduates, including many church leaders, supported ecumenism and reconciliation, even larger numbers of church members in general and students in particular did not. Neither the SCM nor its supporters had succeeded in communicating their enthusiasm for Christian unity at a popular level, and the popular level was where sectarianism had its strength.

The Irish SCM tradition, however, by no means disappeared. In the words of Mari Fitzpatrick, it was not a matter of the ecumenical bubble bursting, but rather of its spreading, as the initiative expanded to other groups. The SCM's ecumenical mantle was taken up by a number of other organizations, including official church meetings like the Irish Council of Churches (ICC), which did not include the Roman Catholic Church, the Irish Interchurch Conference ('Glenstal') which did, and the ICC/Roman Catholic Church Joint Group on Social Questions which in 1976 produced a remarkable report, edited by Cahal Daly and Eric Gallagher, *Violence in Ireland*. The Irish Christian Fellowship (ICF) was in effect a group of SCM senior friends (like 'the Aux' in Britain), and many former SCM members were involved in the work of PACE (Protestant and Catholic Encounter). When Fr Michael Hurley SJ founded the Irish School of Ecumenics in Dublin in 1970, many of his Protestant supporters, in both South and North, had roots in the SCM tradition. But in the North it was especially the Corrymeela Community which carried on that tradition. Founded by Ray Davey in 1965 as a project of the Presbyterian chaplaincy at QUB, the start of the Troubles saw it deliberately expanding to include Roman Catholics in its membership and programmes, which more and more became focused on reconciliation between the two communities. In Martin Rowan's words, Corrymeela 'succeeded in balancing its social concern and its connections with the churches in Northern Ireland'.[42] In all of these different ecumenical ventures (some of which, like the ICF, went back to the 1920s) former members of the SCM took a leading part. Over the years people like Bolton Waller, Archbishop George Simms, Michael Ferrar, Anthony and Richard Hanson, and Brian Harvey from the Church of Ireland, James Rutherford, Jimmie Haire, Ray Davey, Jim Boyd, Carlisle Patterson, John Morrow, Salters Sterling and Alan Martin from the Presbyterian Church, and Robert Nelson and Eric Gallagher from the Methodist Church – all of them SCM people – worked for Christian unity, and were eager especially to bridge the Protestant–Catholic chasm.

By way of a postscript we may note that in 1982, with goodwill from both sides, the Irish SCM separated from the old 'SCM of Great Britain and Ireland', and since then has, with varying success, pursued its own course as a Movement within the WSCF. Worldwide, the SCM has not yet fulfilled its potential in ecumenical relations with the Roman Catholic Church, though in many national Movements there is considerable Roman Catholic participation, at both membership and leadership level, as we shall see.

* * * * * *

In Britain, Australia, Ireland and many national Movements as well as in the Federation, the ecumenical initiative was passing out of the hands of the Movement. It was of course right, as Ambrose Reeves had said, that this initiative should come from the churches themselves. But at a time when the SCM – as an intentional ecumenical community, a real though imperfect *koinonia* – might have pioneered a new way forward for the churches, the Movement appeared to indicate that its priorities lay elsewhere. If only the Federation had been prepared to take up the 1970 challenge of Syndesmos, the Orthodox student organization, which had suggested the creation of a new Federation, formed of the WSCF together with Syndesmos itself, and Roman Catholic representatives – great things might have resulted, both internationally and nationally. But in the political climate of the time, the necessary theological nerve was lacking.

So far as Christian witness in the university was concerned, the SCM's extreme diminution in numbers had an effect which can best be described in terms of deprivation. Whole generations of students were deprived of the kind of lively, inquiring, concerned, worshipping Christian student community which had been so influential in the lives of their parents and grandparents, and which had contributed so much to the life of the Church. At a critical point in their lives students were deprived of the excitement and challenge of belonging to a student community which was also a movement consciously dedicated to wrestling with the Christian faith and to changing the world to the glory of God. The vacuum created by the diminution of the SCM represented a great loss to generations of students – a gap which has yet to be filled.

8

Picking up the pieces (*c.* 1980–2005)

When the stormy waves of the late 1960s and the 1970s subsided, the SCM was still there. In some countries, like India, its work proceeded substantially as before; in other places, and at Federation level, it continued on a greatly reduced scale – reduced in numbers of student members, in finances and in influence on both university and church. In many places it was a case of 'picking up the pieces' of an organization which had lost many, though not all, of its senior supporters. It found itself a small community in the university, vastly overshadowed by the IVF and other even more conservative organizations like Campus Crusade, and – though sympathetically viewed by many university chaplains and radical but perplexed senior friends – virtually out of touch with the leaders of the churches and with the professional theological and biblical expertise which in earlier years had been essential to its existence. As early as 1971 Martin Conway could write sadly, 'It is clear that the SCM is no longer the major organ of Christian community and of effective Christian witness within higher education . . . It has evidently lost any continuous and stable self-understanding.'[1]

Yet it *was* still in existence, and over the past 30 years it has continued to live, and at times to show remarkable vigour. Internationally, the life of the Federation has been maintained in each of its different geographical regions, and also at its inter-regional office (IRO) in Geneva. Space forbids an up to date survey of the whole Movement, but we shall look briefly at some episodes in its life in this most recent of our periods, beginning with Britain and going on to Australia and finally to the Federation itself. It should be borne in mind that the Movement whose life we are now recording is not only much smaller than before 1965, but much less closely related to either church or university. In the words of one of its own reports, the stormy years had been years 'in the wilderness'.[2]

Britain

After the Wick Court venture, the SCM in 1977 moved its headquarters to Birmingham. The Wick period had seen a deliberate move away from the university; but in the reaction which followed a clear decision was made to return to the university scene, and it was realized that this would involve establishing constructive relations with the denominational chaplains.[3] Already during the 1970s the National Student Christian Congress (NSCC) – a body whose leadership was in the hands of the chaplains, though the SCM was also a participant – had decided to make a concerted effort to bring an 'open' Christian presence back into the student world. The SCM took the initiative through Dave Snowden, who in 1976 came to the annual national higher education chaplains' conference proposing that the SCM and the denominational chaplaincies should organize a joint conference for students. Despite a good deal of scepticism on the part of the chaplains, a committee was formed and eventually the 'New Heaven, New Earth' conference took place in 1978 in Manchester, based at St Peter's House, the chaplaincy where Tim McClure was working as Anglican chaplain. No fewer than 400 students attended, and they slept in church halls around the city and travelled in to St Peter's each day to hear the keynote speakers – including the leading Methodist ecumenist Pauline Webb, just back from the WCC's Nairobi Assembly – and to share in workshops and in the community life of the conference. This very successful event led to a series of three more such conferences at two-yearly intervals. They finished in 1983 because it was agreed that the SCM had once again become strong enough and trusted enough to run its own annual conferences. The NSCC had proved to be an important element in the Movement's rehabilitation and in the building of relationships with the denominational chaplaincies, even though at first there was some suspicion on the chaplains' side on account of the apparent oddness of some of the non-student activities of the Wick period.

Clearly there was now a real desire on the part of the SCM to re-enter its proper field of the university, and the setting up of headquarters in the Selly Oak complex of colleges in Birmingham signified a determination to resume the role of a national student movement rather than of a specialized commune. The Movement had also decided that it was time to return to a proper regional structure, with a national headquarters and a full-time general secretary.

And so in 1982, in response to an advertisement in the press, Tim McClure – later Archdeacon of Bristol – was appointed general secretary, fully aware that there were those in the Movement who were not overpleased at what they saw as a return to outmoded structures, headed by a white, male, Anglican cleric. Yet it was clear that a majority of the members had already accepted the need for a new orientation, and were eager to consolidate the Movement's position in the universities and to take up the new challenges.

It could not, however, be a return to the golden age. It was clear that the SCM would no longer have the resources to be a free-standing organization, but that it would need to work in close association with the chaplains: and indeed one reason for McClure's appointment was that he was already working as a higher education chaplain in Manchester, and was familiar with the national chaplaincy networks. The fact of the matter was that the churches' concern for the Christian welfare of students was now being channelled into the work of the chaplains, and the realistic solution for the SCM was to accept that context, contribute its own ethos within it and make this new relationship really work. It was a context in which the SCM, with its open tradition of ecumenism and of mission in the widest sense, could once again make its presence felt and effective: the denominational chaplains were inevitably limited in their outreach, and there was a tendency for them to concentrate on their own, whether in 'MethSoc' or in the cosy Anglican friendliness of sherry after chapel. The wider SCM vision – social, political and theological – was not always in evidence in the work of the chaplaincies; and so the SCM had a real role to play. On the one hand its comprehensive vision could be strengthened and earthed by the fact that the chaplaincies had the status and resources provided for them by the churches; while on the other hand the SCM could inject a new stimulus through its engagement with political and social issues and its conviction that Christian witness was most effective when it was ecumenical.

Tim McClure was general secretary for ten years, from 1982 to 1992, and during that time the number of SCM 'groups' – the term now used instead of 'branches' – more than doubled, from about 40 to more than 100. The growth area was indeed within the chaplaincies: that was where McClure was best qualified to expand the network. Within that context the SCM once more established its role as a *bona fide* student movement with high quality staff providing a Christian challenge to students from all the churches, encouraging them to raise their sights above the purely personal (where the UCCF excelled) and the purely denominational (the context within which the chaplains were tempted to work). The SCM staff in this decade consisted at its maximum of 12 or 13 full-time members, all recent graduates, who looked after Northern, Midland, Western and South-Eastern England, London, Scotland and Wales. Ireland, as we have seen, had in 1982 just become an independent Movement.

There was a programme of annual conferences, usually held at Easter, and in a variety of places, including Aberystwyth, Southampton and Edinburgh. Attendances were smaller than at the great Swanwicks of old, but were still usually between 100 and 150; and conditions in this new back-packing age were sometimes even more spartan than Swanwick had been – sleeping on the floors of church halls, for example. But for many students these were life-changing events. Speakers included

W. H. Vanstone, author of *Love's Endeavour, Love's Expense*; John Bell and Graham Maule, musicians and social activists of the Iona Community; and on one occasion there was a memorable dialogue between two radical theologians, Elizabeth Templeton of Edinburgh, and Don Cupitt of Cambridge, of which the former later said that it was the only time she had ever been called a fundamentalist! A particularly successful conference was organized in Edinburgh in 1985, to mark the seventy-fifth anniversary of the 1910 Edinburgh Missionary Conference, which itself had owed so much – and given so much – to the SCM.

The magazine *Movement* continued and prospered during this period, being edited at various times by Peter Gee, Rainier Holst and Annie Murray. Bible study had not regained the centrality it had held in earlier days, yet the SCM once more found that the very nature of the subjects it wanted to study drove it back to this primary resource. Some of the leading topics discussed were liberation theology, women's issues – for feminism had come firmly and specifically on to the SCM agenda – and sexuality, especially homosexuality; and through tackling these subjects thoroughly and systematically, serious Bible study again became essential. Worship too was important, though frequently informal; and here the music of the Iona Community mediated through John Bell, and South African freedom songs, usually coming via the WSCF, played a significant part. Worship was planned by a small group of students and staff, and was highly creative – 'stunning' was how some participants described it. Not infrequently the worship was eucharistic, though without the careful theological safeguards about intercommunion which in earlier days the Movement had felt it must honour. Yet the theological problems associated with intercommunion were not entirely bypassed, the more so because by now there was always a significant minority of Roman Catholic students present at SCM occasions. A memorable event happened at the Aberystwyth conference when the student and staff group preparing the worship devised a 'eucharist without the eucharist', which stopped short at the point where the eucharistic prayer should have begun, leaving the participants hurt, frustrated and spiritually hungry and thirsty. Someone commented, 'We should have had an archbishop and a cardinal watching this!'[4]

While this revival of life and activity in the SCM was exciting and encouraging, not all the ground lost earlier, when so many of the senior friends had abandoned the Movement, was recovered. The earlier confident and trusting relationship with the churches proved hard to recapture; and the student members of the Movement were not wholly convinced that the leaders of the churches were hearing what they were saying. It was a difficult situation, requiring on both sides a sensitivity which was not always evident. A particularly disappointing situation,

certainly from the student point of view, arose over the prolonged process of study and discussion entitled 'Beyond 1984' which preceded and
introduced the restructuring of the British Council of Churches (BCC)
into Churches Together in Britain and Ireland (CTBI). The SCM was
invited to share in this process, worked hard at producing its own
contribution, and sent a delegation to take part in the discussion. Its
members returned sad and angry, because it seemed to them that the
official leaders of the ecumenical movement – by now, as Ambrose
Reeves had foreseen, restricted firmly within the limits of their respect-
ive churches – had ignored their contribution, and were still, it seemed,
working to an outdated agenda which failed to notice all that had
been happening in the student revolution of the 60s and 70s. Deeply
influenced as the SCM representatives were by post-modern thought,
and disillusioned by institutions, especially large ones seemingly controlled
by elderly male clerics, they felt ignored and marginalized. It seemed to
them that even the brand-new ecumenical structures were destined to
repeat the mistakes of the old ones they replaced.

In the late 1980s, towards the end of McClure's period, an effort was
made, through a major appeal, to raise funds to increase the SCM staff
with a view to its being organically integrated with the denominational
chaplaincies. It was a far-sighted and hopeful vision. The appeal was
launched in connection with the Movement's centenary celebrations in
1989 and was endorsed by archbishops, moderators and ex-moderators,
and some of the great and good of the SCM's past. About a quarter of
a million pounds was raised, part of which paid for additional staff to
promote the SCM in universities and generally raise the profile and increase
the contact with denominational chaplaincies. This strategy met with reasonable success and it seemed to Tim McClure as he left the staff that
the Movement was now in a position to pursue even closer ties with
the chaplaincies. Yet, sadly, the vision of an integrated national student
movement was lost, and the SCM eventually took a different direction.
The Movement, which had once more begun to make an effective contribution to the Christian life of the universities, and had seemed to
be on the verge of great things, was left in a vulnerable position. This
fluctuating pattern of encouraging development and disappointing
decline has tended to be typical of many national SCMs in the 'post-
Storm' period.

The British Movement continues and, ~~at the time of writing,~~ is showing many signs of renewed life. It had recently moved its headquarters from
a hard-to-find annexe often known as 'the shack' at Westhill College, Selly
Oak, Birmingham, and relocated to a shiny new office in Birmingham's
Jewellery Quarter. The SCM was connected with groups and chaplaincies in 50 different universities and colleges – sadly not including either

Cambridge (cradle of the student movement in England) or Oxford. It had three distinguished Patrons: Peter Selby, then Bishop of Worcester, Michael Taylor, formerly Director of Christian Aid and former President of the Selly Oak colleges, and Kathy Galloway, leader of the Iona Community. Liam Purcell was the editor of a lively, reader-friendly magazine, *Movement*, with book, film and music reviews, but also with articles on political, social, ethical and theological issues, including, for example, a 2004 article on the 'Evil Empire' by Tom Wright, Anglican Bishop of Durham, which signalled a wide area of convergence between the radicalism of the SCM and the 'new wave' commitment of so many evangelicals to justice and environmental issues. In 2005 Liam Purcell became national co-ordinator of the British SCM. The current Vision Statement describes the SCM as 'a movement seeking to bring together students of all denominations to explore the Christian faith in an open-minded and non-judgemental environment'. It goes on to say that the Movement is *inclusive*, since 'all people are welcome because our diversity is a gift to be celebrated'; *aware*, because 'we recognise the importance of respect for and openness to other faiths'; *radical*, because 'faith and social justice cannot be separated – Christians must be equipped to engage with contemporary theological, political and social issues'; *challenging*, because 'thinking through and questioning our faith ensures that it remains alive and dynamic'. 'Questioning faith' is a revealing, typical, and convincingly Christian description of the authentic SCM tradition.

Australia

For a picture of the Australian Movement in the final years of the twentieth century we turn to Ian Telfer,[5] who entered Adelaide University in 1991, and from 1995 served as the Movement's general secretary for two years – riding high on the supportive wave of the ASCM's large and enthusiastic centenary 'Gathering' in Canberra in 1996. Like so many others, he had moved to the SCM from the Evangelical Union because of 'the excitement of being in a group of people who were really open'. The SCM at that time was a small but clearly identifiable Christian group working in close connection with other activist groups on a broad range of concerns – solidarity with East Timor, environmental issues, feminism, gay interests, and liberation theology among them. He was very conscious of the change in the atmosphere of the greatly expanded universities: students, and even staff, no longer had the time or energy to think about the great issues of life – ideas, politics, philosophy, religion – but instead concentrated on securing a useful degree so that they could begin to make money. In Australia this was the first generation of students for some decades who had to pay university fees, and they were very much aware that their degrees did not confer any certainty of employment. The sense of being involved in great earth-shaking struggles and their global solutions simply was not there: post-modernism had banished interest in such 'meta-narratives'. Students were indeed interested in personal relationships; the battle for gay and lesbian rights was a real concern, and so was the struggle against racism; but even Marxism was no longer on the agenda, and capitalism was simply an accepted and even appreciated part of life. All these factors combined to produce an extremely materialistic environment in which a paralysing apathy prevailed. The Evangelical Union occupied quite a large place in the university, but was rejected by most students as being narrowly fundamentalist; while the SCM was so small that most people were unaware of its existence.

After a period of considerable optimism and some growth in the mid-1980s, the ASCM had, in the late 90s, again entered a difficult period: like the British Movement, it had gone through a roller-coaster succession of brief 'eras', good and bad, in the period since the 'Storm' of the 1960s. In this situation, Telfer and other SCM leaders believed that the Movement's task was to find a positive language for what radical Christians believe: to reclaim some of the 'middle ground' of the Christian spectrum, not by becoming less radical but by recovering a coherent theological construction to build on, and then to communicate that belief. This led to a move towards closer relations with the National Council of Churches (which, more than the actual churches, had continued to be friendly to the Movement and to give it a representative place in its meetings), and also with the churches themselves: indeed Telfer speaks of the need for a new relationship which would show that the SCM really did care passionately about the churches. This was a note which had not been heard for a long time. Once again the SCM was wanting to be a pioneering body on behalf of the churches – a body with the freedom given by independence, but nevertheless with real concern. For many years the Movement had taken a stance virtually outside the Church, regarding itself as a critic rather than an arm of the Church. Telfer saw this return to the Church as all the more important at a time when the new configuration of the National Council of Churches (with the happy yet in some ways restrictive addition of the Roman Catholic Church) was tending to make it more of an institution and less of a pioneering community of ecumenical people.

For about 30 years the SCM's relationship with the churches had been minimal, and students had been alienated by the whole official church establishment and its authority structures. Telfer realized that a lot had been lost through the diminution of this relationship, and that it needed to be restored. Yet he was convinced that the SCM's stormy struggle had been a necessary one: tough and painful, but ultimately healthy.

One necessary part of the struggle, for example, was connected with sexuality – especially with the place of women in the Movement, and also the need to secure room within it for gay and lesbian people. The time was now ripe, he believed, for a renewal of theology in the SCM, and he regretted that there was no longer a relationship, as there had been earlier, with the theological colleges, whose students and staff had for years provided a strong base of biblical and theological understanding. He pointed out that whereas a perusal of back issues of the old ASCM magazine *The Intercollegian* revealed a constant development of theological thought, the same could not be said about contemporary SCM publications. In the past the SCM had had constructive and easy relationships with leading thinkers in Church and society, but that was no longer so. He admitted that the Movement had turned away from the Bible because the Bible did not seem to echo the students' own experience, and also because they were not being challenged to wrestle with the text as earlier generations had done. He was ready even to use the language of lostness – 'we have lost our way'. But he also pointed out that there was very little in the way of up to date, reliable, scholarly, yet radical and readable Bible study resources to engage the interest of the kind of students who fill the contemporary university. So he looked forward to a recovery of Bible study, and went on to speak of the importance of liturgy, especially the eucharist, and of the need to use theological language, provided it was inclusive and not paternalistic.

There is a moving expression here of a longing to return to 'the great tradition' and yet to do so in a way which retains the experience of life and struggle – the down-to-earth struggle, expressed in action and not merely in word – through which the Movement has been passing. The SCM – the small, post-1970 SCM – went into a far country, into some places where the Church as a whole disdained or feared to go: now the time has come for it to reclaim its heritage; and to share with the rest of the family the experience of the world and its struggles which it has had but many in the Church have not.

The Federation

Changes in the structure of the Federation had already started during the period of the 'Storm', and these continued, influenced partly by opposition in the different national Movements to what appeared to be the bureaucratic centralization of the WSCF staff in Geneva, and partly also by financial difficulties arising from the diminution of support for the work of the Movement, especially in America. At the 1968 WSCF Assembly it was decided to adopt a policy of 'regionalization', with Geneva acting only as the Inter-Regional Office (IRO). The regions (whose boundaries varied somewhat from time to time, as did the location of their head-quarters) eventually came to comprise Africa (with its base in Nairobi, Kenya), the Asia–Pacific area, including Australia and New Zealand (based in Hong Kong), Europe (Budapest), Latin America and the Caribbean (Buenos Aires), the Middle East (Beirut), and North America (long in abeyance, except for Canada, but now actively reopening).

The move away from Bible and theology, so dominant in 1968, had begun to be reversed, and in the European region Bible-reading seminars were held annually between 1976 and 1981, with the focus on what was called 'materialist' Bible-reading, in which special attention was given to the social and political contexts underlying the biblical texts.[6] Gabriele Dietrich, a German theologian living in India, entitled her Bible studies at the 1977 Sri Lanka assembly 'Christian Witness in the Struggle for Liberation'; they gave a serious and comprehensive presentation of 'materialist Bible reading', as did the 1982 book *Before the Cock Crows* (edited by Gerhard Köberlin and published by WSCF Europe, though printed in India).

Christine (Chris) Ledger,[7] then a staff worker of the Australian SCM, attended that 1977 Sri Lanka assembly. It was her first Federation experience, and she was plunged into the deep end by being made minutes secretary. She noticed how, despite the great tradition of Suzanne de Diétrich, the agenda of the meeting was predominantly a male agenda: while there was some input by women and about women, the Federation seemed to be only beginning to be challenged by some of its members to take women's issues more seriously. In 1984 she was elected to the Federation's executive committee, by which time there had been a considerable improvement: there was a women's commission, and about half the executive committee were women.

In 1986 – largely through the advocacy of Asian members of the Movement, who saw the Australian Movement as a sort of bridge between the Asia–Pacific Region (to which the ASCM belonged) and the West – Chris Ledger was appointed to the Geneva staff, where she stayed for almost five years. In that year the Federation had changed its constitution so that, instead of having – as previously – a general secretary (male), and an associate secretary (sometimes but by no means always a woman), there would be two co-secretaries, one man and one woman. She herself was 'the first woman guinea-pig' in that role, her male colleague being Manuel Quintero of Cuba. She notes that while in the 1970s the feminist movement in the Federation had been mainly carried on by women from Europe and America, by 1986 the feminist energy came mainly from so-called 'third world' Movements in Asia, Africa and Latin America. This was largely because the SCM in Britain and most European countries had shrunk to small proportions, and in North

America, although there was considerable strength still in Canada, the Movement in the USA, once so strong, was noticeable by its almost total absence. In ecumenical Christian affairs, the voice of the South was beginning to be heard more clearly and effectively than that of the North.

In Geneva Chris Ledger found that the relationship between the Federation and its WCC neighbour was still a strong one. This link went back historically to the fact that when the WCC was inaugurated in Amsterdam in 1948, largely by people who had been leaders in the Federation, there was an understanding that the WCC would not form a 'student department' (like that of the YMCA), but rather that the WSCF would continue as a parallel ecumenical body, acting as the presence of ecumenism in the student world. This arrangement continued, in cordial co-operation with the WCC's Youth Department, until the restructuring after the 1968 Uppsala Assembly, and thereafter with the Department's somewhat diminished successor groups; and at the Vancouver 1983 Assembly of the WCC, plans were set in motion for an Ecumenical Global Gathering of Youth and Students (EGGYS), which eventually brought together 500 young people in Rio de Janeiro, Brazil in 1993. There was Roman Catholic participation through Pax Romana, and the agenda included issues like poverty, environmental degradation, HIV/AIDS, and drug abuse. The organizing secretary of EGGYS, and of the conference, was Manuel Quintero (Cuba), who from 1986 to 1991 had been Chris Ledger's co-secretary in the WSCF.

Far away from the city of Geneva the WCC/WSCF relationship was also maintained at the regional level by the Christian Conference of Asia (CCA). In 1996 Chris Ledger was appointed associate general secretary of the CCA, based in Hong Kong. She was cheered as she took up her work there on the eve of the British departure from Hong Kong and its incorporation into China by the knowledge that the head of the mainland China Christian Council was Bishop K. H. Ting, who many years earlier had served on the staff of the Federation, and still treasured the SCM tradition which he held to have been essential to his own formation. Chris Ledger knew that when she and K. H. Ting were in communication with people from other countries, sometimes under very difficult circumstances, there would still be what he called 'a level of trust you can build upon. You will not just be meeting with strangers'. And she remembered the title of a book he had written: *No Longer Strangers*.

In 1995 the Federation marked the centenary of its 1895 foundation at Vadstena Castle in Sweden. The celebration took place at an assembly at Yamoussoukro, Ivory Coast, with the theme 'A Community of Memory and Hope – Celebrating God's Faithfulness'. The centenary provided an opportunity for reflection and for the production, in the centennial history project, of a series of publications recalling its history, assessing its achievements, and looking to its future. These included a long-overdue English translation of Suzanne de Diétrich's *WSCF: Fifty Years of History, 1895–1945,* two books of personal recollections by staff members (*A Community of Memory and Hope,* and *Memoirs and Diaries, 1895–1990,* edited by Elizabeth Adler) and *Bible and Theology in the Federation* (edited by Thomas Wieser). Finally, in 1997, came *Seeking and Serving the Truth: The First Hundred Years of the WSCF,* a comprehensive survey of the Federation's history in every continent by Philip Potter and Thomas Wieser, distinguished long-term servants of both the WSCF and the WCC.

Encouraged by the tumultuous story of the past, with its succession of triumphs and failures, miseries and glories, the assembly adopted a revised Constitution, which is still current in 2006, and is remarkable for the faithful yet challenging way in which it recaptures the 'SCM tradition'. The 'Aims' section is worth quoting in full:

> *The aims of the World Student Christian Federation in all its work among members of the academic community shall be:*
> 1. to call them to faith in God – Father, Son and Holy Spirit – according to the Scriptures and to discipleship within the life and mission of the church;
> 2. to help them to grow in the Christian life through prayer, study of the Bible, and participation in the worship and witness of the Church;
> 3. to help them witness to Jesus Christ in the academic community;
> 4. to bring them into fellowship with one another in mutual service and to support efforts to serve all students in their needs;
> 5. to help them to strive for peace and justice in and among the nations;
> 6. to help them to work for the manifestation of the unity of the church;
> 7. to help them to be servants and messengers of God's Kingdom in all the world.

This is the charter under which all the affiliated Movements are required to operate, for the aims and work of each affiliated Movement 'shall be in full harmony with the aims and work of the Federation'. The different regions, however, may describe their own mission in different ways, as, for example, this from the European Region, which describes itself as being 'committed to dialogue, ecumenism, social justice and peace':

> Our mission is to empower students in critical thinking and constructive transformation of our world by being a space for: prayer and celebration; theological reflection; study and analysis of social and cultural processes; and solidarity and action across boundaries of culture, gender and ethnicity. Through the work of the Holy Spirit, the WSCF is called to be a prophetic witness in Church and society. This vision is nurtured by a radical hope for God's Reign in history.

Today (2006) the Federation is once again a large worldwide Movement. In Africa there are no fewer than 25 different national Movements.

Europe has 23 Movements in 18 countries. As in other regions, these Movements – some of them fully 'affiliated', others more loosely 'associated' with the WSCF – do not necessarily operate under the name 'Student Christian Movement'; not a few of them are in fact denominational groups which have chosen to be part of the WSCF. Compared with the golden age, the Federation is now much more loosely structured, has far fewer staff and a much smaller budget. But it continues to be a vibrant Christian fellowship.

In 2004 the WSCF held its general assembly at Chiang Mai in Thailand. The meeting was marked by the diversity of the national Movements. Some were in the recognizably traditional SCM model, like those of India, Indonesia, Burma (Myanmar) and Nigeria, with their large memberships and multiple branches; the Asia–Pacific Region indeed claims to enrol more than 90,000 students every year, and so to be by far the largest SCM in the world. The Indian Movement alone, in 2005, had 10,000 members spread over 13 regions, covering 29 states. The Middle East Region works in close co-operation with the Middle East Council of Churches. In Eastern Europe there has been a virtual explosion of new or revived Movements like those of Belarus, Bulgaria, Croatia and Romania. The Orthodox Syndesmos is still a 'partner organization' with its strength mainly in Eastern Europe. The number of Orthodox and Roman Catholic leaders in the Movement has increased, some of the Orthodox leaders being clergy, while the Roman Catholics are mostly laypeople – from Quebec in Canada, for example, and also from Pax Romana, still part of the WCC-related EGGYS network.

The theme of the Assembly was '*Talitha Cum!* Arise to Life in Abundance!', and the meeting was preceded by both a women's and a men's pre-assembly, the women's meeting having a Bible study on Women and Globalization led by Eilidh Whiteford of Scotland. Among the areas of concern noted for further action, in addition to human rights, global debt and HIV/AIDS, were theology and spirituality, ecumenism and inter-religious dialogue, the theological foundation of the Federation, and the maintenance of the Universal Day of Prayer for Students, as well as the global Day of Prayer for Human Rights. The somewhat arbitrary order of issues described in the Assembly report is perhaps given more focused and more 'SCM traditional' shape in the concluding brief vision statement:

1) The WSCF is a global community of Student Christian Movements committed to dialogue, ecumenism, social justice and peace.
2) Our mission is to empower students in critical thinking and constructive transformation of our world by being a space for:
a) Prayer and celebration
b) Theological reflection

c) Study and analysis of social and cultural processes and
d) Solidarity and action across boundaries of culture, gender and ethnicity.
3) Through the work of the Holy Spirit, the WSCF is called to be a prophetic witness in church and society. This vision is nurtured by a radical hope for God's Reign.[8]

The printed word still holds an important place within the life of the Movement, and the different international regions and national Movements continue to produce a variety of stimulating literature. The European Region, for example, produces an attractive illustrated magazine called *Mozaik* twice a year, with serious, scholarly articles on a variety of issues like interfaith dialogue or 'Latin America and Europe'. Its editor until recently was Szabolcs Nagypal, a young Roman Catholic theologian who works closely with the Bekes Gellert Ecumenical Institute in his native Hungary.

Chris Ledger sees the diversity of form of the Movements affiliated to the WSCF as an enrichment rather than a diminution, and believes that the SCM tradition is needed as much as ever, particularly in view of the way in which the WCC, like national Christian councils everywhere, has inevitably come to represent a more institutionalized ecumenism, limited by the policies of its constituent churches, to each of which all decisions must be referred. She also stresses the Federation's importance as a largely lay Movement, at a time when in some churches informed lay voices are seldom listened to. While communication between the churches is probably easier than ever before, and at the personal level more informal, their mutual relationship has lost much of the intentional ecumenical drive of the 1950s and 60s, and has simply become part of the mainstream culture. It is assumed that the churches get on well with each other, and so people have forgotten how important – and exciting – it is for Christians to come together in order to take real action together, as a committed ecumenical community. For people who have been in the SCM, ecumenism can never be just a theory, or an institution: it must be a lifestyle. And she mentions some of the Australian SCM members who have carried the characteristics of the SCM tradition into their later service of church and society – like Sir Ronald Wilson, especially in his work for the Aboriginal community; or David Gill, of the WCC and the National Council of Churches in Australia; or Mandy Tibbey in the Australian Legal Aid Commission. The Federation, and the national SCMs, can still provide a unique freedom and space for young people to do Christian things their own way without the constraints of church rules, regulations and structures. And in later life such people will carry the SCM tradition with them.

A strategic planning meeting of officers and staff in Geneva (January 2005) was marked by several encouraging features, especially (as we shall see) the long overdue renewal of the Federation's traditional link with the United States. The meeting also recognized the need to reclaim a Christian identity in the largely secular world of the United Nations and Unesco (with both of which the Federation has consultative status through the Economic and Social Council), as well as in non-government organizations. And it was decided to select a special theme each year for biblical and theological reflection, the theme for 2005 being Women.

Behind much of the recent development in the life of the Federation can be discerned the hand of Lawrence (Nana) Brew, a layman and geographer from Ghana, who after being president of the Ghana SCM and then chairperson of the executive for the Africa Region, has recently (2005) completed five years' service at the Inter-Regional Office (IRO) in Geneva.[9] For the first four years he was co-general secretary with Beate Fagerli from Norway; in 2004 she offered to resign to ease financial difficulties, and went on to work for the WCC, while Nana continued as general secretary of the Federation. He speaks of the Movement with both realism and hope. He acknowledges that the SCM lost its way in the period of 'the Storm', and that its 'single issue' politicization led it away not only from its own time-tested structures but even from any kind of structuring: led it in fact in the direction of an individualistic anarchism. This departure, he believes, was fatal for the Federation's relationship with the churches, and led not merely to suspicion of the Movement's volatility, but to a massive reduction in financial support, which has continued into recent times. It also led to the virtual abandoning of the universities: the WSCF was no longer sure if it really wanted to be associated with the universities, whether in fact they were any longer a suitable *pays de mission* for a Movement which prided itself on its radicalism. And in the meantime that field has, in many parts of the world and especially in Europe and the United States, been fully occupied by denominational chaplaincies (usually with ample funding from the churches), as well as by the IFES and other more conservative agencies. So the Movement has been falling short in its two traditional areas of witness: mission and unity. It has also, and sadly, been slow to return to its traditional *praxis* of Bible study and corporate worship. It has been more concerned, as have so many church agencies, with methodology: with the latest techniques of decision-making rather than with the struggle for the truth; for there is still in the Movement an anti–intellectualism, a critique of anything recalling an 'ivory tower' view of the purpose of study.

The whole university situation is very different from what it was before 'the Storm'. In most countries the sheer number of students is overwhelming. Mostly they live off campus, and have little time for any social activities, let alone such things as meetings for Bible study or worship. Christian witness is either denominationally concentrated (and led by ordained chaplains who are no longer students), or it is very conservative; in either case there is a lack of the kind of student freedom which was so important for the SCM – that wrestling with the Word, that working for justice alongside Christians of different traditions, that singing to God's glory, that communion in worship which were the SCM's special gift to the ecumenical movement. Brew notes with regret that many current SCM members have little knowledge of the great history of which they are the inheritors. Yet he is hopeful for the future, and has no hesitation in saying that the Federation needs to reclaim Christ as its basis, as indeed it makes clear in its Aims, which unambiguously call students to faith in God, Father, Son and Holy Spirit, and to witness to Jesus Christ in the academic community. There is no suggestion here of abandoning the Movement's commitment to justice and peace: current concerns – like the ongoing world struggle for justice for women, or the Indian movement for justice for the *dalit* (oppressed) community – are vital, and must be supported. But the Federation's *special* concern is to relate these issues to the gospel, and to bring to them the love and passion, the compassion and forgiveness for which Christ lived and died. He feels that in the current university world the Movement is unique in linking that 'Christ-centre' with politics and the quest for justice, and in giving students the freedom to 'read the Bible with a different eye'. He longs to 'bring back passion' to the university scene – the passion of students committed to Christ, to the Church, to the university, and to Christ's mission of forgiveness, justice, peace and unity.

Brew finds many grounds for hope. In Africa, after a period of weakness – one of whose results has been that many current leaders in the churches have not come through the SCM tradition – the Movement has revived, and is stronger than it has ever been, so that in many places students are grappling with current issues like Aids, political fragmentation, and paramilitary violence, in a fully Christian framework. In both Asia and Africa the Movement has continued to maintain close and encouraging relations with the churches, as it does in Latin America, often with the significant inclusion of the Pentecostal churches. A special cause for thankfulness is the current revival (he would use the word 'rebirth') of the SCM in the North American region, where in 2006 Brandon Gilvin of the Disciples of Christ (USA) has been appointed as regional secretary, operating from an office in Toronto, Canada. This development is linked with events at the Geneva Inter-Regional Office, where the new general secretary (Nana Brew's successor) is Michael Wallace, an Anglican from New Zealand, while the chairperson is the American Methodist Ken Guest, who is already deeply involved in the rebirth of the American Movement.

Encouraging also are relationships with a number of other organizations. The WSCF is a member of the Ecumenical Asia–Pacific Students and Youth Network (EASY Net) which in 2004 organized a large youth gathering in Indonesia on the theme 'Together in Action for Peace and Reconciliation', carrying on a tradition which started with the Amsterdam Youth Conference of 1939. It is also represented on the All Africa Conference of Churches (AACC), as it is on the Christian Conference of Asia (CCA), with which it runs a joint programme each year. In Europe it has strong relations with the Conference of European Churches (CEC), and with the Ecumenical Youth Council of Europe, which is part of CEC. The European University Chaplains Conference is a body which was in fact started by the WSCF in the early 1970s, in an effort to enable denominational chaplains to work together ecumenically. That ideal still continues in the organization, though it is no longer linked to the Federation. Adrian Hastings' question, of course, still needs to be asked – and undoubtedly is asked by all those connected with Christian witness in the university: how can a truly united witness be given by organizations which by their very nature 'consecrate denominationalism'? The SCM from the first has had an inbuilt safeguard against such consecration.

Most important of all these relationships with other organizations, however, is the Movement's continuing, and developing, relationship with the World Council of Churches, demonstrated most recently in its significant presence at the ninth WCC Assembly at Porto Alegre, Brazil, in February 2006, whose theme was 'God, in your Grace, Transform the World'. The WCC had publicized this as a youth assembly, and had arranged for a Youth Pre-Assembly and a Young Ecumenists' Group in order to encourage participation by young people. In addition 'under 30s' were invited to join in the Assembly's 'ecumenical conversations', as well as in worship, Bible study and plenary sessions. WSCF members participated in all these aspects of the Assembly's life, and acted as advisers to the WCC, as leaders in the Bible studies and worship, and in the *Bate Papo* (intergenerational dialogue). A special feature of the Assembly was the ecumenical *Mutirao* – a Brazilian word meaning 'coming together to make a difference' – which provided an informal space for celebrations, exhibits, workshops and seminars open to the public and focused particularly on young people. Four of the *Mutirao*'s workshops were led by WSCF staff and students, and offered the Movement's critical perspectives on issues of gender, migration, students, and, significantly, on 'Empire', the Federation's theme for 2006, with all its implications for a world at that moment deeply divided by military violence in Afghanistan and Iraq, and moving rapidly towards open war in Lebanon.

'Empire' – defined in a recent WSCF document as 'the coherence of economic, cultural, political and military powers that constitutes a global system of domination' – was also the theme of the Universal Day of Prayer for Students, held at Porto Alegre during the Assembly, with a liturgy prepared by the Federation's North American Region. Dr Mercy Oduyoye of Ghana, the theologian and one-time chairperson of the WSCF, who took part in the service, described the WSCF at prayer as 'a living sign of hope', and Carla Khijo of Lebanon, speaking from the perspective of a young female leader of the Movement, called on the WSCF to be part of the struggle for change: 'Let us transform the destructive will of current Empires, for in Christ we have the power that goes beyond politics, economics and arms. We have the power of love, and with this power we can transform the world.'

At the Assembly there was a colourful display highlighting various aspects of the Movement's work, and staffed by students with eye-catching red T-shirts, one of which was presented to the WCC's general secretary, Dr Sam Kobia of Kenya, himself an exemplar of the SCM tradition. Printed on the shirts was the slogan 'World Student Christian Federation: Ecumenism Guaranteed – since 1895'.

We see, then, that the Movement – however much diminished in Europe, America and Australia – still continues its ministry, perhaps in more places than ever before. In Chris Ledger's words:

> Given the limitations of human and financial resources, the movements continue to produce stimulating publications, to explore issues the churches do not dare approach, to engage in political activity, to provide open forums of debate, to care for each other in solidarity. Often a movement is not aware of how much it does achieve.[10]

Looking to the future, Nana Brew believes that the main work of the Federation will continue to be done in the regions, but that the Inter-Regional Office in Geneva will have a significant function of communication and encouragement. He sees the recovery of the centrality of Christ in the Movement's witness as essential – and the recovery of 'passion' in the communication of the gospel. That communication will more and more be done through the electronic media, though *Federation News-Sheet* and *The Student World* will continue the effective tradition of the printed word; and it will be accompanied, on the local level, by the building up of small ecumenical communities of students, exploring the riches of their inherited faith through Bible study and worship, while fully committed to the establishment of justice and peace in the world. And in all this it will be important to maintain, and where necessary recover, the good will and support of the churches.

9

Into the far country

Why did the SCM collapse in 'the Storm'?

We have been following the story of the SCM from its beginnings to
the present day; and as we remember its high moments, and rejoice in
the signs of new life in so many places, we must also ask why, in the
years between about 1966 and 1973, it virtually collapsed, or at least suffered a catastrophic decline. Was Visser 't Hooft right in saying that the
Federation Assembly in Addis Ababa in December 1972–January 1973
marked the most drastic break which had ever occurred in the ecumenical
movement? It is a statement which shows both how highly he estimated
the importance of the Federation, and how deeply he deplored the events
of that Assembly. It is painful for those who love the SCM to ask these
questions, but it is necessary to face them.

Secularization

A major reason for the Movement's decline was certainly the general
secularization of society in the western world in this period. The mid-
1960s in many places saw a percentage decline in church attendance and
membership more marked than at any time before or since. There were
so many other influences which competed with the churches, notably
the vast development of the leisure industry and especially of television,
which more and more absorbed people's free time. The universities shared
in the increasing consumerism of society, and tended to become factories for producing people with the qualifications needed for specific jobs,
rather than being academic communities devoted to the pursuit of truth.
The churches became less and less interesting to students; and as their
study burden increased, the time they could devote to voluntary activities of any kind diminished. They could still be aroused by spectacular
events, like protest marches, but they were no longer 'joiners', no longer
interested in regular meetings for study, discussion or worship.

University chaplains

Ronald Preston, in a 1987 article entitled 'The Collapse of the SCM: A
Case Study', suggests that a major reason for the decline of the SCM
in Britain was the growth of denominational chaplaincies from the 1950s

onwards.[1] The fact that the churches had at last – and rightly – decided seriously to acknowledge and fulfil their obligation to university students meant that they felt obliged to control as well as to contribute. In the words of Andrew Morton, who served successively as a Scottish SCM secretary and as chaplain of Edinburgh University, 'the effect of this on the SCM was to take away potential members and their energies and to spread a culture of dependency which became infectious'.[2] The chaplains, however friendly they might be to the ecumenical ideal, inevitably worked primarily in the interests of their own churches, and Preston points out how this was in direct contradiction of the Lund Principle of 1952, which urged the churches to do together all that conscience did not require them to do separately.[3] He adds that in 1963, when Ambrose Reeves was general secretary, the SCM decided that

> ecumenism had become official and was no longer a matter of pioneering . . . [They] decided to leave ecumenism to the churches and to be where they thought the students were, by working for a new and socialist order of society . . . A gentle decline set in [and] the democratic structure of the SCM proved its undoing.[4]

The revolt against authority

The British SCM's democratic structure had indeed ensured that major decisions were taken by the general committee, which had a student majority. The health of the SCM depended on a successful symbiosis between student members, SCM staff and senior advisers in both the academic world and the churches, and for many years this combination worked extremely well. But in the late 1960s, in the Movement as in the whole student world, there was a dramatic change.

In the 1950s and early 60s many university teachers were cheerfully involved in the SCM as advisers and speakers: there was an atmosphere of calm mutuality between staff and students. In the late 60s and the 70s academic staff began to come under much heavier career pressures, and were less ready to give time and energy to extracurricular activities. So students came under other influences, and Preston bluntly asserts that 'the SCM came under the control of a group of people who followed a Marxist or neo-Marxist political analysis, and represented only a small minority of students. Decline was rapid, and the SCM ceased to exist in most universities.' He continues, 'There was a deliberate attempt to wipe out the historical tradition of the SCM. Radical discontinuity was thought to be necessary . . . Quasi-apocalyptic language was used . . . there was no long-term vision.'[5] Organized bodies had become suspect. In part this was a healthy rejection of external authority associated with hierarchies and élites; but in part also it was the deliberate denigration of social institutions as such, and an inflation of individualism, which would later develop into post-modernism. The targets of the SCM's criticism included not only the university and the churches, but also the WCC – which it accused of pursuing Christian unity at the expense of prophetic witness.[6] Even the Movement itself became a target. Instead of well-organized SCM branches linked to a well-staffed headquarters at Annandale, 'grass-roots participation and instant communal decisions' took over. 'Three years of unstructured activity in a student body can bring it near to collapse', writes Preston. And so it happened.

A 'diffuse belief system'?

Preston's piece was written in response to an article by Steve Bruce in *Religious Studies* entitled 'A Sociological Account of Liberal Protestantism'.[7] Bruce, as a sociologist, aims to study the SCM dispassionately, using the categories of social movement analysis, and comes to the conclusion that its 'liberal Protestantism' – unlike the conservative evangelicalism of the IVF – contained within itself the seeds of its own destruction. He describes the SCM (which he views as simply a manifestation of liberal Protestantism) as having 'a diffuse belief system', and writes, 'liberal Protestantism can be characterised as undogmatic. It was not framed in a series of short and forceful propositions.'[8] In a somewhat simplistic way he virtually equates the SCM's theology with the 'New Light' model of eighteenth-century Scottish and Irish Presbyterianism and with the 'demythologizing' perspective of Bultmann in the twentieth century. One cannot help wondering whether he was familiar with the work of Suzanne de Diétrich and her influence not only on the WSCF but on all the national Movements, including the British.

Bruce contrasts this supposed 'diffuseness' with the much more focused and clear-cut beliefs of the IVF, with its specific doctrinal statement, strong senior leadership and strict conditions of membership involving adherence to the doctrinal statement. But is Bruce right in identifying the SCM with 'liberal Protestantism'? The answer, at least for the 1940s and 50s, must be 'No'. The question is like asking whether the *Church* is liberal or evangelical. No doubt some aspects of liberal Protestantism have at times been influential in the Movement, especially in the 1920s and early 1930s, as names of speakers popular at Swanwick conferences, like C. E. Raven, confirm. But that was only one strand among many others in the Movement's theological make-up. And even in the liberal 1920s the SCM never departed from its commitment to Bible study. In the 1950s the Movement was certainly open to a wide range of hermeneutics: but it always regarded itself as existentially related to and reliant on the Bible. It was also, demonstrably, committed to mission, though 'mission' was – rightly – susceptible of a wide range of interpretation. Most, though not all, SCM staff members of the 1950s consciously repudiated the term 'liberal'. They were much more closely drawn to Barth, Bonhoeffer and, in the English-speaking world, to Dodd, the Niebuhrs, Alan Richardson, Donald MacKinnon and Lesslie Newbigin. Preston names a further galaxy of theologians who at this period were influential in the British SCM, and who could certainly not all be thought of simply as 'liberal Protestant' – Berdyaev, Brunner, Buber, Maritain, Tillich, Donald and John Baillie, Ronald Gregor Smith, A. R. Vidler, William Temple. At its best the SCM always insisted on 'the importance of a vertebrate system of Christian belief' – to use the happy phrase which Visser 't Hooft quotes from his WCC American staff colleague Samuel McCrea Cavert.[9]

As an avowed atheist, Bruce is concerned only to point to the controlling sociological factors for what he views as success and failure: he does not raise the question of truth and integrity. But the search for truth and the practice of integrity were basic to what may have seemed, to some, the restless questioning of the SCM. For that questioning, as the 1951 Declaratory Statement makes clear, though it ranged over the whole field of human inquiry, was focused on, and anchored in, the Bible, the Church, worship and theology. An SCM branch might sometimes seem to be full of questions and problems and complications, which ordinary students could find perplexing. But at the same time it provided a warm fellowship where denominational and social barriers were broken down, where friendships were formed, where conversation on real questions – and especially on questions of the faith – were encouraged, and where prayer was made. And because this was in the context of the university, no limit was set to the questions which could be asked, and the minds of everyone, including the best minds, were stretched to the full. What did *not* happen was the laying down, from above, of a line of belief and practice which members must follow. Yet the effort was always made to point students to the best sources of biblical and theological, social and political scholarship, so that the integrity of their faith could match the academic integrity of their study in their chosen disciplines. And there were usually young members of university or SCM staff who were happy to help in this process without attempting to control it.

The 'single issue'

Far from diffuseness of belief being the reason for the diminution of the SCM, the problem would seem to have been rather that of the 'single issue', which in the mid 1960s was the political issue. The Movement was distracted away from its central commitment to the biblical witness and the sacramental life of the Church.[10] Today there is a comparable danger of homosexuality becoming such a single issue, and of its being combined with a particular doctrine of scripture in such a way that it becomes *the* criterion for accepting or rejecting other Christians. Here the rigour and integrity of biblical hermeneutic will help the followers of Christ towards fellowship rather than division. For the single issue to which they are committed can only be the truth, to know whom is freedom.[11]

In 1962 it was natural for Ambrose Reeves, so recently expelled from South Africa, to concentrate attention on the injustice of apartheid. The whole student world, in so-called 'western' countries at least, was in a state of political turmoil, and the members and leaders of the SCM were part of that world and therefore children of their time. And if Christian convictions impelled a student to attack distant authority structures in South Africa or Latin America, then authority structures nearer home had also to be challenged – even in the churches: even in the SCM itself. It was hard for good Christians to have to admit that Marxist students were doing more for God's reign of justice than they themselves were. And so, in many places, the SCM adopted a neo-Marxist stance. Many members felt (to use a later phrase of M. M. Thomas) that they must 'risk Christ for Christ's sake'.[12] But in fact the focus on a single issue tended to mean insistence on a single solution, which was a departure from the SCM tradition of toleration of different points of view within the one fellowship. It was a capitulation to the very kind of direction from above which the SCM criticized in the IVF.

The result was not all loss. Ambrose Reeves' opposition to apartheid was a not insignificant element in the long process which finally led, in 1995, to the freeing of Nelson Mandela and the establishment of a black majority government in South Africa. A notable factor leading to the fall of the Berlin Wall in 1989 was the leadership of student pastors, in the Bonhoeffer tradition of the old *Studentengemeinden*, who organized peaceful marches and vigils and especially meetings of young people for Bible study and prayer in the churches of Berlin, Leipzig and other cities in East Germany.[13] Student protests throughout the 1980s against the cold war in general and the 'star wars' programme of so-called defensive missiles in particular, in which SCM members in both the USA and Europe often played a leading role, were a definite factor in bringing together Presidents Gorbachev and Reagan in talks which led to the virtual end of both the cold war and the arms race.[14] And the Movement's constant commitment to women's rights, and its participation, at both Federation and national levels, in feminist theology and its implementation, kept it once again ahead of the Church – though not necessarily ahead of some of those whom the Church tended to regard as 'the world'.

Betrayal? Apostasy?

Two further reasons have been put forward for the collapse of the Movement. The first, proposed by many senior supporters of the SCM at the time of the crisis, is that the leaders of the SCM deliberately led it astray – in effect betrayed it. The decline was 'the direct result of the ideology and mismanagement of the nineteen-seventies generation. It is the Catholic Marxists and the alternative lifestyle cohorts who caused the collapse of a once great movement.'[15] The story we have followed, I believe, indicates that this charge is at best only partly true.

The second view is the argument, advanced by some conservative evangelicals, that the SCM was simply unfaithful to the scriptures and to sound evangelical doctrine, and so was bound to collapse sooner or later. Oliver Barclay mentions a pro-SCM senior churchman who commented that the SCM had been expected to sweep the field at the time of the expansion of higher education in the 1960s, but who later reflected that 'we lost and you [the UCCF] won'. And he went on to acknowledge that the growth of the CUs, parallelling the SCM's decline, was due to the CUs' sticking closely 'to Jesus, the Bible, and prayer'.[16] There is some truth in this comment, but it is not the whole truth. The IVF seems to have been strangely unaware of the SCM's real theological position during the 1940s and 50s; or perhaps it was deliberately blind, just as the SCM often seemed to close its eyes to the strengths of the IVF. Be that as it may, the SCM's commitment to biblical theology, its participation in the German Church struggle, and its theological wrestling with the problems of Christian obedience in the university are strangely ignored in Barclay and Horn's history of the CICCU. Some, though by no means all, of the SCM's evangelical critics would tend to add that the SCM's progeny, especially the WCC and all united churches, suffer from the same defect and will all likewise perish. The best refutation of this argument is to point to the SCM's record of Bible study and worship, and its continuance and development in the de Diétrich tradition of the ecumenical movement, later carried forward so effectively by Hans-Ruedi Weber,[17] and still flourishing.

Into the far country?

I should like to advance a different interpretation of the decline. The student-led Movement, with the best of intentions, and with only the peaceful weapons of Ephesians 6, had gone out to do battle with evil, and especially with the evil of political and social injustice and violence. But it had neglected its supply line, and so had become virtually detached from the community life in the body of Christ of which its own life was a part. And so its strength began to fail. One is reminded of the comment of the Scottish poet Edwin Muir on the 'political poets' of the late 1930s, who were faced by the choice of accepting Marxist power: 'They acted honourably, desperately and mistakenly. And Marx provided them with an old-fashioned weapon.'[18] Sincere political witness led to the point where, to adapt phrases from Raymond Panikkar and Karl Rahner, Christ became hidden and Christians became anonymous. There was little left for the world to see. The generosity of the Movement's heart, and its passionate commitment to justice, had prevailed over its wisdom; and its new weapon had turned out to be both old-fashioned and inadequate.

I believe that the SCM *did* make a series of wrong decisions: a near fatal flaw had indeed entered its life, and in its devotion to one aspect of truth, it had imperilled its contact with the source of truth. The SCM had allowed itself to be carried away on a single issue – the political issue. The Movement had often before been involved in politics: for example, the Indian and British SCMs had both been involved – ever since the 'Quit India' campaign of 1942, if not even earlier – in the issue of political independence, as had the Dutch SCM in 1949 over Indonesian independence.[19] In the 1951–53 period the British SCM was deeply committed to political protest over the proposed Central African Federation. But by 1968 the political agenda, and its Marxist analysis, had tended to marginalize all the Movement's other activities in what Oliver Tomkins called 'the totalitarian error of absolutising politics'.[20] The Bible ceased to interest students – even Christian students: they had other things to engross them. And with the Bible went the whole scholarly theological tradition with which the Movement had been so closely identified. And so the Movement lost the support not only of individual friends and generous donors but of the churches themselves. The Movement's approach to mission came to be seen as something purely sociopolitical. The SCM, surprisingly, had allowed itself to be caught in the stance which it deplored in the IVF – the stance of the single issue, the fundamental party line. It adopted a single, clear, partisan commitment, in the same way as the IVF had a single, clear, doctrinal commitment. It was an orthodoxy parallel to that of the IVF and similarly exclusive, even towards other Christian students. The traditional open policy of the SCM had been fractured, as had its close involvement with the great Christian tradition of the Church. Openness had become exclusive. When worship and Bible study decline and cease, when the lifeline to the Church is ruptured, when the ongoing and lively community of study and worship is marginalized, little remains.

In their history of the CICCU, Barclay and Horn make the frank admission that 'we failed to address the wider issues concerning our place in the university'.[21] Does the SCM, in a comparable recognition of failure, need to confess its failure to maintain its firm base in the Bible and the Church? For decades it took pride in being 'church ahead of the Church'. But the time came when its genuine commitment to Christ and to humankind blinded it to the fact that by going so far ahead of the Church 'into the far country', it had seriously damaged its lifeline. One recalls Jesus' parable of the two sons. The one whom the Church has always called the prodigal has indeed travelled to the far country. Gradually he comes to the realization that things have gone disastrously wrong; he repents and returns to his parents' home. And he comes back, not only with repentance but with a load of hard-earned experience, born indeed of error and struggle and hurt, but overruled by a continuing love of home. And now, confessing his sin, and with the forgiveness and blessing of his father, he is ready for renewed life – a life which understands more deeply the world in which he is going to live and witness, with all its suffering and injustice and sheer evil, but also its hope. The father loves both sons and has a future for them both.

The Church has not been good at confessing its failures, and neither has the SCM. In talking to several people who were closely associated with the Movement in the 1960s and 70s I have found what I can only call a conspiracy of silence – a silence which has lasted for 40 years or more. This verdict is borne out by the fact that no comprehensive national history of this period – for example for the British Movement – has yet been published. Some of the people I have spoken to have been eager to attribute blame for the collapse: others have been reluctant to admit that there really was a collapse. And one friend whom I asked if the word 'repentance' was an appropriate one to use in this context, cautiously replied, 'Not as a statement: more as a question'.

The question must be: Does the SCM – in company with the UCCF, and also with the one, holy, catholic and apostolic Church – stand in need of confession, forgiveness and renewed life? The answer is clear. The British SCM has recently taken a significant step in this direction. In the 'History' section of its current (2006) web page, after describing the vast expansion in higher education in the late 1950s and 60s, and noting how the university chaplains were doing virtually the same work as the SCM, it tells how the Movement instead 'threw itself into the social and political questions of the period with a zeal unparalleled in other religious quarters'. And then comes the admission: 'Unfortunately it also moved further and further away from its original Christian standpoint and at the same time distanced itself from many of the very students it existed to serve.' Today the life of all the national Movements takes place within the context of the Aim of the WSCF 'to call [students] to faith in God – Father, Son and Holy Spirit – according to the Scriptures, and to discipleship within the life and mission of the Church'.

In the very frank 1975 report of the British SCM (written in the midst of the Wick Court experiment) comes the sentence, 'We would not like to say that even today SCM has completed its time in the wilderness'. The authors were reviewing the events of the previous 10 years. Today 30 more have elapsed. Forty years in the wilderness? The SCM, and all the other groups and movements which inherit its family likeness, can rejoice in its achievements and its strengths. They should also share in the sadness of its failures, and seek — in that *metanoia*, commonly translated 'repentance' but more accurately meaning change of mind (and heart), which is not only the turning towards God and away from wandering but also the renewal of the mind — to fulfil the task to which God is calling Christians today. And for students that task is to be found above all in their own *pays de mission*, the university.

10

The family likeness

We sometimes ask, of well known movements in the history of the Church, 'Where are its effects still to be seen? What transformations has it achieved in the Church's life?' Such questions can rightly be asked of movements like the Methodist revival, or the Oxford Movement. And they may appropriately be asked of the SCM. Analysing the causes of the SCM's decline in the 1960s, Adrian Hastings says that 'Perhaps it was just because its message had been so widely received that the organisation itself was losing apparent significance'.[1] It is no accident that the first volume of the monumental *History of the Ecumenical Movement* (covering the period 1517–1948, and edited by Ruth Rouse and Stephen C. Neill) has multiple references in its index to the SCM and the WSCF; the second volume (1948–68) has a handful to the WSCF but none to the SCM, while the third volume (1968–2000) has only six altogether, three of which relate, very properly and encouragingly, to the Movement in Africa. In many ways the SCM *has* achieved its major goals. The world *has* been evangelized, in the sense that the gospel has been proclaimed and the Church planted in virtually every country. Significant steps *have* been taken towards Christian unity, and official organs are in place to continue that work. Issues of justice and peace are firmly on the agenda of the churches. I am reminded of the emblem and motto (based on John 12.24) which Fr Michael Hurley SJ chose at the 1970 foundation of the Irish School of Ecumenics – a stalk of wheat with the words *Floreat ut pereat* (*May it flourish in order that* – its task of unity achieved – *it may perish*). Has the SCM indeed reached such a point of achievement? What lasting effects has it left? Does it have any children, to rise up and call it blessed – children bearing the family likeness?

The answer is that the SCM has indeed had lastingly significant effects, and has produced a numerous family of flourishing children. Ronald Preston lists no fewer than nine of those children, including the SCM Press,[2] which, though it no longer belongs to the SCM, still – as the SCM-Canterbury Press – retains the historic name; and Steve Bruce berates the Movement for having allowed most of these children to fly the nest. But in fact the list of children is much longer than Preston or Bruce suggest, and repays examination. In some cases this will involve following the 'post-SCM' career of former staff and members of the

Movement, for they became carriers of the SCM tradition into many areas of Christian life and witness all over the world. It is a mark of the health and strength of the Movement, and of its close and friendly relations with the churches, that many people who were leaders in the SCM in their student days went on to become ecumenical leaders of the churches; leaders also in the field of mission in its many manifestations.

The World Council of Churches

It would be difficult to refute the claim that the SCM is the progenitor of the modern ecumenical movement. Lesslie Newbigin, deploring the events of 1968, could still affirm that the SCM had been 'the most powerful source of new life for the ecumenical movement'.[3] And he paid tribute to its part in his own ecumenical formation when he wrote, 'One of the joys of being born into the Christian faith through the SCM was that one was from the beginning part of an ecumenical family'.[4] It is true that the leaders of the Protestant missionary movement had already, by the very early nineteenth century, realized that missionary co-operation was essential for the evangelization of the world, and before the end of that century sophisticated arrangements for 'comity' (the avoidance of competition in evangelization) were in place, in India and elsewhere. Yet the organization of Edinburgh 1910, and its follow-up in what became the International Missionary Council (IMC) and the Faith and Order and Life and Work movements, were something new, and were all products of the ecumenical co-operation pioneered by Mott, Oldham and others in the SCM and WSCF. Tatlow laboured to secure the participation in the SCM of the Anglo-Catholic wing of the Anglican tradition, and so prepared the ground for Oldham to persuade them to be part of the Edinburgh Conference. The Federation pioneered the participation of the Russian Orthodox Church in the student movement, and after the revolution of 1917 the emigré community in Paris continued and deepened that lively co-operation.

The WCC was for many years largely staffed by people who had worked for the various national SCMs and for the Federation – Wim Visser 't Hooft, Robert Mackie, Suzanne de Diétrich, Francis House,[5] Oliver Tomkins, K. H. Ting, M. M. Thomas, Patrick Rodger, Steven Mackie, Martin Conway, Stanley Samartha,[6] Philip Potter, Emilio Castro, and many others. Both friends and opponents of the WCC often remarked that it was like an SCM for grown-ups – 'the SCM in long trousers'![7] For good or ill the SCM set its mark on the WCC. And that mark was not simply the fact that familiar SCM names were now listed as working in Geneva: the SCM had set its mark on the kind of *koinonia* found among the staff of the WCC. Marie-Jeanne de Haller Coleman comments on the relationships between these first leaders of the WCC in Geneva:

> There was a mutual trust between these people who had, thanks to the SCM, shared freely with one another what made them tick spiritually, their faith, their doubts, their hopes and frustrations, and who had in the process learned a lot about each other's churches' traditions, dropping many mistaken prejudices along the way. This mutual trust was instrumental in getting the World Council of Churches and the International Missionary Council's early negotiations over many hurdles.[8]

But beyond people and *koinonia* there was a demonstrable continuity of methodology. It was the model of representative democracy, with an assembly, an executive, a central staff and travelling secretaries. Basic to it all was a study department, one of whose major tasks was the production of Bible study material. Like it or loathe it, that was the SCM model: and it was a good model. In Thomas Wieser's words, 'Group Bible study became an ecumenical discipline, not only within the Federation and its movements, but also within the WCC'.[9] During the volatile 1960s there was pressure within the WCC to get rid of Faith and Order as a separate entity (as indeed happened to Life and Work). It was Oliver Tomkins who struggled for and achieved the continuing life of Faith and Order, which 'fought back and greatly flourished' in the 1960s.[10] One notable result of this victory was the official participation, from Uppsala 1968, of the Roman Catholic Church in Faith and Order. In this dogged adherence to Faith and Order – demonstrated once again, as we have seen, at the 1983 Vancouver Assembly in the debate on the *Baptism, Eucharist and Ministry* document – the WCC proved wiser than its parent-body, the SCM.

It may help our understanding of the continuance of the SCM tradition in the life of the WCC if we return to the role of M. M. Thomas, who from 1968 to 1975 was Moderator of the WCC's Central Committee, and so, in fact, the senior figure in the whole structure, though working closely with the general secretary (first Eugene Carson Blake and then, from 1972, Philip Potter). These years covered the period of student unrest, and MM was very conscious of what was happening in the SCM, for the student presence was painfully noticeable at the WCC Assemblies in Uppsala (1968) and Nairobi (1975). MM's influence was seen in several ways. First, it was highly significant that the titular head of the WCC – if one dare use such an expression – was both an Asian and a layperson. And MM's passion for justice made him seek to ensure that groups which had hitherto been marginalized in the counsels of the WCC – laypeople, non-westerners, women and young people – were appropriately represented. Second, his Mar Thoma Church background made him sensitive to the traditions and the difficulties of the Orthodox churches which had come into the WCC in considerable numbers at the New Delhi Assembly in 1961, most of them from countries in the Eastern bloc. Third, his opposition to what he saw as American cultural and economic imperialism made him sympathetic to Christians living 'behind the iron curtain', and particularly to those who, like Hromádka, were prepared to co-operate with the authorities so far as they could, and who genuinely believed that Marxism was dealing more effectively with economic and social injustice than was capitalism. (MM modified this view considerably after the suppression of Dubček's 'Prague Spring' in 1968.) Fourth, he took a leading part, with his friend and mentor Paul Devanandan, in developing ecumenical theological thought on the problems of areas of 'Rapid Social Change', following up on the book which they had jointly edited in 1960, *Christian Participation in Nation-building*.[11]

Fifth, MM was largely responsible (under the influence of Devanandan, and later with the help successively of Stanley Samartha and Wesley Ariarajah) for persuading the WCC to take seriously the relationship of the Christian Church to people of other faiths. Gradually, and largely through the pioneering work of Devanandan and MM at CISRS in Bangalore, the word 'dialogue' began to be used specifically in this connection. At first it was used particularly of dialogue between Christians, Hindus and Muslims in their common struggle for a new and better society in India.[12] Devanandan's first organized Hindu–Christian dialogue was held at Nagpur in 1960 on the theme 'The Christian and Hindu Views concerning Man';[13] and the idea soon developed into interfaith dialogue as we now understand it, and attained worldwide currency. Devanandan made an appeal for interfaith dialogue at his plenary address to the WCC Assembly in New Delhi in 1961, but it was not until the Nairobi Assembly in 1975 that representatives of other faiths were invited to participate in a WCC Assembly. When MM was accused of syncretism he replied by saying that he believed in 'Christ-centred syncretism', pointing out that the Church had never been free from syncretism, starting with the fourth Gospel and its use of the Greek term *logos*, and continuing with the absorption of philosophical, legal and cultural structures from many other traditions. Finally came the accusation, especially after the publication of his book *Risking Christ for Christ's Sake*, that he was humanizing and marginalizing Christ. What he was in fact advocating was the practice of dialogue from a position of equality, with no assumption of superiority, and with preparedness to listen or be silent as well as to talk, and readiness to follow the truth wherever it might lead. His detractors said that he had become a humanist: he affirmed that he believed in *true* humanism, the humanism lived and demonstrated by the incarnate Christ. To that end he had already in 1953 written an article for *The Student World* entitled 'The Gospel of Redemption as the Foundation of True Secular Humanism'. And in 1974, after reading John Hick's *God and the Universe of Faiths*, he commented, 'I found his theo-centricity quite inadequate from both the Christian and the anthropological angles, and it was this that gave me the idea for the book *Man and the Universe of Faiths.*' MM's view of the world and of other faiths was nothing if not Christocentric. Indeed his friend Metropolitan Paulose Mar Gregorios (Paul Verghese in SCM days) criticized him for not being sufficiently Trinitarian.[14]

There were many people in the WCC and in the churches who did not want to hear this kind of message. But MM was consistent in all he wrote and said. And also, in the true SCM tradition, he was fully committed to the Bible; to the Church with its life of Word and sacrament; to the Church's mission – both in word and in the witness of justice; and to Christian unity. In this task he was greatly supported by his friends, many of them going back to SCM days. These were friends with whom he could differ, and yet retain their friendship. *My Ecumenical Journey* is full of accounts of arguments with them – Lesslie Newbigin,[15] Paul Abrecht, Visser 't Hooft, Ronald Preston, Reinhold Niebuhr, Pauline Webb, Paulose Mar Gregorios and many others. Yet always they remained friends, members of the one body of Christ.

For MM, the *koinonia* of an ecumenical community, first experienced in the SCM, was of crucial importance. And it was that conviction of the reality and integrity of *koinonia* which supported him when, under his moderatorship, and with the encouragement of the general secretary Eugene Carson Blake, the executive committee of the WCC, at Canterbury in 1969, made the decision to set up the Programme to Combat Racism (PCR). 'It was this personal community', he wrote, 'which became the foundation of the *koinonia* of the churches; and the challenge of *koinonia* of all human beings was also before us in the decision of the committee to fight racism.'[16] Today, years after the ending of apartheid, it is hard to realize how vehemently the PCR was opposed, not only by governments but by churches – in Britain even by the Archbishop of Canterbury, Michael Ramsey, and by the British Council of Churches.[17] Yet MM mentions a letter he received from Lesslie Newbigin saying that the PCR Fund distribution was the most important thing that had happened in the WCC and had helped to convince people that the Church did not automatically side with the *status quo*.[18] Events have vindicated the stand taken by the WCC.

That kind of witness was not maintained without cost, and at times MM was a lonely figure. His courage can be seen in the stand he took during Indira Gandhi's infamous 'emergency' in 1975. When popular anger against her undemocratic and authoritarian style of government boiled over and she declared a state of emergency, abrogating many fundamental rights and imprisoning the leaders of the opposition, MM – as editor of *The Guardian* Christian weekly – decided to oppose her declaration. 'My opposition to it', he wrote, 'was just a natural, almost passive, unheroic response to a political act which cut the ground of the ecumenical Christian concern for human rights and peoples' liberation.'[19] When the government censor disallowed one of his editorials he resigned his editorship and began to duplicate newsletters for private circulation among friends in India and overseas. It was a memorable stand for truth and justice. Much later – in 1991 – and perhaps in belated recognition of his stand at this time – he was appointed governor of the largely Christian northeast Indian state of Nagaland. There too his honesty and outspokenness got him into trouble: he protested against central government corruption, and in 1993 resigned. Years earlier he had written *The Christian in the World Struggle*: his own life was a shining, and costly, example.

Some of the problems which had troubled the SCM also created difficulties for the WCC. During the decade 1980–90 the WCC had three major ecumenical concerns: first, justice, peace and the integrity of creation (JPIC),[20] which included the study on men and women in the Church, and so took feminist theology seriously; second, Faith and Order (culminating in the 1982 agreement *Baptism, Eucharist and Ministry* (*BEM*); and third, interfaith dialogue.[21] As a result, mission and evangelism seemed to many observers to have been marginalized as being only one activity among several others. This meant that some people, especially those hostile or neutral towards the WCC, began to say that evangelism was no longer a concern of the Council, and so had become, by default, the monopoly of the evangelical wing of the churches. A notable exception to this apparent marginalization of evangelism was a WCC document which impressively sought to bring the whole life and witness of the Church together in a biblical and theological synthesis – *Mission and Evangelism: An Ecumenical Affirmation* (1982). In many ways this is a better, and certainly a more prophetic, document than *BEM*, which appeared in the same year and has had much wider publicity. *Mission and Evangelism*, which in the year 2000 was supplemented and updated though not replaced by *Mission and Evangelism in Unity Today* (*MEUT*), was commended by Lesslie Newbigin as 'a splendid document', which 'should set the parameters for ecumenical thinking for many years to come'.[22] While condemning proselytism it finely affirms that 'each person is entitled to hear the Good News' (paragraph 10), and that Christians 'owe the message of God's salvation in Jesus Christ to every person and every people' (paragraph 41). And in *MEUT* comes the notable sentence, 'We cannot point to any other way of salvation than

Jesus Christ: at the same time we cannot set limits to the saving power of God'.[23] *BEM* is indeed a crucial ecumenical statement of what the Church *is*. *Mission and Evangelism* is a no less significant affirmation of what the Church *does*.

M. M. Thomas' younger contemporary (also from the SCM, but from a very different cultural background) Philip Potter (born in 1921) has been described as the most outstanding figure of the third generation of ecumenical leaders[24] (following Mott in the first generation and Visser 't Hooft in the second). Born on the West Indian island of Dominica, he is proud of his mixed cultural heritage – Carib, African, Irish and French – of which he says, 'I contain within me oppressed and oppressors, white and black and yellow'. And in his ecumenical career he has done more than perhaps anyone else to make the WCC a fellowship where racial differences are regarded as an enrichment rather than a problem, and where the centuries-old white, European balance of power has been overcome. After study in Jamaica and London he became a Methodist minister, and spent some time as a missionary in Haiti. From his student days he was a member of the SCM, and at the Oslo Youth Conference of 1947 he represented the Jamaican SCM. From 1948 to 1950 he worked for the British SCM as overseas secretary, and then went on to serve the Federation, from which he graduated to the WCC's youth department (1954–60). In 1967 he became director of the Division of World Mission and Evangelism, finally serving as general secretary of the WCC from 1972 to 1984. A large, athletic man, a fine preacher and expositor of the Bible, he has been truly 'a towering symbol of ecumenical commitment'. Konrad Raiser (general secretary from 1993 to 2003) identifies three of Potter's special insights, which he articulated in good SCM fashion 'ahead of his time and against some resistance'. First comes his understanding of the Church as a pilgrim people with a prophetic mandate; his whole life, in fact – like Mott's or St Paul's – has been spent in the constant journeying of prophetic evangelism, the constant advocacy of the Church's mission. Second comes his commitment to dialogue – 'the universal dialogue of cultures'. Dialogue for him is the essential form of evangelism, 'the form of the incarnate Lord as a servant living among human beings, open and vulnerable to them. It is the way of the cross'. And third comes the scope of his ecumenical vision: it is the scope of Jesus himself:

> The oikoumene to come, the new humanity, is already manifest in Jesus, he who saves, he who is himself authentic, integral, whole human as we are destined to be. He is the pioneer, the representative of this coming oikoumene, and we become part of it when we see Jesus and follow his pioneering, representative steps.[25]

Potter envisages this 'oikoumene to come' as taking the form of the new Jerusalem, the new city, the fulfilment of God's plan (*oikonomia*) to unite all things in Christ. It is a symbol of a new creation and of a culture which is truly human. 'The oikoumene to come, the city to come, is open to all and is full of the variety of the riches of creation, culture, which all the peoples bring. It is the place of the universal dialogue of cultures.'[26]

In 1984 Philip Potter was succeeded as general secretary by Emilio Castro from Uruguay. Both of them come from the SCM tradition, and both have courageously carried forward this vision of a wider scope of mission, a universal dialogue of cultures in Christ's way, a countercul- ture to the new imperial globalization which has begun to dominate the beginning of the third millennium.

Throughout this period the great de Diétrich tradition of Bible study was being maintained by Hans-Ruedi Weber, who was on the WCC staff from 1955 to 1988, and was director of biblical studies from 1971. He ran immensely stimulating training courses all over the world, and produced fine books on biblical exegesis which were not only scholarly and readable, but also used Christian art, ancient and modern, in a way which captured both the imagination and the intelligence.[27] Writing about the WCC's tradition of Bible study, MM gives a roll-call of 'the great Bible study leaders of the ecumenical movement in the '60s and '70s'; he has already spoken frequently of Suzanne de Diétrich and Marie-Jeanne de Haller, and the others, following in that tradition, are Paulose Mar Gregorios, Hans-Ruedi Weber, D. T. Niles and Lesslie Newbigin. They are all SCM people: and all believed that the theology of the ecumenical movement cannot be effective unless it is based on Scripture.

The history of the SCM, glorious as it is, provides cautionary tales for its progeny, especially the WCC and united and uniting churches. No one has outlined the dangers more clearly than Ronald Preston, reflecting, as he did, the views of a distinguished group of friends of the ecumenical movement, including Paul Abrecht, Keith Bridston and Charles West of the United States, Charles Birch and David Gill of Australia and John Francis of Scotland,[28] nearly all of whom had been staff or student members of the Movement in its golden age. Preston criticizes the WCC's tendency in the 1980s and 90s to act from the heart rather than the head – as the SCM did in the 60s and 70s – and to issue public statements on a wide variety of political issues with what he regards as minimal expert consultation; and his insistence on ade- quate undergirding in the professional secular fields involved, as well as in the areas of biblical and theological hermeneutics, must be treated with respect. From the African, Latin American or Pacific perspective, however, criticism of this kind may be seen as oppressive and unjustified. Their own experts, as well as their own people, know where the shoe pinches; Northern heads need to remember that Southern voices represent both hearts *and* heads. Duncan Forrester has made out a strong though sympathetic case against Preston, in which he states, 'What the WCC does have is an ability to speak for the voiceless, and [it] has a positive mandate to do so'.[29]

Yet in the midst of all its activities in the fields of JPIC and interfaith dialogue, the WCC has steadfastly maintained its strength in the areas of Faith and Order,[30] World Mission and Evangelism, and in its continuing emphasis on study, despite the closing of its specific study department after the Uppsala Assembly in 1968. In each of these areas biblical hermeneutics continues to play a decisive role.

At a time when there is talk of an 'ecumenical winter', and world church communions often seem intent on building their own individual empires, the WCC's active commitment to Christian unity is vital. Commenting on how the churches in Britain seemed to regard the WCC as a threat, Newbigin wrote:

> In this situation the Churches fail to hear the judgement which the existence of the WCC implies upon their still jealously guarded denominational sovereignty. Yet nothing can remove from the Gospel the absolute imperative of unity.[31]

The WCC, by reason of its official nature, is bound to be more cautious than the SCM was; and an illuminating insight into the difference between the two is provided by an exchange of letters in 1976, soon after the Nairobi WCC Assembly, between Oliver Tomkins and Philip Potter, veterans of both SCM/WSCF and WCC. Tomkins defines his own, SCM-built outlook as 'a whole cultural temper which value[s] thought above slogans, consensus above confrontation, self-criticism above propaganda, tolerance above crusading'. And Potter, in his reply as general secretary of the WCC, writes, 'We cannot go on behaving as an avant-garde who will be followed in due course'.[32] That, in a nutshell, gives the difference between the SCM and the WCC. The SCM could – and did – act as an avant garde, as 'church ahead of the Church': that was its peculiar calling. The WCC has to be more cautious, as it needs to carry its constituent churches with it.

And that is why the absence of the SCM as a major force is so much felt today: the absence of a pioneering, experimental community of young people fully committed to their own churches yet committed to the eschatological unity of the Church, and prepared to live and worship and witness as a *koinonia* of people who in some strange and wonderful way already experience that unity.

United and uniting churches

The stamp of the SCM is also to be seen in the united churches which were inaugurated in the period between, say, 1947 (Church of South India – CSI) and 1977 (Uniting Church in Australia – UCA). With reference to the CSI, suffice it to mention the contribution to its Plan of Union, and to the theological defence of that Plan, of Lesslie Newbigin[33] and Anthony Hanson,[34] both of whom had served as SCM secretaries. The fact that the Plan of the Church of North India (1970) was designed to overcome many of the Anglican difficulties with the CSI, notably by providing a unified ministry from the beginning, illustrates the SCM tradition of intentional theological debate, undergirded by informed biblical exegesis. As one who was present at the inauguration of the CNI, and took part as a presbyter in the act of unification of the ministry in the Gujarat diocese, I can testify to the biblical and theological wrestling which took place in the process leading up to the inauguration, and especially to the 'scruple-removing' ministry of Donald Kennedy, a former Irish SCM secretary, and later CNI bishop of Bombay, and particularly his careful exegesis of the Greek word *hikanotes* (sufficiency) in 2 Corinthians 3.5 (RSV), 'Our sufficiency is *from* God'.

I should like to examine in rather more detail the Uniting Church in Australia (UCA), not least because it is the church of which I have for many years been a minister. It should be noted that in the church's name the words 'uniting' and 'in' are deliberately chosen: the church makes no extra-territorial claims: it is an open-ended experiment in Christian unity which is intended to encourage others to take part. The UCA is also, probably, the church in whose foundation document (*The Basis of Union*) the hand of the SCM is most clearly seen. It was originally hoped that the Anglican Church would form part of the new church, along with the Presbyterian, Congregational and Methodist churches, and the Anglicans did indeed take part in the negotiations at an early stage. The proposal was that the church should have bishops, linked by a concordat with the Church of South India, to ensure that the bishops shared in the historic episcopate. Difficulties arose, however, mainly on the Anglican side, where there were problems both from Anglo-Catholics and from the conservative evangelical Sydney archdiocese. The negotiations stalled, and the other three churches decided that they should go ahead with union rather than return to the drawing-board.

Many of the members of the Joint Commission on Church Union (of the Presbyterian, Methodist and Congregational churches) which drew up the Basis finalized in 1971 and carried into effect in 1977, had been members or staff members of the SCM, either in Australia or in the UK.

Their work began with two careful studies which prepared the way for union, *The Faith of the Church* (1959) and *The Church: Its Nature, Function and Ordering* (1963), whose authors included SCM people like Davis McCaughey, John Garrett and Bert Wyllie. *The Basis of Union* (1971), in which their work culminated, no doubt reflects the language of the Barthian era – and of the contemporary SCM! But above all it takes the Bible seriously, and the Creeds, and the Fathers, and the Reformers, and John Wesley. In recent years the authority of the Basis has not gone unchallenged (there are anti-authoritarian trends in the Church as well as in the SCM!), and there have been those who have wanted to marginal-ize it, together with the Reformation documents which it safeguards. But the Uniting Church's 1997 Perth Assembly, while failing to give the Basis the degree of 'confessional' authority which many desired, at least affirmed that the Uniting Church, in its life and work 'within the one, holy, catholic and apostolic Church' is 'guided by' its Basis of Union.

The Basis breathes the atmosphere of the SCM of the 1950s, strongly influenced by Barth and the German church struggle, and with a gov-erning emphasis on the Bible, on mission and on Christian unity. A few examples of its wording will indicate the resonance, and the echoes of the British SCM's 1951 Aim and Basis, and especially its accompany-ing Declaratory Statement.

- *On Scripture.* When the Church preaches Jesus Christ, its message is con-trolled by the Biblical witnesses. The Word of God on whom salvation depends is to be heard and known from Scripture appropriated in the worshipping and witnessing life of the Church. (From Para 5)
- *On Preaching.* Christ who is present when he is preached among people is the Word of God who acquits the guilty, who gives life to the dead and who brings into being what otherwise would not exist. (From Para 4)
- *On 'Scholarly Interpreters'.* The Uniting Church acknowledges that God has never left the Church without faithful and scholarly interpreters of Scripture, or without those who have reflected deeply upon, and acted trustingly in obedience to, God's living Word. In particular the Uniting Church enters into the inheritance of literary, historic and scientific enquiry which has characterised recent centuries, and gives thanks for the knowledge of God's ways with humanity which are open to an informed faith. The Uniting Church lives within a world-wide fellowship of Churches in which it will learn to sharpen its understanding of the will and purpose of God by contact with contemporary thought . . . The Uniting Church thanks God for the continuing witness and service of evangelist, of scholar, of prophet

and martyr. It prays that it may be ready when occasion demands to confess the Lord in fresh words and deeds. (Para 11)

• *On Mission and Unity.* In entering into this union the Churches concerned are mindful that the Church of God is committed to serve the world for which Christ died, and that it awaits with hope the day of the Lord Jesus Christ on which it will be clear that the kingdom of this world has become the kingdom of our Lord and of the Christ, who shall reign for ever and ever. (From Para 1, *The Way into Union*).

The Uniting Church declares its desire to enter more deeply into the faith and mission of the Church in Australia, by working together and seeking union with other Churches. (From Para 2)

If the British SCM of the 1950s had been asked to draw up an ideal basis for the reunion of the divided churches of the world, it would have included statements something like that. And it is significant that in recent years the more conservative and evangelical leaders of the Uniting Church in Australia, many of them with an IVF background, have been eager defenders of the Basis of Union, against those who would reduce its explicit commitment to Scripture and tradition.[35]

Davis McCaughey (1914–2005) provided the most clearly identifiable hand behind the wording of the Basis of Union. Many years before, in the early 1950s, his had also been a distinguishable hand behind the revised Aim and Basis and Declaratory Statement of the British SCM. He had grown up in Belfast in the Irish Presbyterian Church, had read English Literature at Cambridge, studied theology in Edinburgh, and served as Irish secretary of the SCM (1937–39). He spent seven effective years in London (1946–53), first at Annandale as study secretary (with Ronald Preston and John Gibbs) and later acting as a consultant for the SCM Press (with Ronald Gregor Smith), the British Council of Churches and various Oldham-inspired groups loosely linked with the Movement. We have seen something of his work in the field of Bible study, of worship (*Student Prayer*), and of what, in the title of his own book, he called Christian obedience in the university. He was also much involved in the development of good relations with the Orthodox churches, and was closely aware of the Church of South India and the theological debate surrounding its Plan of Union. He was in demand as a facilitator of discussion, among his earlier efforts being a report, *The Era of Atomic Power*, for the British Council of Churches, and the Federation Grey Book *The Christian in the World Struggle*, written in collaboration with M. M. Thomas. As a drafter of documents he had few equals, and he knew from experience that churches do not unite without a carefully structured biblical and theological base. Yet he had little sympathy for useless minutiae, and is famously reported to have said, 'Let us cut the regulations in half and throw away half; any half will do!'[36]

McCaughey's subsequent career was a classic example of the SCM tradition in action. In 1953 he became Professor of New Testament Studies at Ormond College, Melbourne (which was then still a Presbyterian institution) and in 1959 became Master of the college. He was soon involved in the negotiations for union between the Australian churches which we have been following, and when the three churches united in 1977 became the first President of the Uniting Church. After retirement, he was in 1986 appointed governor of the state of Victoria, at a point when that public office had fallen into some disrepute. His wife Jean, who had studied medicine in Belfast, was also a product of the SCM, and became well known in Australia for her courageous and vigorous public stand on issues of social justice, especially relating to poverty. She was part of the team headed by Ronald Henderson which produced the report, *Inquiry into Poverty in Australia* (1975); and her book following up its findings, *A Bit of a Struggle: Coping with Family Life in Australia* (1987), was widely read. Together Jean and Davis transformed the hitherto somewhat stuffy office of state governor, opening Government House to the public, and hosting a wide variety of informal meetings of groups from all walks of life – politicians, specialists in medical ethics, university teachers, poets, musicians, even theologians. For those familiar with the story, the stately atmosphere at Government House was often charged with memories of the more spartan surroundings of the Chum Creek campsite in the not-so-distant hills, or of Study Swanwick in Britain, or Gwatt in Switzerland or Nunspeet in the Netherlands or Tambaram in India – or any of the scores of holy places where SCM students and experts were wont as friends to wrestle with their faith and their jobs.

There is a tendency today to criticize united and uniting churches, arguing that they were premature, or that the great uniting wave of the mid-twentieth century has subsided without ever breaking properly. As one who has been a part of two unions – in North India and Australia – I would say rather that these unions faithfully represent the 'church ahead of the Church'; that they required a great deal of nerve (otherwise known as faith) to carry out – a nerve which seemed to fail at crucial moments in places like Britain where it was most needed – and that they are working models, models which have a future, and which will in time develop further, to the glory of God.

The Ecumenical Institute, Bossey[37]

The Château de Bossey, which has frequently figured in this story, is a beautiful early-eighteenth-century mansion near the Lake of Geneva, and about 20 kilometres from that city. In 1945 the provisional committee of the WCC, led by Visser 't Hooft, had decided that a lay training centre was needed for the ecumenical movement, and he and Robert Mackie, both still officers of the WSCF, decided that Bossey was the place. They were able, amazingly, to persuade John D. Rockefeller to support the venture with a donation of a million dollars, and in August 1946, as we have seen, the first conference – the general committee of the Federation – was held in what would soon become known simply as 'Bossey'. Hendrik Kraemer of the Netherlands, lay theologian and expert on Islam, was appointed director and, until he was free to come, the indefatigable Henri-Louis Henriod held the fort. They were joined by Suzanne de Diétrich. It was a formidable trio – all laypeople, all of them coming from the SCM tradition, and all eager to teach the three basic subjects – the Bible, the world and the universal Church. In 1952 the institute opened a graduate school of ecumenical studies, with a five-month course validated by the theology faculty of the University of Geneva. Suzanne de Diétrich's biblical mantle eventually fell upon Hans-Ruedi Weber, who had first visited Bossey as national secretary of the Swiss SCM in 1948. In the years since it was founded thousands of people, most of them lay and most of them young, have had their faith strengthened, their worship deepened, and their commitment to living out the gospel inspired and empowered through the teaching and the experience of 'life together' which they have found at Bossey.

The SCM Press

We have followed the history of the British SCM's enterprise in the world of Christian publishing from its early study outlines on Bible and mission, through the distinguished editorships of Hugh Martin, Ronald Gregor Smith, David Edwards and John Bowden. It maintained its useful work right through the difficult period of 'the Storm', and under John Bowden's management continued to be a major contributor to SCM finances; between 1969 and 1979, for example, the Movement received no less than £100,000 from the Press.[38] John Bowden and Tim McClure wisely founded a separate trust association for the Press, so that it did not suffer through the financial problems of the Movement itself. The decline of the SCM had in fact little effect on the financial fortunes of the Press, which in 1982 actually increased its influence by becoming closely linked with Epworth Press, Sheed and Ward, and Fortress Press (USA).

The initials 'SCM' are still highly significant in the world of theological and religious publications through the ongoing and developing work, as an enterprise quite distinct from the Movement, of what is now the SCM-Canterbury Press. This imprint belongs to Hymns Ancient and Modern Ltd, a company whose history goes back to the 1861 edition of *Hymns Ancient and Modern*; it adopted the 'Canterbury Press Norwich' imprint in 1986, and purchased the SCM Press in 1997. Though not related to the Movement, it continues the SCM tradition of theological and religious educational titles, as well as publishing the *Church Times* and *The New English Hymnal*. And so the great tradition of the SCM Press still continues.

★ ★ ★ ★ ★ ★

In addition to these four 'children' of the Movement – the WCC, united and uniting churches, Bossey and the SCM Press, each of whose careers has involved the creation of an ongoing body or organization – three special SCM areas of concern and achievement must be mentioned: race relations, women's ministry and issues relating to sexuality.

Race relations

From the first the Movement took the line that in Christ there is neither black nor white, Jew nor Gentile. But several national Movements were in a position where race discrimination was part of the surroundings in which they lived; in the United States and South Africa the Movement was always a leader in the struggle against discrimination, and we have seen something of the early work of J. H. Oldham in Britain. The Australian record on race relations is not one of which Australians can be proud; and even in the SCM the question of justice for the Aboriginal community remained marginal for years – partly perhaps because so few Aboriginals were able to attend universities, and for many city-dwelling white students contacts with Aboriginal people were difficult to make. The mission programmes of the churches were well intentioned but paternalistic, though indeed most of the white people who supported Aboriginal rights in the early days came from the churches. From the churches too, in more recent days, have come many of the white Australians who have done most for Aboriginal rights – like the Jesuit Fr Frank Brennan, his fellow Roman Catholic Sir William Deane, Governor General of Australia, and Sir Ronald Wilson of the Uniting Church.

Ron Wilson (1922–2005)[39] was born in Western Australia and had a tough upbringing through losing his mother at the age of four and being separated from his disabled father at seven. He left school at 14 and took his first job as a messenger at the local court. Joining the Royal Australian Air Force in World War 2 he became a Spitfire pilot in Britain, and after the war studied law, and was a member of the SCM, at the University of Western Australia. He later affirmed that the SCM provided the most formative experience in his life, in terms of being a Christian and understanding the faith, having a sense of 'doing' theology, and what it means to be a lay theologian. He appreciated the balance between biblical reflection and social justice activism, and tells how in his later legal work he often found himself wrestling with the Bible when faced with particularly difficult cases. In 1949 he attended a WSCF Asian leaders' training course in Sri Lanka, and met M. M. Thomas, D. T. Niles, Lesslie Newbigin and Philip Potter (still, like himself, a student). In 1963 he became a Queen's Counsel, in 1969 Solicitor General for Western Australia, and from 1969 to 1979 a Justice of the High Court of Australia.

Having sworn to administer justice according to law, he sometimes found that in cases relating to the Racial Discrimination Act he had to give judgements which his Aboriginal friends found hard to accept: if the law had to change, it was only Parliament which could change it. But by 1990, having retired from the High Court, he was free to become president of the Human Rights and Equal Opportunity Commission, where he was an outspoken and courageous advocate of the rights of the Aboriginal community. Together with the Aboriginal leader Mick Dodson he led the famous National Inquiry into the forced removal – by government but with the co-operation of the churches – of Aboriginal children from their families and communities. Ron Wilson and Mick Dodson co-authored the famous report *Bringing Them Home* (1997) which includes dozens of moving human stories comparable to the one brought to the screen in the film *Rabbit-Proof Fence*, in which two young Aboriginal girls far outshine their co-star Kenneth Branagh.

From 1988 to 1991 Ron Wilson served as President of the Uniting Church, and took delight in being the first layperson in that office, believing that he had a special calling to chart the role of the layperson in the life of the Church. He had to suffer for his convictions on race relations, for they were by no means universally popular, and the incoming Howard administration in 1997, with its deep-seated interest in the mining and pastoral industries and its dislike of what it termed 'the black armband' view of history, moved quickly to disable the Human Rights Commission, and to discredit its report *Bringing Them Home*. Critics objected especially to the report's use of the word 'genocide' in this context; but Wilson defended it, affirming that what had happened *was* genocide according to the United Nations definition, and adding that 'we had to name the evil'.[40] Wilson called on the government to make a national apology to the Aboriginal people, and there was wide support for what, in an Aboriginal expression, was called 'Sorry Day'. 'The word

"Sorry" begins the process of healing', he said, 'and what people must realize is that we are not talking about events of long ago. We are talking about the contemporary suffering of a significant section of the Australian people.' The Prime Minister bluntly refused to make the apology. Ron Wilson's courteous, cheerful, and well-informed advocacy of human rights was not diminished, however, and with his Aboriginal and white friends and colleagues he carried most mainline Australian Christians with him. 'I am happy to be seen as "politically correct" ', he said, 'if that means being sensitive to the problems of the disadvantaged and working to overcome them'.[41]

Women's ministry

From the start women took a leading part in the life and leadership of the SCM. Interestingly enough, when the IVF eventually separated from the SCM, the tradition of women's leadership was not carried over into that organization. It was not until 1993, for example, that the CICCU elected a woman president, and as recently as 1996 they decided against having women speakers at their meetings.[42]

It was not like that in the beginnings of the student movement, from which both the SCM and the UCCF are descended. Ruth Rouse was already a staff member of the British Movement when she first met John R. Mott in 1894, and soon became involved in the Federation, of which she became assistant general secretary in 1905. She and Mott formed what Suzanne de Diétrich calls 'a magnificent alliance . . . inspired by the same faith and the same vision of the world',[43] and she went on to become the historian of the first 30 years of the Federation. Suzanne de Diétrich herself was perhaps the most outstanding of a long succession of women leaders in Geneva, including – besides those we have already met – Madeleine Barot of France, Sarah Chakko of India, Audrey Abrecht and Helen Morton of the United States, Margaret Wrong of Canada, Birgit Rodhe of Sweden, Inga-Brita Castren of Finland, Rena Karefa Smart (African–American) and Mercy Oduyoye of Ghana.

In the British Movement Tissington Tatlow would never have been able to achieve what he did without Zoë Fairfield, for many years his most able colleague, to the point where people said that she was the brain behind the Movement, with T simply the brilliant administrator who put her ideas into action. And T himself might never have joined the staff if he had not been 'discovered' by Ruth Rouse, when he was a 22-year-old engineering student at an Irish student conference in 1897.[44] We have seen the work of Winifred Sedgwick in the early years of the British SCM, and there were others, like Lilian Stevenson of the Slade School (sister of the early SVMU volunteer Sinclair Stevenson), who edited the comprehensive report of the 1900 conference on 'Students and the Missionary Problem' (including the postal addresses of the more than 1600 delegates) – a large red volume known to later ages as 'the red elephant'! For several years she was the leader of the whole women's side of the Movement, editing first *The Student Volunteer* and later *The Student Movement* (for six years), and went on to be one of the founders of 'the Aux' in 1912.[45] Lilian Stevenson was a student of art; so were Zoë Fairfield and Winifred Sedgwick, for the study of art and music was one of the ways by which women were first enabled to break into the citadels of higher education. And so too was Emily Scott, of the Dublin Metropolitan School of Art and the Royal College of Art, South Kensington, who became Mrs Tissington Tatlow, and who, though she features only three times in the index to T's massive history, served the Movement with distinction in her own right and was his constant support and enabler. Later names to be remembered include Amy Buller (1921),[46] whose adventures at Cumberland Lodge we shall shortly recall, Helen Macnicol (1929), who trained many women for missionary service at St Colm's in Edinburgh, and Mary Trevelyan (1932), who became the tough guardian spirit of Student Movement House.

Many other women who made a distinguished contribution to the Movement as staff secretaries went on to marry men whose names, in the climate of the times, became better known than those of their wives. But these were really SCM partnerships, like those of Helen Henderson (1930, Mrs Lesslie Newbigin), Ursula Dunn (1935, Mrs Oliver Tomkins), Isabel Megaw (1939, Mrs Donald Kennedy) and Anne Forrester (1950, Mrs Stanley Booth-Clibborn): equal partnerships in everything except fame – and salary.

It is true that the top executive positions in the Movement, as in the Church, were usually held by men; and also true that for much of our period the ordained ministry in most churches was not open to women, so that their subsequent career paths were effectively blocked so far as the churches were concerned. But within the life of the Movement, at both staff and student level, there was a remarkably free camaraderie. In the golden age of the 1950s feminist issues as such had scarcely begun to be discussed: there was more interest in what were usually called 'personal relations'. But Nansie Anderson (Blackie) was raising questions about the status of women in the Church. She was in a tradition already articulated in the Federation in 1933 by Henriette Bodaert of the Netherlands, who wrote, 'Woman cannot simply exist for the sake of men . . . There will be a woman's problem until women and men together have discovered that it takes two sexes to build the world which God means to build'.[47] In a special issue of *The Student World* (1936, pp. 208ff.) her husband, Visser 't Hooft, wrote, 'Man is no more a norm for humanity than woman is. Man and woman together constitute the human being . . . Humanity stagnates if man and woman do not develop in correlation'.[48]

Some churches, notably the Congregational churches in both the USA and Britain, had had women ministers since the 1920s, and the Revd Gwenyth Hubble of the Baptist Church was assistant general secretary of the British SCM from 1939 until after World War 2, going on to be principal of Carey Hall in Selly Oak and later to distinguished service in Canada. But it was the exigencies of the wartime situation in Hong Kong which provided the occasion, in 1944, for the first ordination of a woman to the priesthood in the Anglican communion, and with this historic event the SCM can claim a strong connection. She was the Revd Florence Li. The bishop who took the courageous, if obvious, step of ordaining her was R. O. Hall, who had served as theological college secretary of the British SCM; and the first people to whom he reported it were Tissington Tatlow and Billy Greer (then Bishop of Manchester).[49] All three of them were prepared to act as 'church ahead of the Church'.

The general, church-wide movement for women's ordination, however, did not really take off until the 1960s. When it did, many of those who became well known as leaders in the struggle – like Mary Lusk (Levison)[50] who was the chief wrestler in the struggle with the Church of Scotland, and Margaret Falconer (Webster), executive secretary from its foundation in 1979 of the Movement for the Ordination of Women (MOW) in the Church of England – had served either as leaders of student committees or as staff in the Movement.[51] Women who had enjoyed the free equality between the sexes which the SCM provided felt constrained and frustrated by the gender inequality they found in the churches, and as a result became convinced workers for the proper recognition of women in the Church, and especially for women's ordination.

Sexuality

From the beginnings of the SCM the relationships between men and women ('sexuality' was a term rarely used before the late 1950s) were considerably freer than in most Christian organizations, and Potter and Wieser suggest that the Federation may well have been the first international organization in which women and men related to each other on a basis of formal equality.[52] Men and women on the staff were good colleagues, and enjoyed working together. Many students met their future life-partners in the SCM, perhaps at Swanwick or at a regional or international conference, and it was not for nothing that the initials SCM were sometimes said to stand for 'Society for Courtship and Marriage'. Leila Giles (Bailey) of Australia, writing in 1955, notes interestingly that 'sometimes the fellowship of the SCM is somehow de-sexed', and records an opinion she had heard expressed that 'the very success with which men and women managed to work together unselfconsciously in their SCMs had given them a sort of sexless ideal of man-woman relationship'.[53] In the 1920s and 30s there was considerable reticence about sex, but Herbert Gray's book *Men, Women and God* was widely promoted, and it was customary to have study groups at Swanwick on what still tended to be called simply 'personal relationships'. Leslie Weatherhead's book *The Mastery of Sex* (SCM Press, 1931), went through many editions and dealt with homosexuality in a kindly pastoral but essentially negative way. In the 1950s the subject of sexuality was opened up in a pioneeringly theological book by D. Sherwin Bailey, *The Mystery of Love and Marriage: A Study in the Theology of Sexual Relation* (SCM Press, 1952); and in 1954 Owen and Jenefer Lidwell produced a study outline on marriage which was widely used. By the time the 1990s debate on homosexuality arose, the SCM no longer commanded the public attention it had once attracted. But the small and radical continuing SCM groups – certainly in the Federation, in Britain and Australia – were once again ahead of the churches in their openness to gay and lesbian Christians, in both membership and leadership roles.

The SCM as catalytic agent

The SCM, its staff and members, took an active part in initiating and resourcing many other Christian enterprises. We have already taken note of several of them, especially those connected with Joe Oldham – 'the Moot', *The Christian News-Letter*, the Christian Frontier Council, and the Institute of Christian Education. But there were many more, and we shall look briefly at some of them.

First of all comes the great family of international ecumenical relief organizations which began just after World War 1 when the WSCF, through Conrad Hoffmann, inaugurated European Student Relief, to be followed by International Student Service (later World University Service). The experience gained, the traditions established, and especially the person-nel inspired through this branch of the Federation's work, including that of operating from a base in Geneva, would influence all later comers to the field including Christian Aid and Oxfam. And the ecumenical co-operation involved would establish precedents which would flower in later years in the sharing of resources and expertise with Roman Catholic enterprises like Caritas Internationalis, Cafod, Concern and Trocaire, as well as with the evangelical-based Tearfund.

As part of the world's first internationally organized student move-ment, whose concerns for justice and peace went far beyond its Christian constituency, the SCM in Britain, as we have seen, encouraged and helped the formation there, in 1922, of the National Union of Students. Nor were the Movement's concerns limited to the university scene, for it took an active role in initiating the series of World Conferences of Christian Youth, beginning with Amsterdam in 1939 with its memorable theme '*Christus Victor*', which was to sustain Christian young people of many countries through six years of war; and resuming after the war with Oslo 1947, Kottayam (South India) 1952, and the largest of all, with 1800 delegates, at Lausanne in 1960. Amsterdam 1939 was a joint enterprise of the YMCA, YWCA, WSCF, WCC (then in process of formation) and the World Alliance for Promoting International Friendship through the Churches, and was organized by Denzil Patrick of the British SCM, while Oslo 1947 was organized by Francis House of the Federation staff. These conferences were notable in that they drew on a wider range of young people than the Federation's purely student events, and so avoided to some extent the stigma of being elitist.

Better known today, because it attracts large numbers of young people each year and is a strong force for Christian worship, witness and unity, is the Taizé Community, whose SCM roots are often forgotten. In April 1940 the French-speaking Swiss SCM held a retreat on 'the formation of personality', which led to a movement of students who wanted to pray for peace. The leader of the retreat was Roger Schutz, a young Swiss SCM leader and pastor in the Reformed Church, who later that year founded the Taizé Community, which today is perhaps the best-known centre of ecumenical worship in the world.[54] Many years later (2005) Brother Roger was to become the victim of an assassin as he led prayers in the community he had founded.

An interesting enterprise with strong SCM roots was – and is – Cumberland Lodge. Its virtual founder was Amy Buller, who in 1943 published a book, *Darkness Over Germany*, pointing out that Hitler had risen to power partly because the universities had not realized the dangers implicit in Nazism. Amy Buller, who had been on the SCM staff from 1921 to 1931, envisaged Cumberland Lodge as 'a college based on the Christian faith and Christian philosophy of life, where students could reside for a part of their vacation or at week-ends', and where there would be 'a realisation of a basic Christian philosophy in international as well as national affairs, and in the realm of individual relationships'.[55] Amy Buller and her fellow prime movers, Tissington Tatlow and the Earl of Halifax, had connections in high places, and in August 1947 King George VI granted Cumberland Lodge in Windsor Great Park as a home for 'St Katharine's Foundation'. 'That's the place', said the King, 'for Miss Buller's college.'[56] Amy Buller had been one of the pioneers of the SCM conferences at Swanwick, and dreamed of making Cumberland Lodge 'a permanent Swanwick'.[57] And under its first principal, Sir Walter Moberly, that is virtually what it became; and many SCM people and events – especially in connection with the nature of the university, and with postwar reconciliation with Germany – were welcomed within its walls. Cumberland Lodge still continues in the Buller/SCM tradition.

In 1949 Reinold von Thadden, who in 1938 as chairman of the German SCM had taken a public stand against Hitler's anti-Semitism, set up the first *Kirchentag*, bringing together in Berlin 2000 laypeople, most of them young, drawn from both parts of a divided country. The *Kirchentag*, held every other year, has continued to be an event of great significance, not just for Germany but for the whole *oikoumene*. In June 2003, for example, the *Kirchentag*, meeting in a Berlin now reunited, and for the first time including Roman Catholics – who normally held their own *Katholikentag* – brought together more than 200,000 laypeople for five days, with the blessing of both traditions.[58] Years earlier von Thadden had told Visser 't Hooft, who had shared with him in *Kirchentag* planning, that 'he wanted to bring into the life of every congregation what he had learned and received in the SCM, the WSCF and the WCC about a radical, world-transforming Christianity with an ecumenical perspective'.[59]

Another area in which the SCM did pioneering work, which it was able later to hand over to others, was the field of bioethics and medical ethics.[60] In the early 1960s the British Movement commissioned Andrew Mepham to investigate the needs of medical students, especially with regard to the ethical issues they were liable to meet in their professional life. His survey pointed out that concern for diseased tissue distracted students from the real care of patients, and recommended an 'educational service' to deal with such issues. In response the SCM commissioned one of its staff, Edward Shotter, to implement these ideas in the London medical schools, and as a result the London Medical Group (LMG) came into existence in 1963, with Shotter as director. Leading moral theologians were soon taking part in its debates, like Bishops Mortimer of Exeter and Ian Ramsey of Durham, Dr Jack Dominian from the Roman Catholic Church and Archbishop Anthony Bloom of the Orthodox Church, as well as Dr Immanuel Jakobovits, British Chief Rabbi and author of *Jewish Medical Ethics*. The LMG developed rapidly, and by 1975 had become independent of the SCM.

Melbourne in Australia became the site of a significant and successful early experiment in ecumenical theological education when in 1969 the United Faculty of Theology (UFT) was born, including within its membership Presbyterians, Methodists and Congregationalists (already at that date negotiating for union), Anglicans and, from 1972, the Jesuits.[61] The initiative came from a group of theological teachers who had nearly all been leaders in the SCM in Australia or Britain, including the Methodists Colin Williams and Eric Osborn, the Presbyterians George Yule and Davis McCaughey and, for the Anglicans, Archbishop Frank Woods, who had been a friend of McCaughey's from student days in the Cambridge SCM. The entry of the Jesuits into this scene is an interesting ecumenical story. In 1971 they were anxious to move out of their traditional seminary buildings in Sydney into a situation of urban poverty, and bought a run-down terrace of houses in the Melbourne inner suburb of Carlton (which has since become much gentrified). They still had to find accommodation for their library, and this was offered to Fr Bill Dalton, founding rector of the Jesuit Theological College, by Ormond College, where McCaughey was Master. The two libraries were amalgamated, so becoming the finest theological library in Australia, and the Jesuits became part of the UFT. From the first it was a community of friends rather than a mere institutional faculty. One of the UFT's most intriguing features is that it does not have a constitution. One was indeed drawn up in the 1970s, but finally it was decided not to have a constitution at all, since it would have required the surmounting of possibly insurmountable ecclesiastical hurdles. It was a courageous and risky decision, but it worked, and 35 years later it still works remarkably well; in the words of Fr Tony Macken SJ, 'the fragility and vulnerability of the UFT is its glory'. The fruit of that fragility has been several hundred ordained priests and ministers from the Roman Catholic, Anglican, and Uniting (Reformed and Methodist) traditions who have studied together, worshipped together, argued together and become friends for life, committed to the mission and unity of the Church.

There were other enterprises with independent origins in which former SCM members and staff gave outstanding service, and which recruited many of their new members from among the ranks of the SCM. One can think, for example, of the Iona Community in Scotland, and of the work there of Ralph Morton, Penry Jones, David Lyon, Walter Fyfe, Tom Colvin and Kathy Galloway – most of them former SCM secretaries. Another enterprise, originally envisioned as a follow-up to the inauguration of the WCC, is Scottish Churches' House in Dunblane,[62] set up in 1960 and helped on its way by such SCM veterans as Ian Fraser (its first warden), Archie Craig, Robert Mackie, Isobel Forrester and Patrick Rodger. In Ireland, Ray Davey, first Presbyterian chaplain at Queen's University Belfast and founder and first leader of the Corrymeela Community which has done so much for reconciliation between Protestants and Catholics, was a member of the Queen's University SCM branch in the 1930s. His successor John Morrow began his ecumenical journey through joining the SCM, and writes:

I thank God for the SCM that refused to cosset me from . . . upsetting currents of thought but took up the challenge to wrestle with the issues in order to fashion a faith that had integrity. It was a society that welcomed honest doubt and was patiently open to work through the vexed questions of our time. It did not give me easy answers but it prepared me for the real world and launched me on a journey that continues to this day. [63]

These are just a few examples among many which could have been chosen. For in countries all over the world there are comparable ecumenical enterprises which would never have started without the catalytic influence of people who had experienced the value, and the excitement, of 'unity-towards-mission' in the SCM, and were eager to put it into practice in the wider world beyond the university.

So the SCM tradition is alive and well in the world today. But we should not forget that the SCM itself is also very much alive, even if, in comparison to its past, it is living in somewhat reduced circumstances. And the day could still come when the mother might become once again, in Miltonic phrase, 'fairest of her daughters'.

11

'Church ahead of the Church'

The SCM tradition

The SCM was a spontaneous movement of young people – students – with student leadership, resourced but not controlled by a relatively small number of low-paid graduate staff, only a handful of whom were aged over 30. From the beginning the fact that it was a voluntary organization was vital: it was not imposed on the students by church, academic or state authority, nor was it even the product of an official ecumenical agency like the WCC or a national council of churches. And so it had a measure of liberty, which in the main (though, as we have seen, not always) it used with understanding and sensitivity. Beginning in the 1890s from a non-denominational position (which continued in the IVF after the two parts of the student movement separated) it developed into a consciously *interchurch* community. Never claiming to be a church, but increasingly encouraging its members to be faithful, critical, practising members of their own churches, it was a truly ecumenical community, whose members were committed to Christ, to God's reign, to their own churches, and also to each other and to the Movement itself. It had a strong and definite aim; it looked towards the future fulfilment of God's purpose for the world. That future included both the living of the life 'in Christ' – individually and corporately – and the proclamation of God's reign. Towards that end it advocated, and in a limited yet real way anticipated, the unity of all Christians. It was a dynamic, united community, living from the Word and, albeit in a way constrained by the limitations of the churches, from the sacraments. And it was committed to global mission in the secular world, and particularly to mission in its own cultural environment, the university.

The Movement, often to the consternation of its detractors, encouraged its members to question everything, to take nothing simply on authority. One of its favourite biblical phrases, prominent in the 1951 Declaratory Statement of the British Movement, was St Paul's *logike latreia* (Romans 12.2), which the Authorized Version translates as 'your reasonable service', the Revised English Bible as 'the worship offered by mind and heart', and the New Jerusalem Bible (wonderfully) as 'the kind of worship for you, as sensible people'. The pursuit of truth, the maintenance of academic integrity, 'the service of the mind', was fundamental to the SCM: not second-hand truth, but truth given after long wrestling, like Jacob's wrestling with God. In Gerard Manley Hopkins' words, often quoted in study groups in the golden age,

> O the mind, mind has mountains;
>   Cliffs of fall
> Frightful, sheer, no-man-fathomed.
>   Hold them cheap
> May who ne'er hung there.[1]

It was a privilege, and a demanding one, to be a member of such a dynamic, lively, diverse community of young men and women. The WCC, because of its official, representative character and its top-down structure has never been able to provide exactly that type of community: it is, after all, a council rather than a movement, and that limits its freedom. But neither has any single church – Roman Catholic, Orthodox, Anglican or Protestant – nor any council of churches. Not even united churches – like the Church of North India, to whose formation the SCM had made a notable contribution, and which brought together into one eucharistic fellowship the widest ever spectrum of traditions – could provide such a *koinonia*. The SCM represented, in a single global community, a far broader range of traditions than even that. From the beginning it included members and leaders drawn from virtually all the churches stemming directly from the Reformation – Lutheran, Anglican, Reformed (Presbyterian and Congregationalist), Moravians and Quakers – as well as from the Baptist and Anabaptist churches, whose origins went back earlier than the Reformation, and from the Methodist Church with its eighteenth-century roots. It also, from pre-World War 1 times, included in its membership students from the Orthodox churches, and since the 1960s, to a limited extent, Roman Catholics. And usually its membership was open to students of any faith, or of none, who wanted to explore the Christian faith and share in the life of a Christian community. For the SCM, as 'church ahead of the Church', had a freedom which enabled it to rush in where churches feared to tread.

Martin Conway, in the stormy days of 1971, drew up a list, nostalgic but accurate, of the marks of what the SCM tradition has always sought to do:

- to have, as its central thrust, the purpose of testing out the truth of Jesus Christ and of his calling;
- therefore to give much attention to careful Bible study;
- therefore too to know the community of Christians called to mission-in-unity, patiently being open to all religious heritages and all cultural

backgrounds in order to discover and communicate the catholic and ecumenical identity of Christ;

- to insist on the lay leadership of students and teachers, with chaplains and other ecclesiastics at best serving and provoking others to play a larger part;
- to insist on the appropriate intellectual calibre for Christian discipleship in higher education;
- to be concerned for adventurous thinking and acting, never content with the status quo but always experimenting beyond; (no wonder it has thrown off so many offshoots!);
- yet to cultivate, not least by student leadership, a self-criticism, indeed a sense of humour, that stops anyone taking himself too seriously.[2]

That is a statement which reflects a real *coherence* (a favourite term of Conway's)[3] far different from the 'diffuseness' of which Steve Bruce accused the SCM. And it is a tradition in which students from the widest variety of churches can feel at home, while still taking seriously and lovingly their own tradition. It is a community which can be highly critical of all the churches – the visible manifestations of the Body of Christ – while still loving the Church itself, and taking pride in being part of it.

The two traditions, WSCF and IFES: rivals or partners?

The global movement for unity-towards-mission, so strongly launched at Edinburgh in 1910, has ever since then been balanced, and often opposed, by another movement, equally well-intentioned, which tends to reject official ecumenism in favour of a strictly limited 'spiritual ecumenism', drawing people together, indeed, from different Christian churches, but drawing them into a fellowship which makes demands beyond those of the creeds of the undivided Church – and even the confessions of the Reformation – in its limited definition of certain controversial points of Christian faith and practice. In the history of the SCM this division took the form of separation between the SCM and the IVF, a division which still continues and has even grown more acute as it has acquired global dimensions. Efforts have been made (mainly stemming, it must be said, from the ecumenical side) to overcome this division, but without much success, though here and there the conversation continues. The separation has now exploded far beyond the student context and has greatly weakened the Church's witness. The division is evident at every level of church life, so that the conversation between the two protagonists – ecumenicals and evangelicals, to continue using the traditional yet misleading labels – has become one of the most difficult ecumenical encounters facing the Church. But it is also one of the most important, perhaps the most important of all. It is beyond the scope of this book to deal in detail with that current global encounter,[4] but we may simply note three hopeful signs: the continued reliance on scripture affirmed by the WSCF and the WCC; the increasing commitment to issues of justice, peace and the integrity of creation shown by those united in the fellowship of the 1974 Lausanne Covenant;[5] and the way in which that tradition has moved so effectively into the area of advanced biblical studies, as well as into the fields of history, literature, languages, economics, politics, philosophy and the fine arts, so long regarded as forbidden territory.[6] A glance at the scope of a current Inter-Varsity Press (IVP) publications list makes this clear. The SCM tradition can no longer claim a monopoly in these areas, thank God! And radical Christians, in the political sense, are to be found on both sides of the divide, for it has also become obvious – even to the most blinkered ecumenical! – that political and social radicalism is no monopoly of the ecumenical wing of the Church. Tearfund and Christian Aid were close neighbours and allies in the massive 'Make Poverty History' march which brought together more than 200,000 people in Edinburgh on 2 July 2005. And the political imperialism of the American moral majority has its evangelical opponents who are just as convinced, committed and effective as their ecumenical counterparts.

It is time for the ecumenical–evangelical encounter to become, as indeed it already has in many places, a conversation instead of a stand-off. I long for this conversation, in which I have over the years been engaged in India, Ireland and Australia,[7] to develop and flourish. I can testify to the fact that within the fellowship of the Church, and especially in the context of mission, a true *koinonia* of evangelical and ecumenical can exist. In my missionary experience in India, for example – and I know that there are numerous other such instances – there was a strong representation of both former SCM and IVF members. Of course we differed in many of our views; but we were friends and colleagues, servants of the same Lord, working in the same cause, and often members of the same church – in this case, after 1970, the Church of North India. This difference can be an enrichment to the Church rather than a source of division. Both sides spring from the same roots in the nineteenth-century missionary movement; and the best basis for recovering the unity of that tradition is biblical hermeneutics – a friendly rivalry in scholarly integrity. The two traditions need each other.

It is an irony of history that Lesslie Newbigin, whose name has occurred so often in this story, was at first regarded by evangelicals as a rather dangerous 'liberal ecumenical'. Now, half a century later, he enjoys an almost heroic reputation among evangelicals: not that he ever consciously changed direction, except perhaps in his later and somewhat self-contradictory repudiation of the Enlightenment, but rather that he always persisted in setting the Bible, the Church and the mission of the Church at the centre of his theology. He and many others, like his friend Donald Kennedy of the Church of North India,[8] believed that it is possible to affirm a common ground where evangelicals on the one hand and ecumenicals or 'conciliars' on the other (I prefer those terms to 'liberals' in this context) can meet in a common affirmation of Bible, Church and mission.

The near collapse of the SCM in the 1970s was largely due, as we have seen, not to bad exegesis but to the rejection of exegesis. Today the study of the Bible is once again basic to the life of the WSCF and its affiliated Movements. The SCM has still some way to go before it can recover its former confident access to the world of biblical and theological academic scholarship. But there are signs that it is on the way. The SCM tradition has never ceased to take a leading part in the biblical and theological enterprise, and the Movement itself is realizing that if its voice is to be heard in dialogue it must once again be a voice informed by Bible study of integrity and depth. Differences of interpretation can be tolerated within the one fellowship when people respect not only each other's commitment to Christ, but also the integrity of each other's scholarship.

Meanwhile, is it impossible for followers of the two traditions to endeavour, so far as conscience permits, not only to study the Bible together, but also to worship together? Could not the doors which were shut in London and Edinburgh in the early 1950s be opened, not just at the student level but at the global level? Bible study and worship go together, and it was a true instinct which led the SCM so early to produce those pioneering examples of ecumenical worship *Cantate Domino* and *Venite Adoremus*. For worship is 'realised eschatology'.[9] When we worship together a door is opened in heaven (Revelation 4.1), and beyond our theological divisions we experience the unity to which we are called in Christ. The unity towards which we are called is *not* unity for its own sake, but unity-towards-*mission* – 'that the world may believe'. Edinburgh 1910, so challenging and fruitful in so many ways, nevertheless marked the beginning of the tragic division of an originally shared vision. Might not the 2010 centenary of that great conference mark the beginning of a renewed and once more shared vision?[10] Evangelicals and ecumenicals need each other. God needs them both. And so does the world.

Church ahead of the Church?

The phrase 'church ahead of the Church' has occurred frequently in this story of the SCM. It is an image which goes back at least to Francis

P. Miller, Visser 't Hooft's American friend and colleague from 1921, of whom he wrote that 'the task of the Federation was in his view to pioneer for the Church universal'.[11] In similar vein J. H. Oldham later described his 'Moot' – which he saw as a sort of senior SCM – by saying that its 'central task was to draw together the best Christian minds in a new adventure of thought . . . What mattered was the Church within the Church . . . the essence of the experiment consisted in asking the institutional churches to give the living church a free field.'[12] And Visser 't Hooft himself, writing of his period as general secretary of the WCC, said, 'The WSCF remained the place where one could get a glimpse of the shape of things to come'.[13] In 1970 Charles West of Princeton, disturbed by the Federation's move away from the Church and theology, reminded it, as we have seen, of how for years it had 'functioned as the Church ahead of the Church, as the seed-bed for the theological and social insights which later became the garden which fed the ecumenical movement'. So too Martin Conway, who wrote, 'The tradition of the SCM at its best has always been . . . to pioneer in obedience for the Church as a whole'.[14]

At the beginning of the Movement, groups of students – committed personally to Christ, obedient to his great commission to evangelize the world, well informed, trained, and ready even for martyrdom – challenged their churches to send them overseas as missionaries. Often the churches were slow to respond, but the students kept up the pressure until the churches, or the missionary societies, were shamed into action. The students were barrier-breakers.

There were other barriers. The Student Volunteer Movement in America was an early breaker of the gender barrier when in 1883 Grace Wilder was ready to accept a leadership role side by side with her brother Robert. The racial barrier was surmounted early in the Movement's history, and it was Japanese students, women and men together, who in 1888 challenged their white contemporaries in America to 'make Jesus King'. Later came barriers where the SCM acted as an *agent provocateur*, eventually followed, often reluctantly, by the churches. The barrier between evangelicals and Anglo-Catholics in England was breached before Edinburgh 1910 by Oldham and Tatlow, and by 1911 Mott had brought the Orthodox churches into the fellowship. And so it went on. The barriers which separated the somewhat patrician students of the day from the industrial workers who created their affluence were assailed, if not destroyed. Issues of colonialism and of world peace were addressed. There were, of course, thinkers and writers in the churches who were well ahead of the SCM: but it was the SCM, through its nature as both a movement and a community, which gradually became strong enough to influence the churches and persuade them to act. The SCM was a place where students from many different Christian traditions, or from none, could find themselves welcomed into a community of young people seeking to 'understand the Christian faith and live the Christian life', and so demonstrating to the churches a working model of what the Church, in the purpose of God, can really be.

The SCM did not claim to be a church. Nor, of course, did it claim to be *the* Church. Yet it saw itself as being a part, an active limb, of the Church, and therefore, in today's terminology, 'being Church'. It did not impose doctrinal statements stricter than those of the churches, but rather pointed students to where the churches' statements were to be found, and encouraged them to be faithful members of their own churches, to understand and learn from the traditions of other churches, and to work for the day when all Christians would be 'one, that the world may believe', and beyond that for the day when, 'they will not hurt or destroy on all my holy mountain; for the earth will be full of the knowledge of the LORD as the waters cover the sea' (Isaiah 11.9, NRSV).

Today, once again, there are encouraging signs of life in the SCM, both at the level of the Federation and of the many different national Movements. Yet lovers of the SCM tradition cannot claim that it alone has the monopoly of being 'church ahead of the Church'. And there are those who believe that the era of organized movements, with regular local meetings, summer conferences, and travelling staff, has had its day, and can be effectively replaced by a well-planned internet programme linked to occasional (perhaps annual) spectacular events. Or one can think of mammoth meetings like the German *Kirchentag*; or the Taizé Community in France with its thousands of young people converging every summer; or Greenbelt in England with its great annual summer festival at Cheltenham racecourse; or the Corrymeela Summerfest every second year in Ireland; or NCYC (National Christian Youth Convention) in Australia – a gathering which is not just for university students, but which, recognizing that a high proportion of young people today go on to some form of higher education, has serious but more general programmes on Bible study and social justice issues, using many of the SCM tradition's methods. These are all large events which include a wide range of ages, though it is mainly young people whom they attract. There is no doubt that it is frequently the big event, the music, the glamour, the emotional pressure, the charismatic yet often vague spirituality which is the attraction, rather than that steady 'service of the mind', that 'seeking and serving the truth' which are hallmarks of the SCM tradition. Yet in an age when there are more university students than ever before it is important that they should be actively challenged to engage with the Bible and the Christian tradition at an intellectual level which matches their secular study. The mission to the university needs once more to be carried out *in unity* – ecumenically.

The components for such united 'mission in Christ's way' are all there – the churches, the chaplains, the WSCF, the IFES, the university, the students. Those components need to be brought together 'so that the world may believe' – the world in all its beauty and all its violence and suffering. That was Jesus' prayer. And with the prayer he gave the Spirit – to make the impossible possible.

For more than a century the SCM tradition has been one of the great currents in the life of the Christian Church – sometimes flowing strongly, sometimes seeming to meander aimlessly, sometimes nearly drying up. That after all has been the pattern of the Church's own life. But it is not enough to say, 'The SCM was a great tradition, which started as a student and missionary movement, and ended up crystallized into the shape of the WCC and a group of united churches'. For the original task of evangelism is still unfinished. Millions of students today are *not* being helped to face the challenge of a gospel which makes demands on their intellect as great as and greater than those of their secular studies.

The SCM tradition is a great tradition. There are certain things which it takes with the utmost seriousness. It takes Jesus seriously. It takes the Bible seriously; and the Church; and worship, including the sacraments and prayer. It takes the truth seriously, not dodging any question, and seeking the best standards of academic integrity. It takes evil seriously, but also the goodness of the world, of creation. It takes mission seriously, for Christians owe the message of God's salvation in Jesus Christ – the gospel which everyone has a right to hear – to every person and every people.[15] It takes seriously the pursuit of justice, peace and the integrity of creation, directed towards the universal and liberating Reign of God. It takes Christian unity seriously, for without unity, mission is hampered.

But it refuses to take itself too seriously, knowing that it must be eccentric, never putting itself, or even a favoured church, at the centre; for the centre is Christ, who leads humankind – in joy – to the heart of the triune God.

* * * * * *

At the end of the second book of Bunyan's *Pilgrim's Progress*, the pilgrim's wife Christiana, who, with her children, has followed her husband on the journey from the City of Destruction, comes at last to the river of death. She crosses the river, and enters in at the beautiful gate of the Celestial City. And Bunyan adds,

As for Christiana's children, the four boys that Christiana brought with their wives and children, I did not stay where I was till they were gone over. Also since I came away, I heard one say that they were yet alive, and so would be for the increase of the Church in that place where they were for a time.

The SCM, like Christian and Christiana, has had a strenuous, exhilarating, and difficult pilgrimage. Perhaps it has come to the end of the road. I do not believe that it has. New challenges and adventures lie ahead. And its children – its many children – are alive 'for the increase of the Church' in this place, at this time.

Notes

1 Students evangelizing the world (*c.* 1890–1920)

1 The word 'Movement' is spelt with a capital M when it refers to the body officially known as the Student Christian Movement.

2 Originally 'World's' not 'World'. The main archival sources for the WSCF are at the WSCF Inter-Regional Office, Geneva, Switzerland, and the Yale Divinity School Library, New Haven, CT, USA.

3 The ecumenical leader and pioneer of the Faith and Order Movement, Bishop Charles H. Brent, described it as 'the greatest Movement of spirit of God in modern times'. Quoted in Clarence P. Shedd, *Two Centuries of Student Christian Movements: Their Origin and Intercollegiate Life* (New York, Association Press, 1934), p. 92.

4 Kenneth Scott Latourette, *A History of the Expansion of Christianity* (London, Eyre & Spottiswoode, 1938–45), vol. iv, p. 74.

5 Shedd, *Two Centuries*, pp. 1–31.

6 Ruth Rouse, *The World's Student Christian Federation: A History of the First Thirty Years* (London, SCM Press, 1948), p. 8.

7 Latourette, *History*, vol. iv, p. 79.

8 Shedd, *Two Centuries*, p. 100.

9 Tissington Tatlow, *The Story of the Student Christian Movement of Great Britain and Ireland* (London, SCM Press, 1933), p. 5.

10 For a good description of Drummond's influence on the beginnings of the SCM see *David Cairns: An Autobiography* (London, SCM Press, 1950), pp. 112–16. Cairns comments that neither Moody nor Drummond was officially related to the British College Christian Union (which became the SCM), 'but unquestionably they gave the main spiritual impulse which, with others, was causative in these organisations'.

11 So Rouse, *WSCF*, p. 32.

12 See George Adam Smith, *The Life of Henry Drummond* (London, Hodder & Stoughton, 1899), p. 297.

13 See the chapter 'Evolution and Revelation' in Smith, *Life*, pp. 227–44.

14 For example, 'The power to set the heart right, to renew the spring of action, comes from Christ. The sense of the infinite worth of the single soul, and the recoverableness of a man at his worst, are the gifts of Christ. The freedom from guilt, the forgiveness of sins, come from Christ's cross; the hope of immortality springs from Christ's grave.' Quoted in Smith, *Life*, pp. 7–8.

15 Smith, *Life*, p. 228.

16 Compare his enthusiasm for the then recently founded Boys' Brigade (BB) and its work among underprivileged boys. Smith, *Life*, pp. 440–61.

17 A similar medallion, which formerly hung in Tatlow's office, is now displayed in Scottish Churches' House, Dunblane.

18 Suzanne de Diétrich, *WSCF: 50 Years of History, 1895–1945* (English edn, Geneva, WSCF, 1993), p. 17.

19 Shedd, *Two Centuries*, p. 260.

20 Latourette, *History*, vol. iv, p. 96.

21 Philip Potter and Thomas Wieser, *Seeking and Serving the Truth* (Geneva, WCC, 1997), pp. 6–7.

22 See H. W. Oldham, *The Student Christian Movement of Great Britain and Ireland: Its Origin, Development, and Present Position* (London, BCCU, 1899), chapter 8; David L. Edwards, *Movement into Tomorrow* (London, SCM Press, 1960), pp. 12–15.

23 Tatlow, *Story*, pp. 20–21.

24 Margaret Stevenson, *Do you Remember Sinclair Stevenson?* (Oxford, Blackwell, 1931), pp. 19–20. There were other claimants, including Howard Taylor, as there appears to have been more than one enrolment book! Tatlow, *Story*, p. 21.

25 Tatlow, *Story*, p. 39.

26 The series of annual conferences held at Keswick in the English Lake District begun in the 1870s has a strong missionary tradition, and brings together evangelical speakers and supporters from many different churches under the motto 'All One in Christ Jesus'.

27 See C. Howard Hopkins, *John R. Mott: A Biography* (Grand Rapids, MI, Eerdmans, 1979).

28 De Diétrich, *WSCF*, p. 23.

29 Quoted in de Diétrich, *WSCF*, p. 25, from John R. Mott, *The World's Student Christian Federation: Origin, Achievements, Forecast* (London, SCM Press, 1958).

30 A large collection of literature relating to the WSCF and many different national Movements is held at the Yale University Library.

31 For a good account of the relationship between the YMCA, YWCA and the SCM/WSCF, see Ruth Rouse's section on 'the World Christian Lay Movements' in Ruth Rouse and Stephen C. Neill (eds), *A History of the Ecumenical Movement*, vol. I, 1517–1948 (Geneva, WCC, 1954 and 2004), pp. 599–612.

32 Tatlow, *Story*, pp. 90–1.

33 Tatlow, *Story*, pp. 94–111.

34 John Bowden, 'SCM Press: A Short History', p. 1, in Robert S. Anderson (ed.), *A Step Out of Line: Essays on the Life of the Student Christian Movement* (unpublished typescript, 1982).

35 Bowden, 'SCM Press', p. 1.

36 Robert Boyd (1880–1957), 'While I Remember' (unpublished typescript in possession of the author), p. 26.

37 Boyd, 'While I Remember', p. 27. John G. Paton was the father of Frank Paton, mentioned below.

38 Johannes Heyer, *Memoir* (unpublished typescript in possession of the author).

39 Frank Paton, *The Message of the Student Christian Movement* (Melbourne, SCM, c. 1910), p. 11.

40 Paton, *Message*, p. 13. The language of the period is non-inclusive, yet from the first the SCM included women as well as men.

41 For this section see Tatlow, *Story*, pp. 192–210.

42 Latourette, *History*, vol. iv, p. 99.

43 For J. H. Oldham see Keith Clements, *Faith on the Frontier: A Life of J. H. Oldham* (Edinburgh, T. & T. Clark, 1999); Andrew Morton, 'J. H. Oldham' in Nansie Blackie (ed.), *A Time for Trumpets: Scottish Church Movers and Shakers of the Twentieth Century* (Edinburgh, St Andrew Press, 2005), pp. 3–16.

44 So Latourette, quoted in Rouse and Neill, *History*, vol. I, p. 362.

45 W. Richey Hogg, *Ecumenical Foundations: A History of the International Missionary Council and its Nineteenth-Century Foundations* (New York, Harper, 1952), quoted in a review by Leila Giles, *Student World*, 53/2, p. 207.

46 Charles McLaren in M. Holmes and D. Garnsey (eds), *Other Men Laboured: Fifty Years with the Student Christian Movement in Australia, 1896–1946* (Melbourne, SCM, 1946), p. 5.

47 Oliver Barclay and Robert Horn, *From Cambridge to the World: 125 Years of Student Witness* (Leicester, IVP, 2002); Geraint Fielder, *Lord of the Years: 60 Years of Student Witness, 1928–88* (Leicester, IVP, 1988).

48 The story is told in some detail in Barclay and Horn, *From Cambridge to the World*, pp. 71–8.

49 SCM Archives, Special Collections, Information Services, University of Birmingham, Edgbaston, Section B, annual report 1910.

50 Barclay and Horn, *From Cambridge to the World*, p. 77.

51 Nicolas Zernov in Rouse and Neill (eds), *History*, vol. I, pp. 650–1. A recent account of Nicolay's advocacy of Orthodox membership in the Federation is given by Ian Parsons, *Baron Paul Nicolay: His Legacy to Russia and the World* (unpublished paper, Melbourne, 2005).

52 Rouse, *WSCF*, p. 154.

53 SCM Archives, Section B, annual report 1910.

54 Rouse and Neill, *History*, vol. I, p. 331.

55 Tatlow, *Story*, p. 337.

56 Tatlow, *Story*, p. 236.

57 Tatlow, *Story*, p. 596.

58 Rouse, *WSCF*, p. 174.

59 Rouse, *WSCF*, pp. 126, 129.

60 See B. R. Keith, *The Lives of Frank Rolland* (Melbourne, Rigby, 1977).

61 See John Mackenzie, *Rev F. H. L. Paton, MA, BD: An Apostle of Love* (Melbourne, Presbyterian Church, Collins Street, 1938).

62 Rouse, *WSCF*, p. 192.

63 Rouse, *WSCF*, p. 205.

64 De Diétrich, *WSCF*, p. 42.

65 Tatlow, *Story*, p. 586.

66 Ruth Rouse, *Rebuilding Europe: The Student Chapter in Post-War Reconstruction* (London, SCM, 1925). Most of the information in the following section comes from this source.

67 Rouse, *Rebuilding*, p. 12.

68 De Diétrich, *WSCF*, p. 43.
69 Rouse, *Rebuilding*, p. 86.
70 Rouse, *Rebuilding*, p. 150.
71 Rouse, *Rebuilding*, p. 165.
72 Rouse, *Rebuilding*, p. 168.
73 See Parsons, *Baron Paul Nicolay*, pp. 4–5.
74 Rouse, *WSCF*.
75 Quoted by Robert Mackie in Rouse, *WSCF*, p. 20.
76 Two later volumes, with different editors, have brought the history up to 2004.
77 Tatlow, *Story*, p. 687.
78 Tatlow, *Story*, p. 691.
79 Eric Fenn, *Learning Wisdom: Fifty Years of the SCM* (London, SCM Press, 1939), p. 59.
80 Tatlow, *Story*, pp. 696–7.
81 Tatlow, *Story*, p. 545.
82 For this section see Tatlow, *Story*, pp. 613–31.
83 Fenn, *Learning Wisdom*, p. 73, emphasis added.

2 'Poisoning the student mind'? (*c.* 1920–35)

1 Eric Fenn, *Learning Wisdom: Fifty Years of the SCM* (London, SCM Press, 1939), p. 25.
2 Oliver Barclay and Robert Horn, *From Cambridge to the World: 125 Years of Student Witness* (Leicester, IVP, 2002), p. 53.
3 J. Davis McCaughey, *Christian Obedience in the University: Studies in the Life of the SCM of Great Britain and Ireland, 1930–1950* (London, SCM Press, 1958), p. 27.
4 Geraint Fielder, *Lord of the Years: 60 Years of Student Witness, 1928–88* (Leicester, IVP, 1988), p. 67.
5 David L. Edwards, *Movement into Tomorrow* (London, SCM Press, 1960), p. 24.
6 Quoted in Edwards, *Movement*, p. 25, from F. Donald Coggan (ed.), *Christ and the Colleges: A History of the Inter-Varsity Fellowship of Evangelical Unions* (London, IVF, 1934), p. 17. See also Barclay and Horn, *From Cambridge to the World*, pp. 91–2.
7 Edwards, *Movement*, p. 25.
8 Quoted in Edwards, *Movement*, pp. 26–7. See also Douglas Johnson (ed.), *A Brief History of the International Fellowship of Evangelical Students* (Lausanne, 1964), p. 174.
9 Edwards, *Movement*, pp. 26–7.
10 Basil Meeking and John Stott (eds), *The Evangelical–Roman Catholic Dialogue on Mission, 1977–1984* (Grand Rapids, MI, Eerdmans/Exeter, Paternoster, 1986).
11 Adrian Hastings, *Oliver Tomkins: The Ecumenical Enterprise, 1908–92* (London, SPCK, 2001), pp. 18, 24. Hastings' book on Tomkins is an excellent source for tracing the development of 'the SCM tradition' in the British SCM, the Federation, and the WCC – especially Faith and Order – from the late 1920s until Tomkins' death in 1992.

12 Lesslie Newbigin, *Unfinished Agenda: An Autobiography* (Geneva, WCC, 1985), pp. 9–10.

13 Newbigin, *Unfinished Agenda*, p. 14.

14 I owe this reference to Martin Conway, 'The Fateful 60s' in Robert S. Anderson (ed.), *A Step Out of Line: Essays on the Life of the Student Christian Movement* (unpublished typescript, 1982).

15 I myself lived and worked from 1948 to 1950 in the New College Settlement in the Pleasance, Edinburgh. The settlement model still survived at that point, though it was under challenge.

16 Tissington Tatlow, *The Story of the Student Christian Movement of Great Britain and Ireland* (London, SCM Press, 1933), pp. 339–40.

17 I owe this reference to Martin Conway, 'A Tradition for Tomorrow: The WSCF 100 Years On' (unpublished paper, 1995), p. 7.

18 Tatlow, *Story*, p. 666.

19 For example Rudolf Otto, *Christianity and the Indian Religion of Grace* (Madras, CLS, 1929); J. N. Farquhar, *The Crown of Hinduism* (London, Oxford University Press, 1913).

20 Charles McLaren in M. Holmes and D. Garnsey (eds), *Other Men Laboured: Fifty Years with the Student Christian Movement in Australia, 1896–1946* (Melbourne, SCM, 1946), pp. 14, 21.

21 The material in this section is largely taken from an SCM booklet I edited in 1952 entitled *Theological College Department: Handbook for Representatives in Theological Colleges*.

22 Tatlow, *Story*, pp. 464–5. For a good discussion of the terminology of 'undenominational', 'interdenominational' etc, see Tatlow in Ruth Rouse and Stephen C. Neill (eds), *A History of the Ecumenical Movement*, vol. 1 (Geneva, WCC, 1954 and 2004), pp. 342–3.

23 John S. Peart-Binns, *Ambrose Reeves: A Biography* (London, Gollancz, 1973), pp. 33–5.

24 Tatlow, *Story*, pp. 779–86. See also Nicolas and Militza Zernov, *The History of the Fellowship* (1979) at www.sobornost.org/fellowship_history/html

25 Tatlow, *Story*, p. 748.

26 For Robert Mackie see Nansie Blackie, *In Love and in Laughter: A Portrait of Robert Mackie* (Edinburgh, St Andrew Press, 1995); also Nansie Blackie (ed.), *A Time for Trumpets: Scottish Church Movers and Shakers of the Twentieth Century* (Edinburgh, St Andrew Press, 2005), pp. 53–64.

27 Tatlow, *Story*, p. 674.

28 Robert Mackie, *Tissington Tatlow*, Memorial Service address, SCM, 1957.

29 Fenn, *Learning Wisdom*, pp. 91–2.

30 Charles C. West, 'My Pilgrimage in Mission', in *International Bulletin of Missionary Research*, Oct 2005, pp. 194–8.

3 Through depression, holocaust and war (*c*. 1935–45)

1 In what follows I am mainly dependent on Marjorie Reeves (ed.), *Christian Thinking and Social Order: Conviction Politics from the 1930s to the Present Day* (London, Cassell, 1999).

2 Reeves, *Christian Thinking*, p. 8.
3 Albert Louis Zambone, 'Marjorie Reeves, 1905–2003' in *Christianity Today*, July/August 2004.
4 Reeves, *Christian Thinking*, pp. 35, 40, 67.
5 Reeves, *Christian Thinking*, p. 211.
6 Reeves, *Christian Thinking*, pp. 81–2, 211.
7 Reeves, *Christian Thinking*, p. 49.
8 Reeves, *Christian Thinking*, pp. 80–100.
9 Reeves, *Christian Thinking*, p. 80.
10 Duncan Forrester, 'A Free Society Today?' in Reeves, *Christian Thinking*, p. 219.
11 This incident is recorded in John Davis McCaughey, *Christian Obedience in the University: Studies in the Life of the SCM of Great Britain and Ireland, 1930–1950* (London, SCM Press, 1958), p. 144.
12 Oliver Barclay and Robert Horn, *From Cambridge to the World: 125 Years of Student Witness* (Leicester, IVP, 2002), pp. 130–1.
13 Ronald Preston gives an excellent study of Leslie Hunter, 'A Bishop ahead of his Church', in R. John Elford and Ian S. Markham, *The Middle Way: Theology, Politics and Economics in the Later Thought of R. H. Preston* (London, SCM Press, 2000), pp. 22–9.
14 Adrian Hastings, *A History of English Christianity, 1920–1990*, 3rd edn (London, SCM Press, 1991), p. 439.
15 Preston, 'A Bishop', p. 28.
16 Hastings, *History*, p. 439.
17 See David L. Edwards in Harold C. Fey (ed.), *A History of the Ecumenical Movement*, vol. II, 1948–68 (Geneva, WCC, 1970, 2004), p. 387.
18 References in this section, unless otherwise noted, are from Tissington Tatlow, *The Story of the Student Christian Movement of Great Britain and Ireland* (London, SCM Press, 1933), pp. 804–9. Davis McCaughey (1958) does not deal with the SCM in schools, as his book is limited to the SCM's work in the university.
19 In my last year at school at the Royal Belfast Academical Institution, 1940–41, Grummitt became its principal, after escaping from his previous post in the German-occupied Channel Islands.
20 Tatlow, *Story*, p. 498.
21 Tatlow, *Story*, p. 491.
22 McCaughey, *Christian Obedience*, pp. 149–56.
23 Reeves, *Christian Thinking*, pp. 100–22.
24 Hans-Ruedi Weber, *The Courage to Live: A Biography of Suzanne de Diétrich* (Geneva, WCC, 1995).
25 Also important, especially in the Federation after its publication in French in 1938, was her *Le Dessein de Dieu*, published in John McAfee Brown's English translation as *God's Unfolding Purpose* (Philadelphia, PA, Westminster, 1960).
26 M. M. Thomas, *My Ecumenical Journey* (Ecumenical Publishing Centre, Trivandrum, 1990), pp. 14–15.
27 Philip Potter and Thomas Wieser (*Seeking and Serving the Truth* (Geneva, WCC, 1997), p. 123) quote the phrase but not the attribution to Barth.

28 For an illuminating account of these events, especially as they related to the WSCF, see 'The Church Struggle in Germany' and 'The WCC and the German Church Conflict in 1939' in W. A. Visser 't Hooft, *Memoirs* (London, SCM Press, 1973), pp. 84–99.

29 Eric Fenn, *Learning Wisdom: Fifty Years of the SCM* (London, SCM Press, 1939), p. 121.

30 F. W. Dillistone, *Charles Raven: Naturalist, Historian, Theologian* (London, Hodder & Stoughton, 1975), pp. 218, 277.

31 Dillistone, *Charles Raven*, p. 288.

32 Dillistone, *Charles Raven*, p. 33.

33 Letter (21.12.02) from Dr Owen Lidwell, with a copy of *The Faith: A Study Syllabus on Christian Doctrine*, Oxford University SCM, 1936.

34 John Bowden, 'SCM Press: A Short History', p. 1, in Robert S. Anderson (ed.), *A Step Out of Line: Essays on the Life of the Student Christian Movement* (unpublished typescript, 1982), p. 2.

35 SCM Archives, Special Collections, Information Services, University of Birmingham, Edgbaston, Section B, annual report 1963–64.

36 Potter and Wieser, *Seeking and Serving*, p. 106.

37 Potter and Wieser, *Seeking and Serving*, p. 108.

38 Material in this section is mainly drawn from Eberhard Bethge, *Dietrich Bonhoeffer: A Biography* (London, Collins, 1970). See also Keith Clements, *Bonhoeffer and Britain* (London, Churches Together in Britain and Ireland, 2006).

39 See article by Ans van der Bent in *Dictionary of the Ecumenical Movement*, (Geneva, WCC, 1991), p. 1077. Also Clements, *Bonhoeffer and Britain*, pp. 7–16.

40 Bethge, *Dietrich Bonhoeffer*, p. 294.

41 Bethge, *Dietrich Bonhoeffer*, p. 549.

42 McCaughey, *Christian Obedience*, pp. 83–106.

43 Potter and Wieser, *Seeking and Serving*, p. 152.

44 F. A. Iremonger, *William Temple, Archbishop of Canterbury: His Life and Letters*, abridged edn, ed. D. C. Somervell (London, Oxford University Press, 1948), pp. 204–5. Much of the material in this section is taken from this source.

45 C. Howard Hopkins, *John R. Mott: A Biography* (Grand Rapids, MI, Eerdmans, 1979), p. 638.

46 Iremonger, *William Temple*, p. 227.

47 See Oliver Tomkins, 'The Roman Catholic Church and the Ecumenical Movement, 1910–1948', in Ruth Rouse and Stephen C. Neill (eds), *A History of the Ecumenical Movement*, vol. I, 1517–1948 (Geneva, WCC, 1954, 2004), p. 682.

48 Alan M. Suggate, *William Temple and Christian Social Ethics Today* (Edinburgh, T. & T. Clark, 1987), p. 25.

49 William Temple, *The Church Looks Forward* (London, Macmillan, 1944), introduction.

50 Adrian Hastings, *Oliver Tomkins: The Ecumenical Enterprise, 1908–92* (London, SPCK, 2001), p. 32.

51 Hastings, *Oliver Tomkins*, p. 27.

4 The golden age (*c.* 1945–65)

1 The author was a member of the British student delegation at this meeting.
2 Philippe Maury and Andreas Schanke (eds), *Christian Witness in the Resistance: Experience of Some Members of European SCMs* (WSCF, Geneva, 1947).
3 'Robert Mackie' in Nansie Blackie (ed.), *A Time for Trumpets: Scottish Church Movers and Shakers of the Twentieth Century* (Edinburgh: St Andrew Press, 2005) pp. 53–64. See also Nansie Blackie, *In Love and in Laughter: A Portrait of Robert Mackie* (Edinburgh, St Andrew Press, 1995).
4 Blackie, *A Time for Trumpets*, p. 57.
5 Blackie, *A Time for Trumpets*, p. 62.
6 Blackie, *A Time for Trumpets*, p. 61, emphasis added.
7 Quoted in Blackie, *A Time for Trumpets*, p. 63.
8 The strength of this influence may be seen, for example, in the pioneering 'Federation Grey Book' *The Christian in the World Struggle*, by M. M. Thomas and John Davis McCaughey (Geneva, WSCF, 1951) and in McCaughey's analysis of the British University scene from 1930 to 1950 in *Christian Obedience in the University: Studies in the Life of the SCM of Great Britain and Ireland, 1930–1950* (London, SCM Press, 1958).
9 For example, Lesslie Newbigin in the Church of South India (1947) and Donald Kennedy in the Church of North India (1970).
10 In this they were continuing a fine tradition, for *The Student Movement* counted Eric Fenn, Oliver Tomkins, Alan Richardson and Ronald Preston among its earlier editors.
11 Lesslie Newbigin, *Unfinished Agenda: An Autobiography* (Geneva, WCC, 1985), p. 15.
12 See, for example, M. M. Thomas, *My Ecumenical Journey* (Ecumenical Publishing Centre, Trivandrum, 1990), p. 99, where he mentions a young Hindu woman student who had been helped spiritually by Marie-Jeanne's friendship and had become a Christian.
13 Marie-Jeanne de Haller Coleman in Elizabeth Adler (ed.), *Memoirs and Diaries, 1895–1990* (Geneva, WSCF, *c.* 1995), p. 79.
14 Mentioning the fact that it was unusual, in the 1930s, for men to work under the direction of women, Engel remarks that in the SCM it was simply accepted, and no one even thought of commenting on it.
15 Quoted with permission from a series of recorded and transcribed interviews prepared by Jane Yule for a forthcoming history of the Australian SCM by Associate Professor Renate Howe (cited as ASCM transcript). Interview with Charles Birch.
16 Interview with the Revd David Gill (SCM transcript).
17 Tatlow in Ruth Rouse and Stephen C. Neill (eds), *A History of the Ecumenical Movement*, vol. I, 1517–1948 (Geneva, WCC, 1954, 2004), p. 345.
18 McCaughey, *Christian Obedience*, p. 125.
19 Ruth Rouse, *The World's Student Christian Federation: A History of the First Thirty Years* (London, SCM Press, 1948), p. 301. See also her account of Suzanne Bidgrain's work in Rouse and Neill, *History*, vol. I, p. 632.

20 Ian Bradley, 'How great are these' in *The Tablet*, 10 July 2004, p. 12.

21 *Study and Discipleship Material*, March 1962, in SCM Archives, New College Library, Edinburgh.

22 Other series started under Gregor Smith included the *Library of Philosophy and Theology* and the *Library of Christian Classics*.

23 David L. Edwards, *A Church Built with Books: A Brief Guide to the SCM Press, 1959–1966* (London, SCM Press, 1966).

24 John Bowden, 'SCM Press: A Short History', p. 1, in Robert S. Anderson (ed.), *A Step Out of Line: Essays on the Life of the Student Christian Movement* (unpublished typescript, 1982), p. 2.

25 Strangely, Alan Richardson's introduction does not mention Kittel, though the *Theologisches Wörterbuch zum Neuen Testament* is listed in the abbreviations.

26 Steve Bruce, 'The Student Christian Movement and the Inter-Varsity Fellowship: A Sociological Study of the Two Student Movements' (unpublished thesis, University of Stirling, Department of Sociology, 1980), p. 256.

27 See Keith W. Clements, *The Theology of Ronald Gregor Smith* (Leiden, E. J. Brill, 1986), pp. 11–14, for an account.

28 Marjorie Reeves (ed.), *Christian Thinking and Social Order: Conviction Politics from the 1930s to the Present Day* (London, Cassell, 1999), pp. 9 ff.

29 McCaughey, *Christian Obedience*, p. 157.

30 The story is told in considerable detail in McCaughey, *Christian Obedience*, pp. 157–66.

31 Oliver Barclay and Robert Horn, *From Cambridge to the World: 125 Years of Student Witness* (Leicester, IVP, 2002), p. 54.

32 McCaughey, *Christian Obedience*, p. 160.

33 McCaughey, *Christian Obedience*, p. 163. See also Appendix II, pp. 209 ff, which gives the full text of the 1951 Aim and Basis.

34 *France Pagan?* was the title of Maisie Ward's translation (London, Sheed and Ward, 1949) of *La France, Pays de Mission* (1943) by the Abbés Godin and Daniel.

35 Thomas, *My Ecumenical Journey*, p. 41.

36 Thomas, *My Ecumenical Journey*, p. 55.

37 Thomas, *My Ecumenical Journey*, pp. 8–9.

38 Edwards, *Church Built with Books*, p. 36.

39 Philip Potter and Thomas Wieser, *Seeking and Serving the Truth* (Geneva, WCC, 1997), p. 148.

40 McCaughey, *Christian Obedience*, p. 136.

41 Dietrich Bonhoeffer, *Letters and Papers from Prison*, p. 124, quoted in McCaughey, *Christian Obedience*, p. 140.

42 McCaughey, *Christian Obedience*, p. 140.

43 McCaughey, *Christian Obedience*, p. 199.

44 McCaughey, *Christian Obedience*, p. 201.

45 Thomas and McCaughey, *The Christian in the World Struggle*.

46 Thomas, *My Ecumenical Journey*, pp. 96–7.

47 Compare Paul A. Crow, Jr, *Christian Unity: Matrix for Mission* (New York, Friendship Press, 1982).

48 Material in this section on Marjorie Reeves comes from Albert Louis Zambone, 'Marjorie Reeves, 1905–2003' in *Christianity Today*, July/August 2004 and Brian Mountford (funeral address, 12 December 2003).

49 McCaughey, *Christian Obedience*, p. 120.

50 From her obituary in *The Times*, 4 December 2003.

51 Adrian Hastings, *Oliver Tomkins: The Ecumenical Enterprise, 1908–92* (London, SPCK, 2001), pp. 80–2.

52 Hastings, *Oliver Tomkins*, p. 80.

53 Hastings, *Oliver Tomkins*, p. 83.

54 Donald Allchin in *The Student Movement*, December 1952.

55 Nicolas Zernov, *The Russians and their Church* (London, SPCK, 1964), p. 168, quoted by Ian Parsons, *Baron Paul Nicolay: His Legacy to Russia and the World* (unpublished paper, Melbourne, 2005), p. 5.

56 Hastings, *Oliver Tomkins*, p. 85.

57 For a good account of Tomkins at Lund, see Hastings, *Oliver Tomkins*, pp. 85–6.

58 Potter and Wieser, *Seeking and Serving*, p. 214.

5 Documents, developments, donations (*c.* 1945–65)

1 Cited as *WSCF/IFES Symposium*, Geneva, undated but *c.* 1957.

2 *WSCF/IFES Symposium*, p. 13.

3 *WSCF/IFES Symposium*, p. 19.

4 *WSCF/IFES Symposium*, p. 16.

5 Quotations in this section are from the transcript of this meeting, lodged in the SCM Archives, Special Collections, Information Services, University of Birmingham, Edgbaston, Section A (Annandale), box 263, Relations with IVF.

6 I owe the substance of this paragraph largely to Andrew Morton (conversation on 21 September 2004).

7 Letter dated 3 March 1953 from John Bendor-Samuel (chairman, IVF, London) to David Philpot (president, EUCU, 1953–54). Much of the information in this section comes from the collection of Revd David Philpot, Edinburgh.

8 This reflects the then (1953) Clause 17 of the IVF Constitution: 'In connection with the Fellowship, no joint activities shall be arranged with any religious body which does not substantially uphold the truths stated in the doctrinal basis of the Fellowship.'

9 Letter, 3 March 1953, Bendor-Samuel to Philpot.

10 Letter, 21 May 1953, Michael C. Griffiths, chairman, IVF executive committee 1953–54, to David Philpot.

11 Letter, 11 August 1953, Griffiths to Philpot.

12 Letter, 11 September 1953, Philpot to Griffiths.

13 Letter, 29 June 1953, Philpot to Griffiths.

14 Letter, 15 September 1953, Griffiths to Philpot.

15 Open letter of the Honorary Committee to 'Christian Friends', 19 November 1953.

16 University of Edinburgh: Report on the Mission, Oct 21–Nov 3, 1954 (Philpot Collection).

17 Patrick Rodger later served on the WCC staff, and was successively Bishop of Manchester and Oxford.

18 Report on the Mission, p. 6.

19 M. M. Thomas, *My Ecumenical Journey* (Ecumenical Publishing Centre, Trivandrum, 1990), p. 15.

20 Thomas, *My Ecumenical Journey*, p. 20.

21 Thomas, *My Ecumenical Journey*, p. 23.

22 Thomas, *My Ecumenical Journey*, pp. 10–11.

23 Unless otherwise noted, this section depends on Philip Potter and Thomas Wieser, *Seeking and Serving the Truth* (Geneva, WCC, 1997), pp. 192–6.

24 W. A. Visser 't Hooft, *Memoirs* (London, SCM Press, 1973), pp. 65–70.

25 Adrian Hastings, *Oliver Tomkins: The Ecumenical Enterprise, 1908–92* (London, SPCK, 2001), p. 28.

26 Hastings, *Oliver Tomkins*, p. 28.

27 For a fuller discussion of this period see Hastings, *Oliver Tomkins*, pp. 74–82.

28 Quoted in Potter and Wieser, *Seeking and Serving*, pp. 213–14.

29 I owe the information in this paragraph to Martin Conway.

30 For an account of the 1964 Nottingham initiative, see David L. Edwards, *The Church That Could Be* (London, SPCK, 2002), pp. 116–17.

31 Hastings, *Oliver Tomkins*, pp. 126–9.

32 Kenneth Darke, 'The Trust Association', in Robert S. Anderson (ed.), *A Step Out of Line: Essays on the Life of the Student Christian Movement* (unpublished typescript, 1982), p. 3.

6 'Story of a Storm' (*c.* 1965–80)

1 Lesslie Newbigin, *Unfinished Agenda: An Autobiography* (Geneva, WCC, 1985), pp. 175–6. For a different, and more sympathetic, account of the Strasbourg meeting see David L. Edwards in Harold C. Fey (ed.), *A History of the Ecumenical Movement*, vol. II, 1948–68 (Geneva, WCC, 1970, 2004), pp. 98–403.

2 I owe this information to Dr Salters Sterling.

3 W. A. Visser 't Hooft, *Memoirs* (London, SCM Press, 1973), p. 367.

4 I am indebted for this point to Martin Conway.

5 Philip Potter and Thomas Wieser, *Seeking and Serving the Truth* (Geneva, WCC, 1997), pp. 205–6.

6 Andrew Morton, 21 September 2004.

7 It is interesting to note that Martin Conway, who as a member of the Federation staff happened to be available to attend this meeting, was deliberately discouraged from attending.

8 Martin Conway, *The Christian Enterprise in Higher Education: An Attempt to See Straight in England in 1970* (London, Church of England Board of Education, 1971), pp. 43–4.

9 Letter from Isobel Forrester, senior friend of the Movement, to her daughter Anne Booth-Clibborn, 16 September 1964.

10 John S. Peart-Binns, *Ambrose Reeves: A Biography* (London, Gollancz, 1973), p. 273.

11 See Ian Mackenzie, *I was Invited* (Glasgow, ICS Books, 2003), pp. 126–9.

12 Martin Conway, 'The Fateful 60s', in Robert S. Anderson (ed.), *A Step Out of Line: Essays on the Life of the Student Christian Movement* (unpublished typescript, 1982), p. 6.

13 Peart-Binns, *Ambrose Reeves*, p. 275.

14 Risto Lehtonen, *Story of a Storm: The Ecumenical Student Movement in the Turmoil of Revolution* (Grand Rapids, MI, Eerdmans, 1998).

15 Potter and Wieser, *Seeking and Serving*, pp. 201–44. This account was written before the publication of Lehtonen's book, but takes note of his earlier article with the same title in *Study Encounter* viii/1, 1972.

16 Hans-Ruedi Weber, *The Courage to Live: A Biography of Suzanne de Diétrich* (Geneva, WCC, 1995), p. 135.

17 Potter and Wieser, *Seeking and Serving*, pp. 210–11.

18 Lehtonen, *Story of a Storm*, pp. 53–4; Potter and Wieser, *Seeking and Serving*, pp. 257–8.

19 Lehtonen, *Story of a Storm*, p. 58.

20 Potter and Wieser, *Seeking and Serving*, p. 258.

21 Alistair Kee, 'SCM, Past, Present and Future', in Anderson (ed.), *A Step Out of Line*, p. 1.

22 Lehtonen, *Story of a Storm*, p. 59.

23 Lehtonen, *Story of a Storm*, p. 65.

24 I owe this point to Andrew Morton.

25 Norman Goodall in the Uppsala Assembly report, quoted in Lehtonen, *Story of a Storm*, p. 66.

26 Newbigin, *Unfinished Agenda*, p. 230.

27 M. M. Thomas, *My Ecumenical Journey* (Ecumenical Publishing Centre, Trivandrum, 1990), p. 301.

28 Thomas, *My Ecumenical Journey*, p. 302.

29 Lehtonen, *Story of a Storm*, p. 68.

30 Lehtonen, *Story of a Storm*, p. 68.

31 Lehtonen, *Story of a Storm*, p. 69.

32 Lehtonen, *Story of a Storm*, p. 70.

33 Personal recollection of the author.

34 Lehtonen, *Story of a Storm*, p. 74.

35 Lehtonen, *Story of a Storm*, p. 77.

36 *Federation News*, 1968, No. 4, pp. 6–7.

37 Lehtonen, *Story of a Storm*, p. 84.

38 Lehtonen, *Story of a Storm*, p. 84.

39 Lehtonen, *Story of a Storm*, p. 88.

40 Potter and Wieser, *Seeking and Serving*, p. 231.

41 I owe this point to Dr Salters Sterling, who was also present at Turku and Otaniemi.

42 Potter and Wieser, *Seeking and Serving*, p. 222.

43 Lehtonen, *Story of a Storm*, p. 109.

44 Lehtonen, *Story of a Storm*, p. 111.

45 Lehtonen, *Story of a Storm*, p. 161.
46 Lehtonen, *Story of a Storm*, p. 167.
47 Lehtonen, *Story of a Storm*, p. 173.
48 Lehtonen, *Story of a Storm*, p. 179.
49 Lehtonen, *Story of a Storm*, p. 181.
50 Lehtonen, *Story of a Storm*, p. 181.
51 Lehtonen, *Story of a Storm*, p. 186.
52 Lehtonen, *Story of a Storm*, p. 187.
53 Lehtonen, *Story of a Storm*, p. 187.
54 Lehtonen, *Story of a Storm*, p. 189.
55 Lehtonen, *Story of a Storm*, p. 191.
56 Lehtonen, *Story of a Storm*, pp. 204–5.
57 Lehtonen, *Story of a Storm*, p. 319.
58 Potter and Wieser, *Seeking and Serving*, p. 233.

7 Living under 'the Storm' (*c.* 1965–80)

1 R. John Elford and Ian S. Markham, *The Middle Way: Theology, Politics and Economics in the Later Thought of R. H. Preston* (London, SCM Press, 2000), pp. 30–45.
2 Risto Lehtonen, *Story of a Storm: The Ecumenical Student Movement in the Turmoil of Revolution* (Grand Rapids, MI, Eerdmans, 1998), p. 167.
3 Lehtonen, *Story of a Storm*, p. 122.
4 Steve Bruce, 'The Student Christian Movement: A 19th Century Movement and its Vicissitudes' in *International Journal of Sociology and Social Policy*, vol. 2/i (1982), p. 79.
5 Steve Bruce, 'The Student Christian Movement and the Inter-Varsity Fellowship: A Sociological Study of the Two Student Movements' (unpublished thesis, University of Stirling, Department of Sociology, 1980), pp. 310–14.
6 SCM Archives, Special Collections, Information Services, University of Birmingham, Edgbaston, Section B, box 354, David Head correspondence.
7 SCM Archives, Section A, box 402, Manchester Congress 1969.
8 Members included Stephen Beasley-Murray (Spurgeon's College, London), James Dunn (Edinburgh) and John Howes (Melbourne).
9 SCM Archives, Section B, box 354, David Head correspondence, folder marked '1968–72 Standing Committee'.
10 Alistair Kee, 'SCM, Past, Present and Future' in Robert S. Anderson (ed.), *A Step Out of Line: Essays on the Life of the Student Christian Movement* (unpublished typescript, 1982), p. 1.
11 Philip Potter and Thomas Wieser, *Seeking and Serving the Truth* (Geneva, WCC, 1997), p. 233.
12 Alistair Kee (ed.), *Seeds of Liberation: Spiritual Dimensions to Political Struggle* (London, SCM Press, 1973).
13 Kee, *Seeds*, pp. 1–6.
14 Kee, *Seeds*, pp. 72, 74.
15 Kee, *Seeds*, p. 74.
16 Kee, *Seeds*, p. 112.

17 Kee, *Seeds*, p. 94.
18 Kee, *Seeds*, p. 113.
19 Kee, *Seeds*, p. 114.
20 Kee, *Seeds*, pp. 114–15.
21 Kee, *Seeds*, p. 75.
22 Kee, *Seeds*, p. 86.
23 Kee, *Seeds*, p. 96.
24 For a detailed description of the first two years of the Wick Court experiment, see the Movement's annual report for 1975, which covers the years 1973–75: SCM Archives, Section B, 1975.
25 Lehtonen, *Story of a Storm*, p. 123.
26 The early stages of the conflict with the Trust Association are described in considerable detail in the 1975 annual report.
27 Kenneth Darke, 'The Trust Association' in Anderson (ed.), *A Step Out of Line*, p. 8.
28 Robert C. Mackie, 'Notes on a Journey to Wick, 1976' (typescript in the possession of Steven G. Mackie, Edinburgh).
29 Letter, Mackie to McCaughey, 15 June 1979.
30 Martin Conway, quoted in Lehtonen, *Story of a Storm*, p. 170.
31 Frank Engel, *Christians in Australia: Times of Change, 1918–1978* (Melbourne, Joint Board of Christian Education, 1993), chap. 6.
32 On Frank Engel see the obituary by Renate Howe in *The Age*, Melbourne, 8 September 2006, and ASCM transcript, Frank Engel.
33 Frank Engel, *Australian Christians in Conflict and Unity, 1788–1926* and *Christians in Australia: Times of Change, 1918–1978* (Melbourne, Joint Board of Christian Education, 1993).
34 Frank Engel, *An East Asian Experience of the World Student Christian Federation, 1931–1961* (WSCF Asia Book No 18) (Geneva, WSCF, 1994).
35 Engel, *Christians in Australia*, p. 116.
36 ASCM transcript, Sandy Yule, supplemented by personal conversations.
37 In the Irish context the word 'Catholic' is generally understood to mean *Roman* Catholic, and is so used occasionally in the following section.
38 Martin Rowan, 'The Student Christian Movement of Ireland, 1950–1980: An Ecumenical Experiment' (University of Dublin M Phil (Ecum) thesis, September 1985), pp. 35–6.
39 Rowan, 'Student Christian Movement', p. 58.
40 Rowan, 'Student Christian Movement', p. 39, quoting from *New Creation*, October 1972.
41 Rob Fairmichael, 'Pushing Back the Boundaries' in Anderson (ed.), *A Step Out of Line*, pp. 4–5.
42 Rowan, 'Student Christian Movement', p. 67.

8 Picking up the pieces (*c.* 1980–2005)

1 Martin Conway, *The Christian Enterprise in Higher Education: An Attempt to See Straight in England in 1970* (London, Church of England Board of Education, 1971), p. 42.

2 SCM Archives, Special Collections, Information Services, University of Birmingham, Edgbaston, Section B, annual report 1975, p. 3.

3 For information in this section I am mainly indebted to conversations with the Ven. Tim McClure.

4 A televised worship service at the Irish School of Ecumenics in about 1985 similarly used part of the eucharistic liturgy, and focused constantly on the elements of bread and wine on the table, which were frustratingly left untasted. The connection between the two events is perhaps not entirely fortuitous.

5 ASCM transcript, and personal correspondence with Ian Telfer.

6 Philip Potter and Thomas Wieser, *Seeking and Serving the Truth* (Geneva, WCC, 1997), p. 252.

7 For material in the following section I am indebted to conversations with Dr Christine Ledger, and also ASCM transcript, Chris Ledger.

8 WSCF 33rd General Assembly report (2004), p. 17.

9 For material in the following section I am indebted to conversations with Laurence Nana Brew in August 2005.

10 Chris Ledger in Elizabeth Adler (ed.), *Memoirs and Diaries, 1895–1990* (Geneva, WSCF, c. 1995), p. 217.

9 Into the far country

1 Preston in R. John Elford and Ian S. Markham, *The Middle Way: Theology, Politics and Economics in the Later Thought of R. H. Preston* (London, SCM Press, 2000), pp. 36–9.

2 Andrew Morton, in notes given to the author, 21 September 2004.

3 Preston in Elford and Markham, *Middle Way*, p 38.

4 Preston in Elford and Markham, *Middle Way*, p. 39.

5 Preston in Elford and Markham, *Middle Way*, p. 40.

6 Philip Potter and Thomas Wieser, *Seeking and Serving the Truth* (Geneva, WCC, 1997), p 290.

7 Steve Bruce in *Religious Studies*, September 1984, pp. 140 ff.

8 Steve Bruce, 'The Student Christian Movement: A 19th Century Movement and its Vicissitudes' in *International Journal of Sociology and Social Policy*, vol 2/i (1982).

9 W. A. Visser 't Hooft, *Memoirs* (London, SCM Press, 1973), p. 247.

10 Compare the emphasis of Alexander Schmemann's 1966 book, *The World as Sacrament*, written expressly for the Federation (London, Darton, Longman & Todd).

11 For the centrality of the concept of Christ as truth see 1 Corinthians 2.2 and John 8.32; 14.6. Compare also a book published by the SCM Press in the midst of 'the Storm' – Ernst Käsemann, *Jesus Means Freedom* (1969), pp. 144–153.

12 Note M. M. Thomas' title, *Risking Christ for Christ's Sake: Towards an Ecumenical Theology of Pluralism* (Geneva, WCC, 1987).

13 Dr Ulrich Seidel, a student at the Irish School of Ecumenics just before this period, has confirmed to me the magnitude of this factor in the successful overthrow of the Marxist government in the German Democratic Republic.

14 Potter and Wieser, *Seeking and Serving*, p. 262.

15 Quoted in Bruce, 'The Student Christian Movement', p. 179.

16 Oliver Barclay and Robert Horn, *From Cambridge to the World: 125 Years of Student Witness* (Leicester, IVP, 2002), p. 193.

17 For a penetrating account of this tradition, especially in the years after 1968, see Hans-Ruedi Weber in John Briggs, Mercy Amba Oduyoye and George Tstetsis (eds), *A History of the Ecumenical Movement*, vol. III, 1968–2000 (Geneva, WCC, 2004), pp. 195–215.

18 Edwin Muir, *An Autobiography* (1954; Edinburgh, Canongate, 1993), p. 230.

19 In summer 1949 Harry Daniel and I, as representatives of newly independent India and of Britain, were guests at a conference of the Dutch and Indonesian Movements at Nunspeet, the Netherlands, as they wrestled with the question of Indonesian independence.

20 Adrian Hastings, *Oliver Tomkins: The Ecumenical Enterprise, 1908–92* (London, SPCK, 2001), p. 62.

21 Barclay and Horn, *From Cambridge to the World*, p. 200.

10 The family likeness

1 Adrian Hastings, *A History of English Christianity, 1920–1990* (London, SCM Press, 1991), p. 542.

2 R. John Elford and Ian S. Markham, *The Middle Way: Theology, Politics and Economics in the Later Thought of R. H. Preston* (London, SCM Press, 2000), pp. 33 ff. The other 'children' are: First Conference Estates, Swanwick; the Christian Education Movement; the Auxiliary Movement ('the Aux'); the London Medical Group; Student Movement House; the Higher Education Group; Freshers' pre-sessional Induction Conferences; work with students going into industry.

3 Geoffrey Wainwright, *Lesslie Newbigin: A Theological Life* (New York, Oxford University Press, 2000), p. 12.

4 Lesslie Newbigin, *Unfinished Agenda: An Autobiography* (Geneva, WCC, 1985), p. 28.

5 I have been privileged to read Francis House, *Some Chapters for a House Family Chronicle* (unpublished typescript, 1998).

6 See Stanley Samartha, *Between Two Cultures: Ecumenical Witness in a Pluralist World* (Geneva, WCC, 1996).

7 Adrian Hastings, *Oliver Tomkins: The Ecumenical Enterprise, 1908–92* (London, SPCK, 2001), p. 74.

8 Elizabeth Adler (ed.), *Memoirs and Diaries, 1895–1990* (Geneva, WSCF, c. 1995), p. 80.

9 Thomas Wieser (ed.), *Bible and Theology in the Federation: A Report* (Geneva, WSCF, 1995), p. 4; see also Hans-Ruedi Weber, *The Courage to Live: A Biography of Suzanne de Diétrich* (Geneva, WCC, 1995), pp. 80–2.

10 Hastings, *Oliver Tomkins*, p. 125.

11 M. M. Thomas, *My Ecumenical Journey* (Ecumenical Publishing Centre, Trivandrum, 1990), p. 197.

12 Thomas, *My Ecumenical Journey*, p. 190.

13 Thomas, *My Ecumenical Journey*, p. 194.

14 Thomas, *My Ecumenical Journey*, p. 442.

15 The celebrated controversy between Thomas and Newbigin over Thomas' virtual espousal of 'churchless Christianity' is documented in George R. Hunsberger, 'Conversion and Community: Revisiting the Lesslie Newbigin– M. M. Thomas Debate' in *International Bulletin of Missionary Research* 22 (1998), pp. 112–17. The controversy was set within their deep and enduring friendship.

16 Thomas, *My Ecumenical Journey*, p. 347.

17 Thomas, *My Ecumenical Journey*, p. 370.

18 Thomas, *My Ecumenical Journey*, p. 372.

19 Thomas, *My Ecumenical Journey*, p. 432.

20 See the study by Geraldine Smyth (then Director, Irish School of Ecumenics), *A Way of Transformation: A Theological Evaluation of the Conciliar Process of Mutual Commitment to Justice, Peace and the Integrity of Creation, WCC, 1983–1991* (Bern, Peter Lang, 1995).

21 For an inside description of the development of interfaith dialogue within the WCC, see Stanley Samartha, *Between Two Cultures*, pp. 63–130.

22 Wainwright, *Lesslie Newbigin*, p. 202.

23 *MEUT* para 58, quoted from the earlier San Antonio (1989) and San Salvador (1986) mission conferences.

24 Konrad Raiser in *Ecumenical Review*, October 2001, p. 522.

25 Quoted in Raiser, *Ecumenical Review*, p. 527.

26 Raiser, *Ecumenical Review*, p. 528.

27 See, for example, Hans-Ruedi Weber, *Experiments with Bible Study* (Geneva, WCC, 1981).

28 See 'An Open Letter to Dr Emilio Castro, the General Secretary of the WCC', 27 July 1990, sent by 'a group of friends of the WCC gathered from five continents in Vancouver, 16–27 July 1990'.

29 Duncan B. Forrester, 'Returning Friendly Fire: Ronald Preston and the New Ecumenical Social Ethics' in *Crucible*, 1997, p. 196.

30 A 1952 postcard, written by Oliver Tomkins, asserted that the WCC's Faith and Order Commission was far more important than the Central Committee! (Hastings, *Oliver Tomkins*, p. 114).

31 Newbigin, *Unfinished Agenda*, p. 253.

32 Hastings, *Oliver Tomkins*, p. 164.

33 Lesslie Newbigin, *The Reunion of the Church* (London, SCM Press, 1948), and *The Household of God* (London, SCM Press, 1953).

34 Anthony Hanson, *The Meaning of Unity: A Study on a Biblical Theme* (London, Highway Press, 1954).

35 For an account of this debate see Robert Bos, 'Revolting Fathers: The 1998 Protest by the Basis of Union's Framers', *Uniting Church Studies*, 9/1, March 2003.

36 Quoted from William Emilsen, 'Tribute to Prof. Davis McCaughey', United Theological College, Sydney, 28 March 2005.

37 For Bossey Ecumenical Institute see the entry by Alain Blancy in *Dictionary of the Ecumenical Movement* Nicholas Lossky (ed.) (Geneva, WCC, 1991); Hans-Ruedi Weber, *The Courage to Live*, chapter 10; *Ecumenical Review*, vol. 39/2, April 1987, '40 Years of the Ecumenical Institute'.

38 John Bowden, 'SCM Press: A Short History' in Robert S. Anderson (ed.), *A Step Out of Line: Essays on the Life of the Student Christian Movement* (unpublished typescript, 1982), p. 2.

39 ASCM transcript, Ronald Wilson.

40 Tony Stephens, obituary in *The Age*, Melbourne, 28 July 2005.

41 Obituary in *The Age*, 28 July 2005.

42 Oliver Barclay and Robert Horn, *From Cambridge to the World: 125 Years of Student Witness* (Leicester, IVP, 2002), pp. 184, 186.

43 Suzanne de Diétrich, *WSCF: 50 Years of History, 1895–1945* (English edn, WSCF, 1993), p. 36.

44 Ruth Rouse, *The World's Student Christian Federation: A History of the First Thirty Years* (London, SCM Press, 1948), p. 183.

45 Tissington Tatlow, *The Story of the Student Christian Movement of Great Britain and Ireland* (London, SCM Press, 1933), pp. 190, 286–7.

46 The date in brackets indicates the year of first appointment to the SCM staff.

47 Philip Potter and Thomas Wieser, *Seeking and Serving the Truth* (Geneva, WCC, 1997), p. 117.

48 Potter and Wieser, *Seeking and Serving*, p. 118.

49 For an account of Florence Li's ordination see Margaret Webster, *A New Strength, a New Song: The Journey to Women's Priesthood* (London, Mowbray, 1994), pp. 68–77.

50 Mary Levison, *Wrestling with the Church: One Woman's Experience* (London, Arthur James, 1992).

51 See Margaret Webster, *A New Strength*.

52 Potter and Wieser, *Seeking and Serving*, p. 117.

53 Potter and Wieser, *Seeking and Serving*, p. 185.

54 Potter and Wieser, *Seeking and Serving*, p. 145. For the story of Brother Roger and the Taizé Community see Kathryn Spink, *A Universal Heart: The Life and Vision of Brother Roger of Taizé*, revised edn (London, SPCK, 2006).

55 Marjorie Reeves (ed.), *Christian Thinking and Social Order: Conviction Politics from the 1930s to the Present Day* (London, Cassell, 1999), p. 134.

56 Reeves, *Christian Thinking*, p. 134.

57 Reeves, *Christian Thinking*, p. 131.

58 Paul Oestreicher in *The Tablet*, 7 June 2003, p. 31.

59 W. A. Visser 't Hooft, *Memoirs* (London, SCM Press, 1973), pp. 224, 340.

60 Material in this section is drawn from Prof. Kenneth Boyd's chapter on 'The Development of Bioethics and Medical Ethics in the UK', from his forthcoming book *The History of Bioethics*. I am also indebted to Prof. and Mrs Patricia Boyd for further information in this section.

61 Ian Breward, '*Holding Fast and Letting Go': A History of the UFT* (UFT Commencement Lecture) (Melbourne, 1999).

62 See Ian Fraser, *Ecumenical Adventure: A Dunblane Initiative* (Dunblane, Action for Churches Together in Scotland, 2003).

him*

✗ 'him' correct in submitted version!

63 John Morrow, *On the Road of Reconciliation: A Brief Memoir* (Dublin, Columba Press, 2000), pp. 15–16.

11 'Church ahead of the Church'

1 These lines from Hopkins were quoted in the widely used booklet *Study Groups and their Leadership*, 1950. See J. Davis McCaughey, *Christian Obedience in the University* (London, SCM Press, 1958), p. 193.
2 Martin Conway, *The Christian Enterprise in Higher Education: An Attempt to See Straight in England in 1970* (London, Church of England Board of Education, 1971), p. 47.
3 Conway, *Christian Enterprise*, p. 52.
4 But see David L. Edwards and John R. W. Stott, *Essentials: A Liberal–Evangelical Dialogue* (London, Hodder & Stoughton, 1988) for a considered discussion; and, for a recent account, Martin Conway on 'the prime evangelical critique' in John Briggs, Mercy Amba Oduyoye and George Tstetsis (eds), *A History of the Ecumenical Movement*, vol. III, 1968–2000 (Geneva, WCC, 2004), pp. 440–4. See also a recent parallel to the Edwards and Stott book in Marcus Borg and Tom Wright, *The Meaning of Jesus: Two Visions* (London, HarperCollins, 2000).
5 Compare, for example, their commitment to relief work and social justice through Tearfund; their engagement with Roman Catholics, especially in the area of mission (for example, the ERCDOM Report of 1982); their productive engagement with the WCC at successive Assemblies – Vancouver 1983, Canberra 1991, Harare 1998, Porto Alegre 2006.
6 Compare Oliver Barclay and Robert Horn, *From Cambridge to the World: 125 Years of Student Witness* (Leicester, IVP, 2002), pp. 152 and 158.
7 For example, through the work of the Christian Unity Working Group of the Uniting Church in Australia. See Robin Boyd, 'Worship and Reconciliation: An Australian Perspective' in *Irish Theological Quarterly* 66 (2001), pp. 259–68, especially pp. 265–6.
8 Donald Kennedy had the distinction of being the only non-Indian consecrated as a diocesan bishop in the CNI.
9 I owe this insight to Prof. Jeff Silcock of Adelaide. See his paper, 'Worship as Realised Eschatology', presented to the Uniting Church/Lutheran dialogue group, Australia, November 1997.
10 Compare Kenneth Ross, 'Edinburgh 2010: Kairos for Christian Mission?' (unpublished paper presented at Edinburgh University's Centre for the Study of Christianity in the Non-Western World, 14 February 2006).
11 W. A. Visser 't Hooft, *Memoirs* (London, SCM Press, 1973), p. 38.
12 Adrian Hastings, *Oliver Tomkins: The Ecumenical Enterprise, 1908–92* (London, SPCK, 2001), p. 34.
13 Visser 't Hooft, *Memoirs*, p. 357.
14 Conway, *Christian Enterprise*, p. 50.
15 Quoted from *Mission and Evangelism: An Ecumenical Affirmation* (Geneva, WCC, 1982), paras 10 and 41.

Index

The titles 'Student Christian Movement' and 'World Student Christian Federation' are not listed in the Index, as they occur with such frequency throughout the book. Women's names are listed under their surname at the time of their membership in the Movement: their married surnames are added in brackets.

Index

Oldham, J. H. 11–13, 17, 35, 38–40, 44, 49, 53–4, 56, 64, 68, 73–4, 90, 157, 170, 175, 185
Orthodox churches 14, 34, 65, 77–9, 109–10, 157–8, 167, 185
Orthodox Theological Faculty of St Sergius, Paris 36, 78
Osborn, Eric 178
Overseas Service (UK) 69
Overseas Service Bureau (Australia) 120

Paisley, Ian 124, 127
Paton, David 70, 72
Paton, Frank H. L. 9, 17
Paton, John G. 8
Paton, William (Bill) 10, 34, 39, 50, 56
Patterson, Carlisle 123, 128
Paul, C. S. 18
Paulose Mar Gregorios 160, 163
Pax Romana 94–5, 125, 139, 141
Peursen, Cornelis van 99
Phillips, Don 124
Philpot, David 87–9
Phipps, Simon 61
Piercy, Penelope 44, 46
Polhill-Turner, A. T. 6
political issues 13, 22–3, 29–30, 39, 41–2, 45–51, 54–5, 70–3, 75, 78–103, 105–11, 113–17, 121–3, 126–8, 145–6, 150–1
Political Stance of SCM, The 1969 113, 126
Pope John XXIII 93
Potter, Philip 53, 79, 102, 140, 157–8, 162–4, 171, 174
prayer 2, 4, 7–9, 11, 23–4, 45, 52, 63–4, 66, 79, 82, 85–6, 101, 140–1, 146
Preston, Ronald 40–2, 60, 64, 66, 72, 147–50, 156, 160, 163–4, 167
Programme to Combat Racism (PCR) 21, 106, 160

Pückler, Count 9
Purcell, Liam 135

Quintero, Manuel 138–9

Raiser, Konrad 65, 162
Ramsey, Michael 78, 160
Raven, Charles 45–6, 53–4, 149
Read, David H. C. 88–9
Reeves, Ambrose 31, 34, 99, 101, 112, 129, 134, 148, 151
Reeves, Marjorie 11, 39–40, 44, 75, 108
Religious Book Club (RBC) 47
Richardson, Alan 46, 52, 68, 150
Robinson, John A. T. 70, 99, 103
Rodger, Patrick 56, 88, 157, 178
Rodhe, Birgit 172
Ross, Una 120
Rouse, Ruth 10–11, 14, 17–22, 78, 156, 172
Routley, Eric 65
Rowan, Martin 125, 128
Russian Orthodox SCM in Exile 14, 20–1, 34, 36, 56, 65, 78, 80, 157
Rutherford, James 128

Samartha, Stanley 157, 159
Sartre, Jean-Paul 98
Sayers, Dorothy 39, 54
Scarlett, Eric 29–30, 40
Schmemann, Alexander 78
Schutz, Roger 95, 176
SCM in Dispersion 51–2
SCM in schools 42
SCM Press 23, 35, 40, 46–7, 50–1, 66, 80, 156, 167, 169–70
SCM–Canterbury Press 156, 169
Scott, Emily (Tatlow) 173
Scottish Churches House 59, 178
Sedgwick, Winifred 10, 43, 172–3

Selby, Peter 135
Shaull, Richard 102, 108, 110
Sheffield Industrial Mission 41, 70
Shotter, Edward 177
Singh, Lilavati 17, 90
'single issue' 118, 150–5
Smith, Stanley 4
Snowden, Dave 131
Sobornost journal 34
Society for Promoting Christian Knowledge (SPCK) 2
SODEPAX (Society, Development and Peace) 105
Söderblom, Nathan 30⅜
Southcott, Ernest 70
Speer, Robert E. 11
Sproxton, Vernon 42
Sterling, Salters 124–5, 128
Stevenson, J. Sinclair 6
Stevenson, Lilian 172–3
Stewart, James S. 86, 88
Studd, C. T. 4, 7, 12
Studd, J. K. 3, 12
Student Movement House 18, 36, 52
Student Movement magazine, The (GB&I) 40, 46, 60, 64, 69, 78, 172–3; Movement magazine 127, 133, 135
Student Outlook magazine, The 90
Student Prayer 1950 64, 167
Student Volunteer magazine, The 6, 22, 172
Student Volunteer Missionary Union of GB&I (SVMU) 6, 7, 24, 26, 35, 68
Student Volunteer Movement for Foreign Mission (SVM) (US) 3, 5, 11, 68, 102, 185
Student World journal, The 47, 52, 59, 71, 94, 146
Suggate, Alan 54
Swain, Patricia 42

211

World Conf. of Chr. Youth 59